SACRED CHRONOLOGY
of the HEBREW KINGS

SACRED CHRONOLOGY
of the HEBREW KINGS

*A harmony of the reigns of the kings of Israel and Judah,
and how the chronologies and histories of ancient Egypt
and Mesopotamia synchronize with their reigns*

Dan Bruce

THE PROPHECY SOCIETY

2013

Sacred Chronology of the Hebrew Kings
Copyright © 2013 Dan Bruce
All rights reserved.

No content from pages 13-144 may be reprinted, reproduced, or utilized in any form by any electronic, mechanical, or other means now known or hereafter invented, including photocopying and recording, nor can it be made available to the public in any information storage or retrieval system, without written permission from the author.

The Prophecy Society
www.prophecysociety.org
770-679-0633
*Monday-Friday, 10am-6pm
Eastern Time*

ISBN 978-1489509048

First Edition (Revised October 1, 2013)

Printed in the United States of America

Portions of this book were privately distributed to selected scholars for review under the title *Daniel Unsealed* in 2011 (ISBN 978-0-9816912-1-3). This release is "for the record" and supersedes all previous releases.

Corrections and responses to readers' questions, as well as results of biblical research that has become available after going to press, can be found in the "Book Notes" section of the website listed above. Questions and comments can be sent by e-mail to: daniel@prophecysociety.org

Cover photo: The front cover features a public-domain photograph of the oil-on-canvas painting "Saul and David" (*ca.* 1655-1660) by Rembrandt Harmenszoon van Rijn. The original painting is on permanent display at the Mauritshuis, The Hague, South Holland, in the Netherlands.

Donations Appreciated

If you feel that you have been somehow spiritually enlightened and blessed by reading this book and would like to make a small donation to help advance the Bible research and outreach ministry of the author, you can do so at: http://www.prophecysociety.org/aboutus.html

Contents

Preface: Chronology and History	1
Chapter One: About Kingdoms Chronology	3
• Champollion's Discovery	5
• Rawlinson's Eclipse	7
• Thiele's Mysterious Numbers	9
Chapter Two: A New Kingdoms Chronology	13
• Anchoring the Kings in History	14
• The Kingdoms Harmonized	19
• What about Bûr-Saggilê?	30
• What about Shishak?	35
• Which Way is Better?	40
Chapter Three: Kings of United Israel	41
• Saul of Israel (1,086-1,046 BCE)	41
• David of Judah and Israel (1,046-1,006 BCE)	44
• Solomon of Israel (1,006-967 BCE)	47
• Rehoboam of Israel (967-961 BCE)	50
Chapter Four: Kings of Israel and Judah	51
• Jeroboam of Israel (961-940 BCE)	52
• Rehoboam of Judah (961-944 BCE)	52
• Abijah of Judah (944-942 BCE)	57
• Asa of Judah (942-900 BCE)	58
• Nadab of Israel (940-939 BCE)	61
• Baasha of Israel (939-916 BCE)	61
• Elah of Israel (916-914 BCE)	62
• Zimri of Israel (914 BCE)	62
• Omri of Israel (914-904 BCE)	63
• Ahab of Israel (904-883 BCE)	64
• Jehoshaphat of Judah (900-875 BCE)	66
• Ahaziah of Israel (883-882 BCE)	67
• Joram of Israel (882/879-867 BCE)	67
• Jehoram of Judah (875-868 BCE)	67
• Ahaziah of Judah (868-867 BCE)	70
• Jehu of Israel (867-840 BCE)	70
• Athaliah of Judah (867-861 BCE)	72
• Joash of Judah (861-822 BCE)	73

Contents

- Jehoahaz of Israel (840-824 BCE) — 74
- Jehoash of Israel (825/824-808 BCE) — 74
- Amaziah of Judah (822-794 BCE) — 75
- Jeroboam II of Israel (808-768 BCE) — 76
- Uzziah of Judah (805/794-754 BCE) — 77
- Zachariah of Israel (768 BCE) — 80
- Shallum of Israel (767 BCE) — 80
- Menahem of Israel (767-757 BCE) — 80
- Pekah of Israel (758/757-738 BCE) — 81
- Pekahiah of Israel (757-755 BCE) — 81
- Jotham of Judah (757/754-738 BCE) — 81
- Ahaz of Judah (742-727 BCE) — 81
- Hoshea of Israel (731-721 BCE) — 82

Chapter Five: Kings of Judah — 83
- Hezekiah of Judah (727-698 BCE) — 83
- Manasseh of Judah (698-643 BCE) — 87
- Amon of Judah (643-641 BCE) — 89
- Josiah of Judah (640-609 BCE) — 89
- Jehoahaz of Judah (609 BCE) — 92
- Jehoiakim of Judah (609-598 BCE) — 92
- Jehoiachin of Judah (598-597 BCE) — 92
- Zedekiah of Judah (597-586 BCE) — 92

Chapter Six: Pharaohs of Egypt and the Hebrew Kings — 93
Chapter Seven: Kings of Assyria and the Hebrew Kings — 109
Appendix One: Timekeeping in Ancient Israel — 123
- Sabbath and Jubilee Years — 127
- Verifying the Sabbath and Jubilee Tables — 132

Appendix Two: Synchronized Bible Timeline — 135
- Date of the Exodus — 135
- Abraham to Solomon (2,162-1,002 BCE) — 139
- Moses in Egyptian History? — 141
- The Exodus to the Divided Kingdoms (1,442-961 BCE) — 142
- Hiram and the Kings of Tyre — 144
- Date of Creation — 146

Index of Names — 147

Reader's Notes

FORMAT FOR DATES: Dates for events occurring in history before October 4, 1582 CE on the Julian calendar are displayed as proleptic Gregorian dates, followed by a BCE or CE era notation. Dates for events occurring in history after October 15, 1582 CE are displayed as standard Gregorian dates, usually without the CE era notation. Unless noted otherwise, proleptic Gregorian dates shown in this book were generated by using the *Jewish Calendar Conversions in One Step* calendar-conversion utility created and made available by Stephen P. Morse on his website (www.stevemorse.org).

EGYPTIAN DATES: Dates for reigns of pharaohs in Dynasties 20-26 of Egypt follow the chronology established by Kenneth A. Kitchen (Personal and Brunner Professor Emeritus of Egyptology and Honorary Research Fellow at the School of Archaeology, Classics and Egyptology, University of Liverpool, England) in the 2004 edition his book *The Third Intermediate Period in Egypt (1100-650 BC)* published by Aris & Phillips.

ASSYRIAN DATES: Dates for reigns of kings of the Neo-Assyrian Empire shown in this book are non-traditional, but based on traditional dates accepted by scholars and published by historian Jona Lendering on his website Livius.org (www.livius.org), which credits Jean-Jacques Glassner (Director of Research for Archaeological Sciences of Antiquity at the French National Centre for Scientific Research) and his book *Chroniques Mésopotamiennes,* 1993 edition. The dates used herein have been modified from those dates in two ways: (1) by adding twenty-eight years to the reigns of Assyrian kings prior to Pul/Tiglath-pileser III, this modification based on identification of the year for the Bûr-Saggilê eclipse as 791 BCE, and (2) by moving the reigns of Shalmaneser III and all prior Assyrian kings back in time an additional two-years to account for the reign of Ashur-danin-pal. The reasons for making both modifications are explained in the text.

ASSYRIAN SOURCE TEXTS: The English-language edition of the Glassner book *Chroniques Mésopotamiennes,* 1993 edition, published as *Mesopotamian Chronicles* by the Society of Biblical Literature in 2004, has been used as a source for quoting some ancient texts. In addition, the 2008 Eisenbrauns edition of Hayim Tadmor's book, *The Inscriptions of Tiglath-Pileser III, King of Assyria,* has been used to identify and interpret some events in the reign of that Assyrian king.

Reader's Notes

HEBREW CHRONOLOGY: The *Seder Olam Rabbah* (סדר עולם רבה, translation: "The Long Order of the World") preserves the rabbinical interpretation of Bible chronology as derived from the Hebrew Scriptures and Jewish tradition. The first edition was compiled *circa* 160 CE, with authorship credited to Rabbi Yose Ben Halafta, a fourth-generation Tanna and scholar of *halakha* and *aggadah* who studied under Rabbi Akiba. The version used as a reference for this book is the English-language translation and commentary by Heinrich W. Guggenheimer, *Seder Olam* (2005 edition) published by Rowman & Littlefield Publishers, Inc.

HEBREW SOURCE TEXT: Unless noted otherwise, Hebrew words and phrases are copied from the Masoretic text of the Hebrew Scriptures as presented in *Biblia Hebraica Stuttgartensia* (5th, revised edition, 1997; based on manuscript Firkovich B19A, the "Leningrad Codex," housed in the National Library of Russia in Saint Petersburg) published by Deutsche Bibelgesellschaft, the German Bible Society.

HEBREW TO ENGLISH: Meanings of Hebrew words and phrases, unless stated otherwise, are based on definitions found in *The New Brown, Driver, Briggs, Gesenius Hebrew-English Lexicon: with an Appendix Containing the Biblical Aramaic* (revised edition, 1996) published by Hendrickson Publishers.

ECLIPSE DATA: Descriptions of lunar eclipses and solar eclipses are based on astronomical calculations derived by using software developed by Fred Espenak of the Goddard Space Flight Center and made available to the public by the National Aeronautics and Space Administration (NASA) on its "NASA Eclipse Web Site" (eclipse.gsfc.nasa.gov).

SCRIPTURE QUOTATIONS: The King James Version is the version used for quotations unless noted otherwise. That version has been chosen primarily because, as a document residing in the public domain, its use greatly simplifies copyright considerations and permissions. Its familiarity to both Jewish and Christian readers, the relative consistency in the way it translates Hebrew, Aramaic, and Greek words into English, and the large number of study aids and commentaries based on that version were also important considerations. Scripture quotations embedded in the text are usually displayed in italics, followed by a version-used notation in parenthesis. Long quotations are usually set apart in block text.

Abbreviations

AEC	Assyrian Eponym Canon
aka	Also known as *(with a name)*
Au	Author's translation or paraphrase
b.	Born in *(with year of birth)*, e.g., b. 1921
BCE	Before the Common Era *(same as B.C.)*
BHS	Denotes Hebrew (Masoretic) text reproduced verbatim from the *Biblia Hebraica Stuttgartensia (Leningrad Codex)* published by Deutsche Bibelgesellschaft (German Bible Society).
ca.	Latin *circa* - about *(with year)*, e.g., ca. 1920
CE	In the Common Era *(same as A.D.)*
d.	Died in *(with year of death)*, e.g., d. 1951
ESV	*English Standard Version*
KJV	*King James Version*
LXX	Septuagint, using *The Septuagint with Apocrypha: Greek and English* by Sir Lancelot C. L. Brenton, 1982 edition.
MT	Masoretic Text
NASB	*New American Standard Bible*
NT	New Testament
OT	Old Testament
p.	Page or pages *(with numbers)*, e.g., p. 62 *or* p. 62-65
r.	Reigned *(with year or years of reign)*, e.g., r. 519-524
Strong's	Denotes a reference number from *Biblesoft's New Exhaustive Strong's Numbers and Concordance with Expanded Greek-Hebrew Dictionary* published by Biblesoft, Inc. and International Bible Translators, Inc.

Symbols

♛	King of Israel or Judah
♕	Ruler of Israel or Judah (but not king)
▲	Pharaoh of a Dynasty of Egypt
♚	King of the Neo-Assyrian Empire

PREFACE

Chronology and History

Almost universally in modern times, the Bible has been rejected by scholars, including many conservative Bible scholars, as a trustworthy source text for the study of ancient chronology. Secular fields of study, primarily Geology and Archaeology, have all but assigned any chronology based on the biblical text to the academic dust bin. The purpose of this book is to reverse that trend—to show that the Bible is still the single most dependable source text available for doing serious chronological study of ancient times. It does so by using the details about the Hebrew kings provided in the biblical text to construct a precise historical timeline for that period, one that can be used not only for understanding Bible times, but for calibrating ancient contemporaneous chronologies as well.

The scope of this book is limited primarily to a detailed examination of the chronology of the Hebrew kings. Chapter One gives a synopsis of past efforts to harmonize the chronology of the kings. Chapter Two sets forth a new harmonized chronology of the kings, one based on Scripture only, with the reigns of the kings and chronological notes displayed diagrammatically side-by-side for easy comparison. Chapters Three, Four, and Five discuss the pertinent chronological details given in the Bible for each king—first, for the kings of United Israel, then for those in the kingdoms of Israel and Judah, and finally for those in the kingdom of Judah after the demise of the kingdom of Israel—and they explain how that information can be interpreted to create a harmonized kingdoms chronology. In Chapter Six, the reigns of the pharaohs of Egypt are synchronized with the reigns of the Hebrew kings who reigned concurrently. In Chapter Seven, the reigns of the kings of the Neo-Assyrian Empire are synchronized with the Hebrew kings. At the end of this book, an expanded Bible timeline shows how the chronology of the kings can be used to align the remainder of the sacred chronology from the birth of Abraham onward.

The methodology used to arrive at the kingdoms chronology presented in this book is based on two important differences that distinguish the resulting dates for the reigns of the Hebrew kings from those published in all prior sacred chronologies. First, the chronology of the kings presented herein is derived solely from the Hebrew Bible, the *Tanakh*, without depending on a secular chronology, such as the one defined by the Assyrian Eponym Canon combined with an astronomical observation, to anchor it in time. Second, it achieves exact harmonization of the reigns of the kings of Israel and Judah with one another, then synchronizes the chronologies of surrounding civilizations with that harmonized chronology, all without having to disregard any of the biblical text or assume scribal emendation or error. It should also be noted that the chronology of the Hebrew kings introduced in this book is based on a source text—the Bible—that is recognized as having the highest degree of transmission accuracy of any ancient document, with the accuracy of its chronological details confirmed by numerous cross-references recorded in the biblical text. Thus, the resulting chronology of the kings of Israel and Judah can be considered to be the most accurate regnal chronology that has come down from ancient times, which means that all other chronologies and histories, especially those of ancient Egypt and Mesopotamia, can best be understood when synchronized to agree with the chronology derived from the Bible rather than the other way around.

For those who may feel that any book devoted to discussing the chronology of the Hebrew kings is nothing more than a secondary pursuit, either not meriting serious academic consideration or not lending itself to spiritual enrichment, a few words of wisdom from a 19th-century scholar are worth repeating:

> "The chronology of the period of the kings of Judah and Israel has formed a fruitful subject of discussion in all subsequent ages. Works have been written on this epoch from the time of the Greek kings of Egypt until now, and yet we are unable, after the lapse of two thousand years, to settle the leading dates. The difficulties which stand in the way have led some to throw on one side entirely the chronological question; this result is unfortunate because history cannot be satisfactory without chronology" - GEORGE SMITH, *The Assyrian Eponym Canon* (London: Samuel Baxter and Sons, 1875; p. 2)

Indeed, secular history cannot be satisfactory apart from chronology, nor can Bible history be satisfactory without having an accurate timeline of biblical events with which to give it context. In fact, having a true chronology of biblical times is key for fully discerning biblical truth. It is your author's hope that the harmonized chronology of the Hebrew kings presented in this book will help to reestablish the Bible, at least in the realm of biblical scholarship, as the most authoritative ancient chronological source text, and that it will provide students, teachers, scholars, and religion professionals with a trustworthy timeline that can be used with confidence to achieve a more accurate interpretation of sacred history and a better understanding of the Bible's message for mankind today.

CHAPTER ONE

ABOUT KINGDOMS CHRONOLOGY

In 1945, writing in the *Bulletin of the American School of Oriental Research*, the esteemed archeologist and Bible scholar W. F. Albright introduced an essay on biblical chronology with these words: "For many years I have occupied myself periodically with the somewhat thankless task of reconstructing the chronology of Judah and Israel between the death of Solomon and the Fall of Jerusalem."[1] His statement reveals the inherent frustration that anyone who has expended years of effort in trying to reconstruct the reigns of the Hebrew kings eventually comes to feel. Albright's statement also goes directly to the heart of the matter. Anyone attempting to reconstruct the chronology of the kings must know where in time to start and where in time to end. In other words, he or she must define a time frame into which the reigns of the kings of Israel and Judah will exactly fit. On one end of that time frame must be the date when the divided kingdoms began after the death of Solomon. On the other end must be two dates, one for the fall of Samaria, signifying the end of the northern kingdom of Israel, and another for the fall of Jerusalem, signifying the end of the southern kingdom of Judah. After the beginning and ending points for the time frame have been fixed, the chronological information about the kings—all of it as specified in the Books of 1 and 2 Kings, 1 and 2 Chronicles, and the prophets—must then be harmonized so that the reigns fit within those end points. Furthermore, the chronology obtained from the biblical text must be in general agreement with other chronologies recognized by secular history. As anyone who has tried will affirm, reconstructing a chronology of the Hebrew kings that meets all of those requirements is a daunting task.

The modern history of "kingdoms chronology" (your author's term for the branch of biblical studies that deals with locating the reigns of the kings of Israel and Judah in history) begins with the publication of *Annales Veteris Testamenti*[2] in 1650 and *Annalium pars posterior* in 1654, both authored by Archbishop James

---

[1] W. F. Albright, "The Chronology of the Divided Monarchy of Israel" (*Bulletin of the American Schools of Oriental Research*, No. 100; December, 1945); p. 16-22.

[2] The full title of Ussher's monumental work is *Annales Veteris Testamenti, a prima mundi origine deducti, una cum rerum Asiaticarum et Aegyptiacarum chronico, a temporis historici principio usque ad Maccabaicorum initia producto* (Annals of the Old Testament, deduced from the first origins of the world, the chronicle of Asiatic and Egyptian matters together produced from the beginning of historical time up to the beginnings of Maccabes).

Ussher, Primate of the Church of Ireland. Ussher's books are best known for setting a specific date and time for the creation of the world, but, in developing his continuous chronology for the entirety of Bible history, he had to specify dates for the reigns of the Hebrew kings. Like all kingdoms chronologists since, Ussher faced challenges pertinent to the chronology of the divided monarchy period. The first challenge he had to face was that of which source text to use. The figures given for the number of years in the reigns of the kings differed in the source texts available to him. For instance, some figures given in the Septuagint differed from those found in the Masoretic text. As a biblical literalist, that was a major problem for Ussher, one which he solved by relying exclusively on the Masoretic text. This book follows his example unless noted otherwise.

A second, and not as easily solved, challenge was to figure out how to identify the year when the kingdom of United Israel divided into the two kingdoms of Israel and Judah. Ussher found a continuous sequence of years given in the Masoretic text between Abraham and the entry of the children of Israel into the land of Canaan, so he simply added the years together to arrive at a chronology for that period. That continuous sequence came to an end after the children of Israel entered the land, and the Bible did not pick up with a new sequence until the time of Saul and the kings of Israel and Judah that followed him, then it ended when the Hebrew Scriptures were completed *circa* 400 BCE. Because of the discontinuities in the chronology of the Jews after that date, no certain anchor point could be identified to pinpoint the beginning of the kingdoms period. So, Ussher had to rely on cross-referencing the reigns of the Hebrew kings with what was known from the secular history of the surrounding nations to arrive at a starting date for the division of United Israel into its two successor kingdoms. Considering that he did not have the benefit of modern archaeological scholarship (or perhaps because of that circumstance), Ussher made a remarkably accurate contribution to the field of biblical chronology,[1] and his chronology is still being used by some branches of fundamentalist Christianity today. This book rejects Ussher's overall chronology and some of the methodology he used to define the time period of the Hebrew kings, but it embraces his belief that the biblical text is accurate and dependable.

---

[1] As is always the case with biblical research, especially when working with chronological questions, Ussher benefitted from the work of many other scholars, and from the work of his predecessor chronologists, such as Rabbi Jose ben Halafta (2nd century CE, probable author of *Seder Olam Rabbah*), Venerable Bede (673-735 CE), and Joseph Justus Scaliger (1540-1609, an early scholar of Persian, Babylonian, Jewish and Ancient Egyptian history).

Chapter One: About Kingdoms Chronology

Champollion's Discovery

The Ussher chronology was the gold standard among scholars for almost two-hundred years with its authority being unquestioned. As the arts and sciences blossomed in the universities of Europe, however, the authority of the Bible began to give way to human reasoning and scholarship that derived its authority from a long process of academic research and peer review. For the first time, scholars, especially those versed in the discoveries and theories of the new science of Geology and its speculations about the age of the Earth, began to feel that they had an empirical basis for challenging the faith-based Ussher chronological interpretation of the biblical text. The reevaluation of the Ussher dates for the divided monarchy gained momentum in 1822 with one of the most far-reaching developments in the field of biblical studies—the decipherment of Egyptian hieroglyphics by Jean-François Champollion. The effect of that event on the field of kingdoms chronology cannot be overemphasized. Prior to the publication of Champollion's translation of the Rosetta Stone hieroglyphs, along with his phonetic dictionary and principles of grammar, the artifacts and monuments of ancient Egypt had successfully secreted a treasury of historical knowledge. No one could understand the inscriptions, and no one could use them to synchronize the details of Egyptian history with the details of biblical history. Thank to Champollion, that synchronization seemed possible.

Immediately after the publication of Champollion's breakthrough linguistic research, scholars began to head for the ruins of Egypt, most of them looking not only to discover and reveal the secrets of the pharaohs to a history-hungry world, but many of them were aggressively seeking physical evidence of the accuracy of the biblical narrative concerning the things of Egypt. Champollion himself was not immune to the lure of exploring the unknown glories of the Nile River cultures. In July of 1828, he boarded a ship for Cairo, leading what was called the Franco-Tuscan Expedition. It was his one and only visit to Egypt, financed by the grand-duke of Tuscany, Leopold II, and the King of France, Charles X, with the announced purpose of validating and perfecting his system of translating hieroglyphs. During his three-plus years in Egypt, Champollion, together with his expedition partner and fellow philologist, Ippolito Rosellini, examined and translated hundreds of monuments and inscriptions found in the Nile Valley and elsewhere in Egypt. Then, when he reached Karnak, Champollion made the discovery of his young life. An account of the discovery was published in an 1857 edition of *Harper's New Monthly Magazine*, written by the 19th-century travel writer and journalist William Cowper Prime and supposedly based on a first-person account by Champollion himself, who reported:

> "There is on the south wall of the temple of Karnak a sculptured group, in which a god is represented as offering to a king a host of captured cities and countries. The king's name was known as Sheshonk, or Shishak, as our translation of the Old Testament has it; but although a hundred scholars had seen the rows of captives, no one of them had read here any thing by which to connect this with the Scripture history. Champollion landed at Karnak on his way to Upper Egypt, and remained an hour or two in the vast halls that are the wonder of modern wanderers. But his keen eye was not idle, and as he passed this group, reading name by name in it silently, he started [sic] astonished at the blindness of his friends who were before him, and read aloud to them the name Melek Aicdah, or the King of Judah. The oval in which it was inclosed represents a fortified place, and the sign at the bottom, as I have before remarked, represents a country. It was like a voice out of the ancient ages, that sound among the ruins of Karnak, as the great scholar read the story of the son of Solomon on the wall of his conqueror's temple. It was the greatest, as it was almost the first of the new discoveries, and a tribute to the truth of God's revelation that at once consecrated and sealed the truth of the scholar's investigations and their results. That wall at Karnak is the most interesting spot among the fallen temples of the land of the Pharaohs. While other records have been effaced, that one seems to have been kept expressly that the world might discover it."[1]

The two hours that Champollion spent at Karnak standing before the reliefs located on the Bubastite Portal outside the Temple of Amun—triumphal scenes depicting the military campaign in Canaan by the pharaoh Shoshenq I—were minutes that would change the world's perception of Bible history. Champollion identified the real-life Shoshenq I as the biblical Shishak, an interpretation that electrified the world of scholarship. Kingdoms chronologists were ecstatic, of course. At long last, there was physical evidence that could possibly allow scholars to pinpoint the year of the rending of the kingdom of Israel from Rehoboam and the subsequent beginning of the divided monarchy. After all, if Shishak invaded Judah in Rehoboam's fifth year, then all that was needed to identify the year of the division was to locate the reign of Shoshenq I in history. Using

---

[1] William Cowper Prime, "From Thebes to the Pyramids" (*Harper's New Monthly Magazine*, Volume XIV, December, 1856, to May, 1857); p. 468.

the chronological information in the writings of the ancient Egyptian historian Manetho and other ancient writers, the reign of Shoshenq I was tentatively pegged to a year occurring somewhere between 980 BCE and 908 BCE. Still, the lack of exactitude about the years for the reign of Shoshenq I (now assumed to be Shishak) disappointed kingdoms chronologists. The inability to precisely date his reign meant that they could not use it to arrive at an exact date for the rending of the kingdom of United Israel from Rehoboam. Fortunately for kingdoms chronologists, a way to date the reign of Rehoboam would soon come from a non-Egyptian source, namely, the rapidly maturing field of Assyriology.

Rawlinson's Eclipse

The artifacts and ruins of ancient Mesopotamia were essentially closed to pre-18th-century western scholars while those lands languished under Moslem rule. The few scholars studying ancient Mesopotamian cultures prior to then had to content themselves with information gleaned from a limited collection of classical writings, many of which had dubious historical value. In the late 1700s, exploration societies in Europe began gaining access and sending expeditions to Mesopotamia to collect artifacts and study inscriptions at the ancient sites. The first recorded archeological excavation in Mesopotamia was led by Abbé Beauchamp, papal vicar general in Baghdad. His memoirs, published in 1790, created intense interest in anything Mesopotamian among European scholars and soon generated archeological expeditions to the Middle East. Systematic excavation of Mesopotamian sites was begun in 1842, with major discoveries being reported annually. Over time, fields of specialization developed to deal with the plethora of new information. One of those specialized fields was Assyriology, which would be of special importance to the study of Bible chronology.

The most important Assyrian discovery pertaining to kingdoms chronology was made public by Sir Henry Rawlinson in 1867. Among the cuneiform tablets that had been brought back from Nineveh and stored in the British Museum, Rawlinson found and deciphered four lists of eponyms[1] that comprise what has come to be called the Assyrian Eponym Canon. In the Neo-Assyrian Empire, each year was named after its *limmu*, a title given to a royal official who would preside over that year's New-Year Day celebrations. Each of Rawlinson's four lists

---

[1] *Definition*: An eponym is a person from whom something is said to take its name.

was incomplete, but they overlapped one another to reveal a continuous and unbroken record of the number of years in the reigns of all of the kings of the Neo-Assyrian Empire. In the account of the ninth year of Ashur-dan III was mention of a solar eclipse during the eponymy of a man named Bûr-Saggilê. Rawlinson determined that the eclipse had occurred on June 15, 763 BCE.[1] For the first time, calculating a date for the beginning year in the reign of Rehoboam of Judah was made possible by using Rawlinson's astronomically anchored and thus assumed-certain chronology of the Neo-Assyrian kings. The Rawlinson chronology was used to date the reign of Rehoboam, as follows:

> "With regard to the year when these occurrences took place, some new chronological data are afforded by a recent discovery of Sir H. Rawlinson by which certain Assyrian dates are fixed with astronomical certainty. A chronicle upon a brick tablet in the British Museum, makes distinct mention of an eclipse, the exact date of which has been fixed, and from it the relative dates of the events chronicled can be exactly known. It results from this that a battle in which Ahab, king of Israel, and his allies, were defeated by the king of Assyria happened in the year B. C. 853, and supposing this to be the battle recorded in the books of kings and Chronicles, where Ahab lost his life, the last year of Ahab's reign is hereby fixed. This happened in the 17th year of Jehoshaphat king of Judah, and taking the regnal years of his predecessors Asa, Abijah, and Rehoboam as 41, 3 and 17 as given by the Hebrew records, it follows that Rehoboam's first year must have been about B. C. 930."[2]

The annals and inscriptions on various steles had revealed that the Assyrian king Shalmaneser III fought a battle at Qarqar in his sixth year, and that he had battled against a coalition of kings that included Ahab of Israel. It was known from 1 Kings, chapter 22, verse 35, that Ahab was killed in battle at Ramoth-gilead. That action was assumed by scholars to have been part of the Battle of Qarqar, or, at the least, a separate battle somehow associated with the Qarqar campaign. By such reasoning, Ahab's final year was equated with the year of the Battle of Qarqar. Biblical chronologists could thus pinpoint the reign of Ahab by equating his last

---

[1] Henry Creswicke Rawlinson, "The Assyrian Canon Verified by the Record of a Solar Eclipse, B.C. 763" (*The Athenaeum: Journal of Literature, Science and the Fine Arts*; number 2064; May 18, 1867); p. 660-661.

[2] C. W. Goodwin, "On an inscription by Takelot II" (*Ägyptische Sprache und Alterthumskunde*, published by Professor Dr. R. Lepsius of Berlin; March, 1868); p. 28.

regnal year at Ramoth-gilead with the sixth regnal year of Shalmaneser III. Since Shalmaneser's sixth year could be identified as the year 853 BCE by counting back in time ninety eponyms from Rawlinson's 763 BCE date for the Bûr-Saggilê eclipse, and since that year was assumed to be Ahab's final regnal year, kingdoms chronologist could count back from Ahab's last year to Rehoboam's first year as king of Judah to identify the year when the kingdom of United Israel had divided into two kingdoms. That year was initially calculated to have been 930 BCE.

The result of being able to identify the year for the beginning of the divided kingdoms, combined with knowing their ending years (*circa* 722 BCE for Israel and *circa* 586 BCE for Judah), provided the time frame necessary for Bible scholars to begin making a serious attempt to harmonize the reigns of the Hebrew kings. Finally, the long-sought kingdoms chronology seemed to be within reach. Still, chronologists would have to wait almost a century before the next big advance in understanding—a credible system for harmonizing the reigns—was introduced.

Thiele's Mysterious Numbers

Edwin R. Thiele would be the person who would make that advance. Born in Chicago in 1895, he grew up in an age when men and women of letters and science still honored the Bible as a repository of wisdom and truth, and that attitude was reflected in his biblical studies and research. After graduating from Emmanuel Missionary College (later renamed Andrews University) with a Bachelor of Arts degree in ancient languages, Thiele served as a Seventh-day Adventist missionary to China for twelve years. In 1932, he returned to America to pursue advanced studies in graduate school at the University of Chicago. Five years later, in 1937, he received a Master of Arts degree, then proceeded to complete his doctoral work, being awarded a Doctor of Philosophy in Biblical Archaeology degree in 1943. His doctoral dissertation—finished sometime in 1942, the year of your author's birth—was published in book format in 1951 under the title *The Mysterious Numbers of the Hebrew Kings*.[1] Today, that book, updated and revised by Thiele over the course of thirty-two years and three editions, is widely accepted by many biblical and secular scholars as the definitive work on the chronology of the Hebrew kings.

---

[1] Edwin R. Thiele, *The Mysterious Numbers of the Hebrew Kings* (1st ed.; New York: Macmillan, 1951; 2d ed.; Grand Rapids: Eerdmans, 1965; 3rd ed.; Grand Rapids: Zondervan/Kregel, 1983).

Early in his academic career, Thiele became interested in finding a way to harmonize the reigns of the Hebrew kings. He began his research with knowledge of the general framework into which the reigns had to fit. The anchoring of the Assyrian reigns listed on the Assyrian Kings List accomplished by Rawlinson had allowed kingdoms chronologists to identify the year 931/930 BCE as the probable date for the start of the reigns of Rehoboam of Judah and Jeroboam of Israel. The Kings List had also allowed the identification of the year 722/721 BCE as the date for the fall of Samaria to Sargon II, the event which ended the northern kingdom of Israel. In addition, it had allowed scholars to align the chronology of the Neo-Babylonian Empire with that of the late Neo-Assyrian Empire, making it possible to identify the year 587/586 BCE as the date for the fall of Jerusalem to Nebuchadnezzar II of Babylon. So, by the time of Thiele's initial efforts to reconcile the reigns of the kings, the chronological framework into which they had to fit, give or take a year or so on either end, was well established by biblical scholars. The real challenge for Thiele, as it had been for all kingdoms chronologists in the years since Rawlinson's chronology had been published, became that of getting all of the reigns of the kings of Israel and the kings of Judah to line up as specified by the chronological cross-references given in the biblical text. Thus, the task of harmonizing the reigns is where Thiele focused his attention.

Thiele limited his research by using only the Masoretic text, recognizing from his own early struggles to harmonize the reigns of the kings that the differences in chronological data found in other source texts, such as the Septuagint, were probably nothing more than ancient attempts to do the same. He also made a deliberate attempt to distance himself from what he termed "certain preconceived opinions" held by kingdoms chronologists of his day, and instead to try to "ascertain just what the Hebrews did in the matter of chronological procedure." Over the course of his studies, Thiele tried to put himself into the mind of the ancient scribes, to think as they thought. By so doing, he was able to discern that the kingdoms of Israel and Judah had used different methods for recording their chronologies. One kingdom had used the accession-year system for counting its regnal years, the other had not. One had begun the year in Nisan, the first month of the Jewish year, while the other had begun its year in Tishri, the seventh month. Thiele hypothesized that both had used coregencies from time to time, although he did not always find support for his assumed coregencies in the biblical text. Additionally, he found that the years of rule in a coregency were sometimes counted in the total regnal years for a king, sometimes not. Over time, as he

Chapter One: About Kingdoms Chronology

refined his chronology by using his new insights, Thiele was able to show where the kingdoms scribes were inconsistent in the way they recorded details about their kings. But, despite the fact that his work was original and provided new insights about the reigns of the kings, Thiele ultimately chose to rely on a secular anchor—the date for the Bûr-Saggilê eclipse that had been determined by Rawlinson almost a century earlier—for anchoring his chronology in time.

When it was published, Edwin Thiele's harmonized chronology for the reigns of the Hebrew kings was generally applauded by secular scholars and religious professionals across academic and theological spectrums, but his system did come with an important caveat. Thiele himself, in the first paragraph of the concluding section of his book, offered the following assessment of his research and its results:

> "The vital question concerning the chronological scheme set forth in these pages is whether or not it is a true arrangement of reigns of Hebrew kings. Certainly, this system has brought harmony out of what was once regarded as hopeless confusion. But is it necessarily the true restoration of the original pattern of reigns? At the least this research shows that such a restoration is possible. However, we must accept the premise of an original reckoning of reigns in Israel according to the nonaccession-year system with a later shift to the accession-year method; of the early use in Judah of accession-year reckoning, a shift to the nonaccession-year system, and then a return to the original accession-year method; of the need to begin the regnal year in Israel with Nisan and with Tishri in Judah; of the existence of a number of coregencies; ***and of the fact that at some late date—long after the original records of the kings had been set in order and when the true arrangement of the reigns had been forgotten—certain synchronizations in 2 Kings 17 and 18 were introduced by some late hand twelve years out of harmony with the original pattern of reigns***. When all of this is understood, we see that it may be possible to set forth an arrangement of reigns for the Hebrew kings in which there are both internal harmony and agreement with contemporary history" (*Mysterious Numbers*, 1983 edition, p. 205; emphasis added).

Today, anyone familiar with the field of kingdoms chronology will agree that Thiele did a masterful job of harmonizing the reigns of the Hebrew kings, of bringing harmony out of confusion. Time has shown that most of the harmonization principles he stated above are valid. Yet, Thiele himself revealed the one glaring weakness of his system, the requirement that a portion of the biblical text be disregarded as unreliable. In the final analysis, Thiele found that he had to ignore chronological details in 2 Kings, chapters 17 and 18, to allow his system to fully harmonize and thus be considered true. The decision to ignore portions of the biblical text was a serious compromise on his part. Furthermore, it was unnecessary. The reigns of the Hebrew kings can be harmonized without having to forsake any of the chronological details preserved in the Bible. The remainder of this book will be devoted to demonstrating how just such a harmonized kingdoms chronology can be achieved and used.

Key dates in the chronologies published by respected kingdoms chronologists				
Name of Chronologist	Published	Kingdoms Divide	Fall of Samaria	Fall of Jerusalem
Orthodox Judaism[1]	---	794 BCE	none	420 BCE
James Ussher (d. 1656)[2]	1650	975 BCE	722/721 BCE	588 BCE
W. F. Albright (d. 1971)[3]	1953	922 BCE	721 BCE	587 BCE
Edwin R. Thiele (d. 1986)[4]	1983	930 BCE	723/722 BCE	586 BCE
John Hayes and Paul Hooker[5]	1988	927/926 BCE	722 BCE	586 BCE
Jeremy Hughes[6]	1990	937 BCE	724 BCE	587 BCE
Gershon Galil[7]	1996	931/930 BCE	722 BCE	586 BCE
John Rogerson[8]	1999	931 BCE	722/721 BCE	587 BCE
M. Christine Tetley[9]	2005	981 BCE	719 BCE	---
Rodger C. Young[10]	2005	932/931 BCE	723 BCE	588 BCE
Floyd Nolen Jones[11]	2007	975 BCE	721 BCE	586 BCE
Leslie McFall[12]	2008	931 BCE	723 BCE	586 BCE

[1] Orthodox Judaism bases it chronology on chronological references in *Seder Olam Rabbah* (2nd century CE).
[2] James Ussher, *Annals of the World* (London, 1650) [updated and republished as, *Annals of the World: James Ussher's Classic Survey of World History*; ed. Larry and Marion Pierce, Green Forest, Arkansas: Master Books, 2003].
[3] W. F. Albright, "The Chronology of the Divided Monarchy of Israel" (Bulletin of the American Schools of Oriental Research, No. 100, 1945; p. 16-22); "New Light from Egypt on the Chronology and History of Israel and Judah" (Bulletin of the American Schools of Oriental Research, No. 130, 1953; p. 4-11).
[4] Edwin R. Thiele, *The Mysterious Numbers of the Hebrew Kings*. 3rd edition (Grand Rapids, Michigan: Zondervan, 1983) [reprinted: Grand Rapids, Michigan: Kregel, 1994; first edition, 1951].
[5] John H. Hayes and Paul K. Hooker, *A New Chronology for the Kings of Israel and Judah and Its Implications for Biblical History and Literature* (Atlanta: John Knox Press, 1988) [reprinted: Eugene, Oregon: Wipf and Stock, 2007].
[6] Jeremy Hughes, *Secrets of the Times: Myth and History in Biblical Chronology* (Journal for the Study of the Old Testament Supplement Series, No. 66; Sheffield: Journal for the Study of the Old Testament Press, 1990) [reprinted: Library of the Hebrew Bible/Old Testament Studies; London: Continuum, 2009].
[7] John Rogerson, *Chronicle of the Old Testament Kings: The Reign-by-Reign Record of the Rulers of Ancient Israel* (London: Thames & Hudson, 1999).
[8] Gershon Galil, *The Chronology of the Kings of Israel and Judah* (Studies in the History and Culture of the Ancient Near East, 9; Leiden: E.J. Brill, 1996).
[9] M. Christine Tetley, *The Reconstructed Chronology of the Divided Kingdom* (Winona Lake: Eisenbrauns, 2005).
[10] Rodger C. Young, "Tables of Reign Lengths from the Hebrew Court Recorders" (Journal of the Evangelical Theological Seminary 48/2; June, 2005; p. 225–48).
[11] Floyd Nolen Jones, *The Chronology of the Old Testament* (Green Forest, Arkansas: Master Books, 2007).
[12] Leslie McFall, "Chronology of the Hebrew Kings" (2008, published online at http://www.btinternet.com/~lmf12/HEBREW_REVISED_KINGS.pdf).

CHAPTER TWO

A New Kingdoms Chronology

The greatest obstacle to achieving a harmonized chronology for the reigns of the kings of Israel and Judah has always been that of identifying the year that the kingdom of United Israel divided into two separate kingdoms. Without that vital piece of information, no time frame can be defined into which the reigns of the Hebrew kings will precisely fit. In 1867, when Sir Henry Rawlinson identified the year of the Bûr-Saggilê eclipse as 763 BCE, thus anchoring the reigns of the kings of the Neo-Assyrian Empire in time, the obstacle seemed to be have been removed. Scholars were able to use that Assyrian alignment to cross-date the reign of Ahab of Israel with the sixth year of Shalmaneser III and calculate the date of Ahab's death as the year 853 BCE. Counting back the number of regnal years specified in the Bible for each of the kings of Judah who preceded Ahab, chronologists were then able to calculate that the year 930 BCE was the first year in the reign of Rehoboam, and thus the year the united kingdom divided.[1]

Once 930 BCE had been identified as the first year in the reign of Rehoboam of Judah, that date seemed to synchronize with Egyptian history. In the decades since Champollion, Egyptologists had determined that Shoshenq I invaded Canaan *circa* 925 BCE, an event coinciding with the fifth year of Rehoboam as calculated using Rawlinson's chronology. Since Champollion had decades earlier identified Shoshenq I as the biblical Shishak, the pharaoh who came against Jerusalem and took the Temple treasures in the fifth year of Rehoboam, the various chronological pieces seemed to be synchronizing nicely. A century later, when Thiele began developing his chronology for the Hebrew kings, he based his work on the foundation laid by Rawlinson and Champollion and others, and ended up making his chronology fit into the time frame that had been established by Assyriology and confirmed by Egyptology. In essence, Thiele made his "mysterious numbers" agree with the secular scholarship of his day. To do so, he had to postulate scribal emendations to the original biblical text. In the sixty-plus years since Thiele introduced his chronology, that compromise approach, which forced the chronology of the Bible to conform to secular chronology, thus calling into question the accuracy of the biblical text, has prevailed in scholarly circles. However, that secular-based approach is no longer necessary.

---

[1] Most reference Bibles published in recent years use 931 BCE as the first year of Rehoboam.

In 2008, your author, while putting the finishing touches on a commentary expounding the chrono-specific predictive prophecies in the Book of Daniel, discovered a Bible-based way to identify the year that the kingdoms of Israel and Judah began functioning as separate kingdoms. The information was sequestered in Daniel, chapter 4, and it allowed the development of a sacred chronology that depended on chronological details given only in the biblical text. For the first time, sacred chronology was freed from reliance on either Assyrian or Egyptian chronology for anchoring the reigns of the Hebrew kings. Additionally, exact harmonization of the reigns of the kings could be achieved without having to disregard any of the biblical text. A complete explanation of the prophecies in Daniel is set forth in the book, *Daniel Unsealed*,[1] and includes a full exposition of the the fourth chapter of Daniel, a chapter that can be used to identify with precision the date that the kingdom of Unified Israel was rent from Rehoboam. A synopsis of that exposition is recounted in the section that follows.

Anchoring the Kings in History

The Book of Daniel contains seven chrono-specific predictive prophecies that were revealed to the prophet Daniel in Babylon prior to the return of the Jews to Jerusalem *circa* 536 BCE. At the time they were revealed, the prophecies were meant to explain to the returning Jewish remnant exactly what would happen to their descendants in the future. The fourth chapter of Daniel contains an allegorical prophecy about a great tree, which represents Israel.[2] In the allegory, a kingdom is rent from an allegorical king. In order to identify the real-life king and the date of the rending of the kingdom from him, one must employ chronological information from several of the prophecies recorded in Daniel. Before applying the chronology from those chapters, though, let us start by examining the allegory itself, which is recorded in chapter 4, verses 10-16:

> *"Thus were the visions of mine* [the allegorical king's] *head in my bed; I saw, and behold a tree in the midst of the earth, and the height thereof was great. The tree*

---

[1] Dan Bruce, *Daniel Unsealed* (The Prophecy Society, 2013); latest edition available as a print-on-demand book from CreateSpace at https://www.createspace.com/4288792.

[2] The allegorical symbolism of the tree and chronological intent of Daniel's vision becomes clear by recalling the words of the prophet Isaiah *"... for as the days of a tree are the days of my people ..."* (Isaiah 65:22b; KJV).

grew, and was strong, and the height thereof reached unto heaven, and the sight thereof to the end of all the earth: The leaves thereof were fair, and the fruit thereof much, and in it was meat for all: the beasts of the field had shadow under it, and the fowls of the heaven dwelt in the boughs thereof, and all flesh was fed of it. I saw in the visions of my head upon my bed, and, behold, a watcher and an holy one came down from heaven; He cried aloud, and said thus, Hew down the tree, and cut off his branches, shake off his leaves, and scatter his fruit: let the beasts get away from under it, and the fowls from his branches: Nevertheless leave the stump of his roots in the earth, even with a band of iron and brass, in the tender grass of the field; and let it be wet with the dew of heaven, and let his portion be with the beasts in the grass of the earth: Let his heart be changed from man's, and let a beast's heart be given unto him; and let seven times pass over him" (KJV).

Then, in verses 20-33, which are quoted below in truncated form with pertinent chronological information shown in bold italics, the interpretation of the allegorical king's dream is given to the him by an allegorical Daniel:

"The tree that thou sawest ... It is thou, O king ... This is the interpretation, O king ... they shall drive thee from men, and thy dwelling shall be with the beasts of the field, and they shall make thee to eat grass as oxen, and they shall wet thee with the dew of heaven, and **seven times shall pass over thee***, till thou know that the most High ruleth in the kingdom of men, and giveth it to whomsoever he will. And whereas they commanded to leave the stump of the tree roots; thy kingdom shall be sure unto thee, after that thou shalt have known that the heavens do rule ... All this came upon the king Nebuchadnezzar.* **At the end of twelve months** *he walked in the palace of the kingdom of Babylon. The king spake, and said, Is not this great Babylon, that I have built for the house of the kingdom by the might of my power, and for the honour of my majesty? While the word was in the king's mouth, there fell voice from heaven, saying, O king Nebuchadnezzar, to thee it is spoken;* **The kingdom is departed from thee.** *And they shall drive thee from men, and thy dwelling shall be with the beasts of the field: they shall make thee to eat grass as oxen, and* **seven times shall pass over thee***, until thou know that the most High ruleth in the kingdom of men, and giveth it to whomsoever he will. The same hour was the thing fulfilled upon Nebuchadnezzar: and he was driven from men, and did eat grass as oxen, and his body was wet with the dew of heaven, till his hairs were grown like eagles' feathers, and his nails like birds' claws"* (KJV).

In the allegory, there are three pieces of chronological information that provide a timeline of events. The first states that the king, called Nebuchadnezzar in the allegory, has been walking in the palace for twelve months. The second states that the kingdom is taken from him at the end of the twelve months. The third states that seven times are decreed to pass over him while he is banished to live among the beasts of the field and birds of the air. Applying that to the actual history of the Jewish people, it takes no great feat of interpretation to discern that the initial events of the allegory are looking back from the time of the exile to the events associated with the judgement of God that resulted in the rending of the kingdom of United Israel from Rehoboam, as described in 1 Kings, chapter 12. It is also easy to see from our viewpoint today that the later events of the allegory are referring to the repeated dispersals of a disloyal Jewish nation—the kingdom people—among the peoples of the non-Hebrew nations, which are represented allegorically by the beasts of the field and the birds of the air. It is also apparent from the allegory that the real king who had his kingdom rent, Rehoboam, was required to have been king for twelve full months before the kingdom was rent from him and the "seven times" of judgement on Israel began.

Understanding the meaning of the cryptic phrase "seven times" is the key to identifying the date of the rending of the kingdom from Rehoboam. Traditional expositions of the fourth chapter of Daniel tends to incorrectly interpret the "seven times" as seven years, and equate the Nebuchadnezzar in the allegory with the historical Babylonian king, Nebuchadnezzar II, who is supposed to have gone mad and dwelt among the beasts of the field and birds of the air for the postulated seven-year period. However, there is no historical record of the real Nebuchadnezzar or any of his successors going mad and acting in such a manner, and there is certainly no evidence that a real-life Babylonian king ever worshipped the God of Israel, as required by verses 34-37. Instead, the "seven times" are best understood as a chrono-specific prophecy about the history of the Jewish people. The correct way to interpret the word "time" and the phrase "seven times" is fully explained in *Daniel Unsealed*,[1] but will be briefly recounted here using Timeline 2.1 on the opposite page.

The Hebrew word "time" מוֹעֵד (BHS, Strong's OT: 4150), when used as a chronological unit as it is in Daniel, chapter 12, verse 7, "… *it shall be for a time, times, and an half*" (KJV), means 228 Passovers. Thus, the 3½ "times" (shown

---

[1] Bruce, *Daniel Unsealed*, Chapter Three, p. 33-40.

Chapter Two: A New Kingdoms Chronology

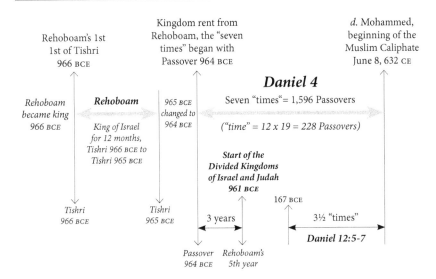

Timeline 2.1 - The Chronology of Daniel 4

on Timeline 2.1 above) is a time period containing (3½ x 228 =) 798 Passovers. The interpretation of the twelfth chapter of Daniel, using that formula, demonstrates that the period of 798 Passovers began with the desecration of the Temple by the Seleucid king Antiochus IV in 167 BCE and ended with the death of the self-proclaimed prophet Mohammed and start of the Muslim Caliphate in 632 CE (all three events are important as chronological end points in this discussion). The period of "seven times" specified in Daniel, chapter 4, is assumed to be contiguous with the period of 3½ "times" in Daniel, chapter 12, thus sharing the same ending date, 632 CE. Calculating back "seven times" (7 x 228 =) 1,596 Passovers from 632 CE, the date the kingdom was rent from Rehoboam is revealed to be Passover, 964 BCE. The biblical text, in 2 Chronicles, chapters 11-12, records that Rehoboam struggled for three years to reunify the kingdom after the rending, but that in his fifth year as king of Israel, Shishak of Egypt invaded Jerusalem. It was at that time that the separate kingdoms were made permanent, identifying the year 961 BCE as the date for the start of reigns of the kings of Israel and Judah in history (see pages 52-56). On pages 18-28 that follow, a harmonized chronology for the kings of Israel and Judah is displayed, using, instead of the traditional 931/930 BCE date as the starting year for the divided kingdoms, the year 961 BCE. As you will see, the reigns harmonize precisely by using the time frame defined by that date.

Chronological References for the Kings of Israel and Judah

King (I = Israel, J = Judah)	1 and 2 Kings	2 Chronicles	Prophets
I - Jeroboam	1 Kings 14:20	none	none
J - Rehoboam	1 Kings 14:21	2 Chronicles 12:13	Daniel 4
J - Abijah	1 Kings 15:1-2	2 Chronicles 13:1-2	none
J - Asa	1 Kings 15:9-10	none	none
I - Nadab	1 Kings 15:25	none	none
I - Baasha	1 Kings 15:33	none	none
I - Elah	1 Kings 16:8	none	none
I - Zimri	1 Kings 16:15	none	none
I - Omri	1 Kings 16:16, 23	none	none
I - Ahab	1 Kings 16:29	none	none
J - Jehoshaphat	1 Kings 22:41-42	none	none
I - Ahaziah	1 Kings 22:52	none	none
I - Joram	2 Kings 1:17	none	none
J - Jehoram	2 Kings 8:16-17	2 Chronicles 21:20	none
J - Ahaziah	2 Kings 8:25-26	2 Chronicles 22:2	none
I - Jehu	2 Kings 10:36	none	none
J - Athaliah	2 Kings 11:13	none	none
J - Joash	2 Kings 12:1-2	2 Chronicles 24:1	none
I - Jehoahaz	2 Kings 13:1	none	none
I - Jehoash	2 Kings 13:10	none	none
J - Amaziah	2 Kings 14:1-2	2 Chronicles 25:1	none
I - Jeroboam II	2 Kings 14:23	none	Amos 1:1
J - Uzziah	2 Kings 15:1-2	2 Chronicles 26:3	Amos 1:1
I - Zachariah	2 Kings 15:8	none	none
I - Shallum	2 Kings 15: 13	none	none
I - Menahem	2 Kings 15:17	none	none
I - Pekah	2 Kings 15:23	none	none
I - Pekahiah	2 Kings 15:27	none	none
J - Jotham	2 Kings 15:32-33	2 Chronicles 27:1	none
J - Ahaz	2 Kings 16:1-2	2 Chronicles 28:1	none
I - Hoshea	2 Kings 15:30, 17:1	none	none
J - Hezekiah	2 Kings 18:2,13	2 Chronicles 29:1	Isaiah 36:1
J - Manasseh	2 Kings 21:1	2 Chronicles 33:1	none
J - Amon	2 Kings 21:19	2 Chronicles 33:21	none
J - Josiah	2 Kings 22:1	none	none
J - Jehoahaz	2 Kings 23:31	2 Chronicles 36:2	none
J - Jehoiakim	2 Kings 23:36	2 Chronicles 36:5	none
J - Jehoiachin	2 Kings 24:8	2 Chronicles 36:9	none
J - Zedekiah	2 Kings 24:18, 25:8	2 Chronicles 36:11	Jeremiah 52:12

Chapter Two: A New Kingdoms Chronology

The Kingdoms Harmonized

The kingdom of United Israel divided into the separate kingdoms of Israel and Judah in 961 BCE. The reigns of the kings of the two kingdoms can be harmonized with one another by using the details about the reigns provided in the Books of 1 and 2 Kings, 2 Chronicles, and the prophets by assuming that the following accounting practices were employed by the ancient kingdoms scribes:

1) The kingdom of Israel used regnal years that began on the 1st of Nisan (the first month), and the portion of a king's reign occurring before his initial 1st of Nisan was counted as Year One in his reign (the non-accession-year system).

2) The kingdom of Judah used regnal years that began on the 1st of Tishri (the seventh month), and the portion of a king's reign occurring before his initial 1st of Tishri was not counted as a numbered year in the king's reign but was considered to be an unnumbered accession year (the accession-year system).

3) In both kingdoms there were instances in which a king and his successor coreigned. The years in the successor king's coreign were sometimes included in the total years recorded for his reign, but sometimes not.

4) The kingdom of Israel experienced periods in which two claimants for the throne controlled separate parts of the kingdom of Israel at the same time.

5) The kingdom of Israel switched to the accession-year system after 768 BCE, but omitted an accession year in the reign of Pekah since he was a rival king already ruling from Gilead when he usurped the throne in Samaria.

6) The kingdom of Judah sometimes omitted counting an accession year if there was a less-than-smooth transition from the reign of one king to another.

Fortunately, there is only one way that the reigns will harmonize if none of the biblical data is disregarded or considered inaccurate, so scribal methodologies and idiosyncrasies can be discerned in the process of harmonizing them.

On pages 21-29, the reigns of the thirty-eight kings (and one queen) of the period of the divided kingdoms are shown harmonized and displayed side-by-side for comparison. In addition to the harmonized chronology provided in this chapter, the chronology pertaining to each Hebrew king is discussed in detail in the three chapters that follow this chapter. Chapter Three, beginning on page 41, discusses the kings in the kingdom of United Israel. Chapter Four, beginning on page 51, discusses the kings in the period of the divided kingdoms of Israel and Judah. Chapter Five, beginning on page 83, discusses the kings in the kingdom of Judah after the fall of Samaria and the end of the kingdom of Israel.

Chronology of the Kings of Israel and Judah

King (I = Israel, J = Judah)	Regnal Years	Reigned for ...	Synchronization (reign began in ...)
I - Jeroboam	961-940 BCE	22 years	5th year of Rehoboam as king of United Israel
J - Rehoboam	961-944 BCE	17 years	5th year of Rehoboam as king of United Israel
J - Abijah	944-942 BCE	3 years	18th year of Jeroboam
J - Asa	942-900 BCE	41 years	20th year of Jeroboam
I - Nadab	940-939 BCE	2 years	2nd year of Asa
I - Baasha	939-916 BCE	24 years	3rd year of Asa
I - Elah	916-914 BCE	2 years	26th year of Asa
I - Zimri	914 BCE	7 days	27th year of Asa
I - Omri	914-904 BCE	12 years	27th year of Asa
I - Ahab	904-883 BCE	22 years	38th year of Asa
J - Jehoshaphat	900-875 BCE	25 years	4th year of Ahab
I - Ahaziah	883-882 BCE	2 years	17th year of Jehoshaphat
I - Joram	882/879-867 BCE	12 years	18th year of Jehoshaphat (*Jehoram of Judah served as his regent for first two years*)
J - Jehoram	875-868 BCE	8 years	5th year of Joram
J - Ahaziah	868-867 BCE	1 year	11th year of Joram (*or 12th year of Joram using a non-accession year system*)
I - Jehu	867-840 BCE	28 years	probably anointed as king in Gilead in 868 BCE
J - Athaliah	867-861 BCE	6 years	usurped throne after death of Ahaziah
J - Joash	861-822 BCE	40 years	7th year of Jehu
I - Jehoahaz	840-824 BCE	17 years	23rd year of Joash
I - Jehoash	825/824-808 BCE	16 years	37th year of Joash
J - Amaziah	822-794 BCE	29 years	2nd year of Jehoash
I - Jeroboam II	808-768 BCE	41 years	15th year of Amaziah
J - Uzziah	805/794-754 BCE	52 years	27th year of Jeroboam II (*or when Uzziah was 27 years old during the reign of Jeroboam II*)
I - Zachariah	768 BCE	6 months	38th year of Uzziah (Azariah)
I - Shallum	767 BCE	1 month	39th year of Uzziah (Azariah)
I - Menahem	767-757 BCE	10 years	39th year of Uzziah (Azariah)
I - Pekah	758/757-738 BCE	2 years	52nd year of Uzziah (Azariah)
I - Pekahiah	757-755 BCE	20 years	50th year of Uzziah (Azariah)
J - Jotham	757/754-738 BCE	16 years	2nd year of Pekah
J - Ahaz	742-727 BCE	16 years	17th year of Pekah
I - Hoshea	731-721 BCE	9 years	12th year of Ahaz
J - Hezekiah	727-698 BCE	29 years	3rd year of Hoshea
J - Manasseh	698-643 BCE	55 years	none
J - Amon	643-641 BCE	2 years	none
J - Josiah	640-609 BCE	31 years	none
J - Jehoahaz	609 BCE	3 months	none
J - Jehoiakim	609-598 BCE	11 years	none
J - Jehoiachin	598-597 BCE	3 months	none
J - Zedekiah	597-586 BCE	11 years	reign ended in 19th year of Nebuchadnezzar II

Chapter Two: A New Kingdoms Chronology

Kings of Israel and Judah, 966-930 BCE

(years shown in center column are proleptic Gregorian years; A = accession or partial year; sabbath years in bold type)

Kingdom of Israel (after 961 BCE) (regnal years counted Nisan to Nisan)	START HERE YEAR BCE	United Kingdom (966-961 BCE) Kingdom of Judah (after 961 BCE) (regnal years counted Tishri to Tishri)
Rehoboam rejected as king by northern ten tribes; three years of realignment begin →	--- 966 --- 965 --- 964 --- 963 --- 962	A ← ♛ **Rehoboam** (966-961) *see page 50* 1st 2nd ← *Kingdom rent from Rehoboam* 3rd 1st yr. *in 964 BCE, Levites and priests* 4th 2nd yr. *moved to Judah, Judah secured* 5th 3rd yr. *for the next three years* [1]
♛ **Jeroboam** (961-940) → 1st yr. 1st *see page 52* 2nd yr. 2nd	961 **960**	1st ♛ **Rehoboam** (961-944) 2nd *see page 52*
3rd yr. 3rd	959	3rd *Kingdoms are divided after*
4th yr. 4th	958	4th *Shishak (the future pharaoh*
5th yr. 5th	957	5th *Shoshenq I commanding the*
6th yr. 6th	956	6th *army of pharaoh Siamun)*
7th yr. 7th	955	7th *campaigns in the 5th year*
8th yr. 8th	954	8th *of Rehoboam, establishes*
9th yr. 9th	**953**	9th *Jeroboam as king of Israel,*
10th yr. 10th	952	10th *Rehoboam remains King of*
11th yr. 11th	951	11th *Judah and probably becomes*
12th yr. 12th	950	12th *a vassal of Egypt* [2]
13th yr. 13th	949	13th
14th yr. 14th	948	14th [1] See 2 Chronicles 11:16-17
15th yr. 15th	947	15th [2] See 2 Chronicles 12:1-2
16th yr. 16th	**946**	16th
17th yr. 17th	945	17th/A ← ♛ **Abijah** (944-942) *see page 57*
18th yr. 18th	**944**	1st
19th yr. 19th	943	2nd
20th yr. 20th	942	3rd/A ← ♛ **Asa** (942-900) *see page 58*
21st yr. 21st	941	1st
♛ **Nadab** (940-939) 22nd yr. 22nd/1st	940	2nd
see page 61 →		
♛ **Baasha** (939-916) 23rd yr. 2nd/1st	**939**	3rd
see page 61		
24th yr. 2nd	938	4th ← *During 942-937 BCE, Asa*
25th yr. 3rd	937	5th 1st yr. *purified the land and fortified*
26th yr. 4th	936	6th 2nd yr. *Judah, which was granted ten*
27th yr. 5th	935	7th 3rd yr. *years of rest from the threat*
28th yr. 6th	934	8th 4th yr. *of war until 926 BCE when*
29th yr. 7th	933	9th 5th yr. *Zerah the Ethiopian, leading*
30th yr. 8th	**932**	10th 6th yr. *an Egyptian army of pharaoh*
31st yr. 9th	931	11th 7th yr. *Sheshonq I, attacked Asa and*
32nd yr. 10th	930	*Judah from the south*

Kings of Israel and Judah, 929-893 BCE

(years shown in center column are proleptic Gregorian years; A = accession or partial year; sabbath years in bold type)

Kingdom of Israel
(regnal years counted Nisan to Nisan)

Kingdom of Judah
(regnal years counted Tishri to Tishri)

Israel notes	Israel regnal		YEAR BCE	Judah regnal		Judah notes
Baasha (cont.)	33rd yr.	11th	929	12th	8th yr.	Asa (cont.)
Baasha attacked Judah and fortified Ramah in the 36th year after the kingdoms were divided [1]	34th yr.	12th	928	13th	9th yr.	
	35th yr.	13th	927	14th	10th yr.	
	36th yr.	14th	926	15th		← Asa repelled attack by Zerah [2]
		15th	**925**	16th		[2] Ethiopians and Lubims led by Zerah attack Judah in the thirty-sixth year after the kingdoms divided, Asa defeats Zerah, then celebrates victory in Jerusalem in his fifteenth regnal year, swears an oath to be obedient to God; see 2 Chronicles 15:9-15.
[1] It was impossible for Baasha to have attacked Judah in the thirty-sixth year of Asa since Baasha died in Asa's twenty-sixth regnal year; see 1 Kings 16:7-8.		16th	924	17th		
		17th	923	18th		
		18th	922	19th		
		19th	921	20th		
		20th	920	21st		
		21st	919	22nd		Baasha blockaded Judah in the thirty-sixth year after the kingdoms divided, Asa bribed Benhadad I of Syria to attack Baasha, causing Shoshenq I to invade [4]
♛ Zimri (914) for 7 days see page 62		22nd	**918**	23rd		
		23rd	917	24th		
♛ Elah (916-914) see page 62		24th/1st	916	25th		
		2nd/A/1st	915	26th		
♛ Omri (914-904) see page 63		2nd	914	27th		[4] The invasion by Shoshenq I of Egypt in 925 BCE, as recorded on a temple wall at Karnak, is usually equated with the invasion of the Bible's Shishak of Egypt during the fifth regnal year of Rehoboam, but chronologically it is better explained as a move by Shoshenq to aid his ally Baasha of Israel, who attacked Judah in 925 BCE but was then attacked by Benhadad I of Syria after Asa appealed for help; Shoshenq's army bypassed the southern kingdom to move into the Jordan valley and then into the cities of the north to counter the move south into Isreal by Ben-Haddad (see 1 Kings 15; also see discussions on page 35-40).
		3rd	913	28th		
		4th	912	29th		
Omri defeated Tibni, became sole ruler in 31st year of Asa [3]		5th	**911**	30th		
		6th	910	31st		
		7th	909	32nd		
Omri began his rule from Samaria in 909 BCE, during the 33rd year of Asa, reigned there for ~ 6 years		8th	908	33rd		
		9th	907	34th		
		10th	906	35th		
		11th	905	36th		
♛ Ahab (904-883) see page 64		12th/1st	**904**	37th		
		2nd	903	38th		
		3rd	902	39th		← Asa diseased in his feet
[3] The Seder Olam says that the struggle between Omri and Tibni for sole rule of the northern kingdom of Israel was resolved in favor of Omri after four years.		4th	901	40th		
		5th	900	41st/A		← ♛ Jehoshaphat (900-875) see page 66
		6th	899	1st		
		7th	898	2nd		
		8th	**897**	3rd		← In his 3rd year, Jehoshaphat sent officials and priests to the cities of Judah for a public reading of the Law, indicating a sabbath year beginning in Nisan of the year 897 BCE (see 2 Chronicles 17:7-9)
		9th	896	4th		
		10th	895	5th		
		11th	894	6th		
		12th	893	7th		

Kings of Israel and Judah, 892-856 BCE

(years shown in center column are proleptic Gregorian years; A = accession or partial year; sabbath years in bold type)

Kingdom of Israel
(regnal years counted Nisan to Nisan)

Kingdom of Judah
(regnal years counted Tishri to Tishri)

Israel		YEAR BCE		Judah
Ahab (cont.)	13th[1]	892	8th	Jehoshaphat (cont.)
	famine 14th	891	9th	
[1] The *Seder Olam* says that a three-year famine began in Ahab's thirteenth year, followed by two-plus years of war with Benhadad II, followed by three years of peace, followed by the war against Ramoth-gilead.	famine 15th	**890**	10th	
	famine 16th	889	11th	Shalmaneser III (889-854?)
	war 17th	888	12th	1st — BATTLE OF QARQAR
	war 18th	887	13th	2nd — The Battle of Qarqar occurred in the summer of 883 BCE; an account is recorded on the Kurkh Monolith, which mentions Ahab as being a participant, although the Bible says that Ahab was wounded and died after a Battle at Ramoth-gilead in 883 BCE (see discussion of the life and reign of Ahab on page 64).
	peace 19th	886	14th	3rd
	peace 20th	885	15th	4th
♛ **Ahaziah** (883-882) *see page 64*	peace 21st	884	16th	5th
	22nd/1st	**883**	17th	6th
♛ **Joram**[2] (882/879-867) *see page 67*	2nd / R	882	18th	7th
♕ **Jehoram of Judah** (R = regent) *see page 67*	R	881	19th	8th — Elijah the prophet died in the nineteenth year of Jehoshaphat according to the *Seder Olam*.
	R	880	20th	9th
♛ **Joram** rules Israel as king (no regent), *see page 67*	R	879	21st	10th
	A 1st	878	22nd	11th
	1st 2nd	877	23rd	12th
	2nd 3rd	876	24th	13th
[2] Joram was apparently not of age to rule when Ahaziah died, so Jehoram of Judah, who was married to Ahab's daughter and Ahaziah's sister Athaliah, served as his regent for two-plus years.	3rd 4th	**876**	25th/A	14th ← ♛ **Jehoram** (875-868) *see page 67*
	4th 5th	875	1st	15th
	5th 6th	874	2nd	16th
	6th 7th	873	3rd	17th
	7th 8th	872	4th	18th ← — BLACK OBELISK
	8th 9th	871	5th	19th — The obelisk shows Jehu bowing and paying tribute to Shalmaneser III in his eighteenth regnal year, 871 BCE.
	9th 10th	870	6th	
	10th 11th	**869**	7th	
	11th 12th	868	8th/A/(1st) ←	♛ **Ahaziah** (868-867)[4] *see page 70*
♛ **Jehu** (867-840)[3] *see page 70*	1st	867	(2nd)	♕ **Athaliah** (867-861) usurped throne in same year Ahaziah was killed, *see page 72*
	2nd	866	(3rd)	
	3rd	865	(4th)	
[3] Jehu, a captain in Israel's army, was sent by Joram to pay tribute to Shalmaneser III's eighteenth year, 871 BCE (tribute payment is recorded on the Black Obelisk but is not mentioned in the Bible); then, in 867 BCE, Jehu was anointed as king by a prophet sent from Elisha (2 Kings, 9-10), and was thereafter recognized as king of Israel by the army in Ramoth-gilead; he then traveled to Jezreel to kill Joram of Israel and Ahaziah of Judah; Jehu's regnal years are counted from the time he began to reign from Samaria as king in 867 BCE.	4th	864	(5th)	
	5th	863	(6th)	
	6th	**862**	1st (no AY) ←	♛ **Joash** (861-822) *see page 73*
	7th	861	2nd	
	8th	860	3rd	[4] Ahaziah became king in the twelfth year of Joram when using the non-accession year counting in Israel, or in the eleventh year of Joram when using the accession-year counting of Judah; the Bible has instances of both for the reign of Ahaziah.
	9th	859	4th	
	10th	858	5th	
	11th	857	6th	
	12th	856		

– 23 –

Kings of Israel and Judah, 855-819 BCE

(years shown in center column are proleptic Gregorian years; A = accession or partial year; sabbath years in bold type)

Kingdom of Israel (regnal years counted Nisan to Nisan)	Israel Year	YEAR BCE	Judah Year	Kingdom of Judah (regnal years counted Tishri to Tishri)
Jehu (cont.)	13th	855	7th	Joash (cont.)
	14th	854	8th	
	15th	853	9th	
	16th	852	10th	
	17th	851	11th	
	18th	850	12th	
	19th	849	13th	
	20th	**848**	14th	
	21st	847	15th	
	22nd	846	16th	
	23rd	845	17th	
	24th	844	18th	
	25th	843	19th	
	26th	842	20th	
	27th	**841**	21st	
♛ Jehoahaz (840-824) → see page 74	28th/1st	840	22nd	
			23rd	← Joash began renovating the Temple in his 23rd year [2]
	2nd	839	24th	
	3rd	838	25th	
	4th	837	26th	
	5th	836	27th	
	6th	835	28th	
	7th	**834**	29th	
	8th	833	30th	
	9th	832	31st	
	10th	831	32nd	
	11th	830	33rd	
	12th	829	34th	
	13th	828	35th	
	14th	**827**	36th	
	15th	826	37th	
♛ Jehoash (825/824-808) [1] → began two-year coreign in the 37th year of Joash, became sole ruler in the year 824 BCE (and his regnal years are counted from that year), see page 74	16th/(1st)	825	38th	
	17th/(2nd)	824	39th	
	1st	823		
	2nd	822	40th/A	← ♛ Amaziah (822-794) see page 75
	3rd	821	1st	
	4th	**820**	2nd	
	5th	819	3rd	

[1] Jehoash coreigned with his father for two years, according to the *Seder Olam*. When Adad-nirari III of Assyria resumed his western campaigns in Syria in 827 BCE, the power of Syria was weakened, so Jehoash was able to free Israel from Syrian control in 824 BCE, coinciding with Adad-nirari's campaign against Manṣuate in the Lebanon valley (*Massyas* according to Strabo 16:2, 18); at that time, the king of Assyria also attacked Damascus, defeated the Syrian armies, and exacted a heavy tribute from Benhadad III, the king of Syria. - *adapted from the online article titled "Jehoash" at www.jewishvirtuallibrary.org*; also, see 2 Kings 13:5; payment of tribute to Adad-nirari III by Jehoash recorded on the Tel-al-Rimah Stele discovered in 1967.

[2] The *Seder Olam* records that Joash began renovating the Temple during his twenty-third regnal year, 155 years after Solomon completed the Temple in 996 BCE, and 218 years before Josiah began renovating the Temple in his eighteenth regnal year, which began in 623 BCE.

Kings of Israel and Judah, 818-782 BCE

(years shown in center column are proleptic Gregorian years; A = accession or partial year; sabbath years in bold type)

Kingdom of Israel *(regnal years counted Nisan to Nisan)*	Israel yr	YEAR BCE	Judah yr	Kingdom of Judah *(regnal years counted Tishri to Tishri)*
Jehoash (cont.)	6th	818	4th	Amaziah (cont.)
	7th	817	5th	
	8th	816	6th	
Elisha the prophet died in the tenth year of Jehoash of Israel according to the *Seder Olam*. --->	9th	815	7th	
	10th	814	8th	
	11th	**813**	9th	
	12th	812	10th	
	13th	811	11th	
	14th	810	12th	
	15th	809	13th	
♛ **Jeroboam II (808-768)** --->	16th/1st	808	14th	
see page 76	2nd	807	15th	
	3rd	**806**	16th	
	4th	805	(17th)/1st — 16 yo.	<--- Uzziah 16 years old, began serving as king in his father's place after Amaziah had fled to Lachish (see 2 Chronicles 25:27)
	5th	804	(18th)/2nd — 17 yo.	
	6th	803	(19th)/3rd — 18 yo.	
	7th	802	(20th)/4th — 19 yo.	
	8th	801	(21st)/5th — 20 yo.	
	9th	800	(22nd)/6th — 21 yo.	
	10th	**799**	(23rd)/7th — 22 yo.	
	11th	798	(24th)/8th — 23 yo.	
	12th	797	(25th)/9th — 24 yo.	
	13th	796	(26th)/10th — 25 yo.	
	14th	795	(27th)/11th — 26 yo.	
Amaziah died in fifteenth year after death of Jehoash, --->	15th	794	(28th)/12th — 27 yo.	♛ **Uzziah (794-754)**[1]
who died in 808 BCE	16th	793	(29th)/13th — 28 yo.	Uzziah 27 years old, became sole ruler of Judah during the reign of Jeroboam II,[2] see page 77
	17th	**792**	14th	
Bûr-Saggilê solar eclipse on --->	18th	791	15th	
June 24, 791 BCE	19th	790	16th	
	20th	789	17th	
	21st	788	18th	
	22nd	787	19th	
	23rd	786	20th	
	24th	**785**	21st	
	25th	784	22nd	
	26th	783	23rd	
	27th	782	24th	

[1] Uzziah is also called Azariah.
[2] Uzziah became sole ruler of Judah in the twenty-seventh year of his life, not in the twenty-seventh regnal year of Jeroboan II of Israel as incorrectly translated in KJV; see 2 Kings 15:1.

Kings of Israel and Judah, 781-745 BCE

(years shown in center column are proleptic Gregorian years; A = accession or partial year; sabbath years in bold type)

Kingdom of Israel
(regnal years counted Nisan to Nisan)

Kingdom of Judah
(regnal years counted Tishri to Tishri)

Israel	Year BCE	Judah
Jeroboam II (cont.)		Uzziah (cont.)
28th	781	25th
29th	780	26th
30th	779	27th
31st	**778**	28th
32nd	777	29th
33rd	776	30th
34th	775	31st
35th	774	32nd
36th	773	33rd
37th	772	34th
38th	**771**	35th
39th	770	36th
40th	769	37th
♛ Zachariah¹ (768) → 41st/A	768	38th
♛ Shallum² (767) ⇒ 1st/A/A	767	39th
♛ Menahem³ (767-757) 1st	766	40th
2nd	765	41st
3rd	**764**	42nd
4th	763	43rd
5th	762	44th
6th	761	45th
7th	760	46th
8th	759	47th
☗ Pekah (king in Gilead) → 9th/ (1st)	758	48th
♛ Pekahiah (757-755) → 10th/A/(2nd)	**757**	49th/1st ← ♛ Jotham (757/754-738)
1st/(3rd)	756	(50th)/2nd
♛ Pekah (758/757-738) → 2nd/(4th)	755	(51st)/3rd
5th	754	(52nd)/4th
6th	753	5th
7th	752	6th
8th	751	7th
9th	**750**	8th
10th	749	9th
11th	748	10th
12th	747	11th
13th	746	12th
14th	745	13th

Accession Year System in Israel
Starting with Zachariah in 768 BCE, the kingdom of Israel adopted the accession-year system for counting regnal years (but it was not always followed as indicated below); the Nisan-to-Nisan system of counting the months was retained.

see page 80 (for all three kings shown above)

¹ Zachariah reigns 6 months starting in the thirty-eighth year of Uzziah into the thirty-ninth year.
² Shallum reigns for one month in the thirty-ninth year of Uzziah.
³ Menahem pays tribute to Pul, king of Assyria, between 767-757 BCE.

see page 81

king in Gilead in 758 BCE; king in Israel in 755 BCE, 52nd year of Uzziah,⁴ *see page 81*

⁴ Both Pekahiah and Pekah had control of large parts of Israel after Menahem died in 757 BCE, and each claimed the throne of Israel until Pekah murdered Pekahiah in 755 BCE and became the sole ruler as king in Samaria; his regnal years are counted from the year he began claiming the throne as king in Gilead, 758 BCE; numerous cities in Israel were annexed by Tiglath-pileser III during Pekah's reign.

2nd year of Pekah in Gilead, Jotham began judging Judah as king in place of Uzziah, who had become a leper, *see page 81*

Chapter Two: A New Kingdoms Chronology

Kings of Israel and Judah, 744-721 BCE

(years shown in center column are proleptic Gregorian years; A = accession or partial year; sabbath years in bold type)

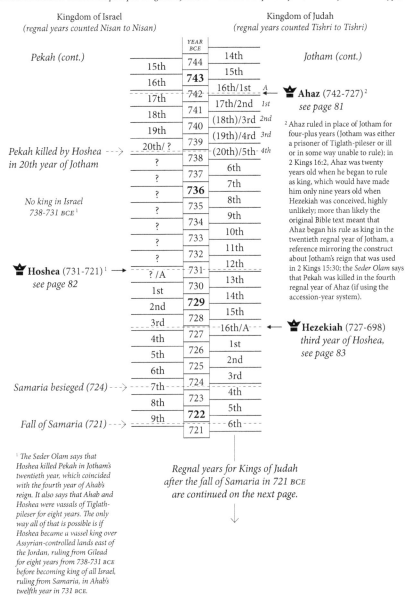

[1] *The Seder Olam says that Hoshea killed Pekah in Jotham's twentieth year, which coincided with the fourth year of Ahab's reign. It also says that Ahab and Hoshea were vassals of Tiglath-pileser for eight years. The only way all of that is possible is if Hoshea became a vassal king over Assyrian-controlled lands east of the Jordan, ruling from Gilead for eight years from 738-731 BCE before becoming king of all Israel, ruling from Samaria, in Ahab's twelfth year in 731 BCE.*

Regnal years for Kings of Judah after the fall of Samaria in 721 BCE are continued on the next page.

– 27 –

Kings of Judah after the fall of Samaria, 727-654 BCE

(years shown in left column are proleptic Gregorian years; A = accession or partial year; sabbath years in bold type)

(regnal years counted Tishri to Tishri)

YEAR BCE			YEAR BCE		
727	A	← ♛ **Hezekiah** (727-698)	690	8th	Manasseh (cont.)
726	1st	became king in third	689	9th	
725	2nd	year of Hoshea, Temple	688	10th	
724	3rd	cleansed and Passover	**687**	11th	
723	4th	kept in his first year,	686	12th	
722	5th	see page 81	685	13th	
721	6th	←--- Fall of Samaria (721)	684	14th	
720	7th		683	15th	
719	8th		682	16th	
718	9th		681	17th	677-673 BCE: Remaining
717	10th		**680**	18th	Jews in kingdom of Israel
716	11th		679	19th	deported to Assyria by
715	12th		678	20th	Esarhaddon and replaced with foreigners.
714	13th	←--- Hezekiah's life-threatening	677	21st	
713	14th	illness, when God gave him	676	22nd	←--- Manasseh taken captive
712	15th	fifteen extra years of life	675	23rd	to Babylon by captains of
711	16th		674	24th	Esarhaddon in 677 BCE[1]
710	17th	←--- b. Manasseh (710)	**673**	25th	[1] Year is based on a passage
709	18th	1 yo.	672	26th	in the *Seder Olam* that says
708	19th	2 yo.	671	27th	Manasseh was taken captive in his twenty-second regnal year;
707	20th	3 yo.	670	28th	see 2 Chronicles 33:11.
706	21st	4 yo.	669	29th	
705	22nd	5 yo.	668	30th	
704	23rd	6 yo.	667	31st	
703	24th	7 yo.	**666**	32nd	
702	25th	8 yo.	665	33rd	
701	26th	9 yo. ←--- Sennacherib's invasion, future pharaoh Taharqa	664	34th	
700	27th	10 yo. leads Shebitku's army out	663	35th	
699	28th	11 yo. of Egypt to oppose him	662	36th	
698	29th/A	12 yo. ← ♛ **Manasseh** (698-643)	661	37th	
697	1st	13 yo. see page 87	660	38th	
696	2nd		**659**	39th	
695	3rd		658	40th	
694	4th		657	41st	
693	5th		656	42nd	
692	6th		655	43rd	
691	7th		654	44th	

Chapter Two: A New Kingdoms Chronology

Kings of Judah after the fall of Samaria, 653-586 BCE

(years shown in left column are proleptic Gregorian years; A = accession or partial year; sabbath years in bold type)

(regnal years counted Tishri to Tishri)

YEAR BCE				YEAR BCE			
653	45th		Manasseh (cont.)	616	24th	11th	Josiah (cont.)
652	46th			615	25th	12th	
651	47th			614	26th	13th	
650	48th			613	27th	14th	
649	49th		←--- b. Josiah	612	28th	15th	
648	50th	*1 yo.*		611	29th	16th	
647	51st	*2 yo.*		610	30th	17th	
646	52nd	*3 yo.*	♛ **Amon** (643-641)	609	31st/A	18th	←♛ **Jehoahaz**
645	53rd	*4 yo.*	assassinated before	608	1st/A	19th	(609)[1]
644	54th	*5 yo.*	the 1st of Tishri in year	607	1st	20th	♛ **Jehoiakim**
643	55th/A	*6 yo.*	641 BCE, throne empty	606	2nd	21st	(609-598)
642	1st	*7 yo.*	until assassins are	605	3rd	22nd	both, see page 92
641	2nd/?	*8 yo.*	killed by the people,	604	4th	23rd/1st	←-- Nebuchadnezzar II
640	A	*9 yo.*	see page 89	**603**	5th	2nd	(r. 605-562) became
639	1st		←♛ **Josiah** (640-609)	602	6th	3rd	king shortly after the
638	2nd		made king by the	601	7th	4th	Battle of Carchemish;
637	3rd		people sometime	600	8th	5th	the city of Jerusalem
636	4th		after 1st of Tishri	599	9th	6th	and Solomon's Temple
635	5th		in year 641 BCE,	598	10th	7th	burned in 19th year
634	6th		see page 89	597	11th/A/A	8th	of Nebuchadnezzar
633	7th			**596**	1st	9th	←♛ **Jehoiachin**
632	8th		The Babylonian Talmud	595	2nd	10th	(598-597)[2]
631	9th		(tractate Arakin 12b) says	594	3rd	11th	♛ **Zedekiah**
630	10th		that Solomon's Temple was	593	4th	12th	(597-586)[3]
629	11th		destroyed in the third year	592	5th	13th	both, see page 92
628	12th		of a sabbath cycle, a cross	591	6th	14th	
627	13th		check confirming that the	590	7th	15th	[4] The Babylonians withdraw
626	14th	*1st*	year 586 BCE was the year	**589**	8th	16th	from Jerusalem in 588 BCE
625	15th	*2nd*	that the Babylonian army	588	9th	17th	when the army of Egypt
624	16th	*3rd*	destroyed the Temple.	587	10th	18th	threatened, but returned in
623	17th	*4th*		586	11th	19th	587 BCE to renew the siege
622	18th	*5th*	←--- Jeremiah began to				(see Jeremiah 37:7-8).

(right column annotations, continued:)

626 *1st sabbath yr.* ←--- Jeremiah began to prophesy to Judah for twenty-three years in Josiah's thirteenth year (Jeremiah 25:3)

588 *1st yr.* --- Siege of Jerusalem (589) (10th month of 9th year)[4]

586 *3rd yr.* --- Fall of Jerusalem (586) (4th month of 11th year)

621	19th	*6th*	←--- Hilkiah found Book
620	20th	*7th*	of the Law during repair
619	21st	*8th*	of the Temple in Josiah's
618	22nd	*9th*	eighteenth regnal year;
617	23rd	*10th*	as a result, celebration of the "Great Passover" took place in 622 BCE

[1] Jehoahaz ruled for 3 months in 609 BCE, including a month of Tishri to begin a regnal year, before being deposed by pharaoh Necho and exiled to Egypt.

[2] Jehoiachin was king for 3 months and 10 days in late 598 BCE until early 597 BCE, but not in a month of Tishri.

[3] Zedekiah was appointed king by Nebuchadnezzar sometime before Tishri in 597 BCE and had a short accession year before his first Tishri later that year.

What about Bûr-Saggilê?

The Kurkh Monolith identifies Ahab of Israel as a participant in the coalition that fought against Shalmaneser III in the Battle of Qarqar. The Black Obelisk states that Qarqar took place in the sixth year of Shalmaneser, which is traditionally identified as 853 BCE by counting back the ninety eponyms (assuming one for each year) listed on the Assyrian Eponym Canon between the Bûr-Saggilê eclipse (which Sir Henry Rawlinson placed in 763 BCE) and the Battle of Qarqar in the sixth year of Shalmaneser. The kingdoms chronology in this book indicates that Ahab reigned from 904-883 BCE (see pages 22-23) and that the Battle of Qarqar happened in 883 BCE, not 853 BCE. So, there is a thirty-year difference between the date of Ahab at Qarqar in this book and the traditional date for Ahab at Qarqar derived by scholars from calculations based on Rawlinson's 763 BCE date for the Bûr-Saggilê eclipse. Which is correct?

The answer depends on the placement of the Bûr-Saggilê eclipse in history, and that is subjective, a matter of interpretation. The only mention of the eclipse is recorded in the Assyrian Eponym Canon, in the ninth year of Ashur-dan III during the eponymy when Bûr-Saggilê was *limmu*, and reads as follows:

> "During the eponymy of Bûr-Saggilê, governor of Gūzanā, revolt in Libbi-āli; in Siwan, eclipse of the sun" ... Glassner, *Mesopotamian Chronicles*, p. 171.

That brief inscription provided the only data on which Rawlinson made his identification of 763 BCE as the year of the Bûr-Saggilê eclipse. Notice that the AEC inscription does not say whether the eclipse was total, as Rawlinson assumed, or partial, an equal possibility, nor does it say where the observation was made (Nineveh was assumed by Rawlinson and your author). It simply says that a "bent sun" (Au) was observed, that it happened in the month of Siwan (or Simanu), which always occurred in the proleptic Gregorian months of May and June, and that it happened when Bûr-Saggilê was the *limmu*. That is all that can be known for sure from the ancient Assyrian records.

The 763 BCE date chosen by Rawlinson featured a partial solar eclipse of 0.987 magnitude. It was observable in Assyria, and occurred on June 15, 763 BCE. However, there is another possibility, an eclipse visible in Nineveh twenty-eight years earlier—a partial solar eclipse of magnitude 0.737 on June 24, 791 BCE—and it also totally agrees with the above textual description used by Rawlinson to identify

Chapter Two: A New Kingdoms Chronology

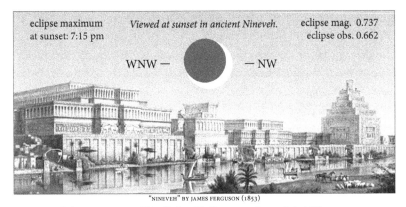

"NINEVEH" BY JAMES FERGUSON (1853)

Diagram 2.2 - The Solar Eclipse on June 24, 791 BCE

his eclipse date. Some will object that the 763 BCE eclipse, with its greater magnitude (almost a full eclipse), was the more spectacular choice to have been recorded in the Canon. However, the magnitude is irrelevant, since the only requirement is that the man Bûr-Saggilê had to have been *limmu* in the year of the eclipse, something equally possible for either date from our viewpoint today since the years when Bûr-Saggilê lived are not known, and were unknown by Rawlinson as well.

As for the 791 BCE eclipse, it was certainly spectacular enough to be recorded in the Canon. It displayed a crescent (bent?) sun diminishing as it set. The sight of the sun being eclipsed as it was setting must have been impressive. Rawlinson's 763 BCE eclipse was at its maximum during mid-morning, so it would have dimmed (but not darkened) the land, then in a few minutes everything would have returned back to normal. In the 791 BCE event, maximum eclipse occurred at sunset. The ancients watching the sun set and eclipse simultaneously would have had all night to ponder if it would reappear whole the next morning. That is speculation, of course, but the point being made is that the 791 BCE eclipse was noteworthy enough to warrant being recorded. Adding additional support for preferring the 791 BCE date is the fact that the Assyrian kings chronology, when adjusted twenty-eight years back in time by using that date as the year for the Bûr-Saggilê eclipse, more closely aligns with the harmonized chronology of the Hebrew kings in almost all instances.

However, moving the Bûr-Saggilê eclipse back twenty-eight years does not achieve exact alignment between the Hebrew and Assyrian chronologies in every instance. One more adjustment is necessary, since Assyrian inscriptions claim that Ahab was defeated at Qarqar in Shalmaneser III's sixth regnal year, saying:

[*from the Kurkh Monolith*] "I destroyed, devastated [the king of] Karkar ... [he] brought twelve kings[1] to his support; they came against me to offer battle and fight: 1,200 chariots, 1,200 cavalry, and 20,000 soldiers belonging to Hadad-ezer of Damascus; 700 chariots, 700 cavalry, and 10,000 soldiers belonging to Irhuleni of Hama; ***2,000 chariots, and 10,000 soldiers belonging to Ahab, the Israelite***"[2] [*and from the Black Obelisk*] "In my sixth year, I crossed the Euphrates ... and received gifts from all the kings of Hatti. At that time Hadad-ezer of Damascus, and Irhuleni the Hamathite, along with the kings of Hatti and the seacoast, relied on each other's strength and came out against me to engage in battle ... I fought with them and was able to defeat them."[3]

Adding twenty-eight years to the traditional dates for Shalmaneser III yields 881 BCE as his sixth regnal year, which is two years after the death of Ahab according to the Hebrew chronology used in this book. Thus, Shalmaneser's reign must be moved back two more years, but can such an adjustment be justified from Assyrian history? Yes, it can be. Shalmaneser's eldest son, Ashur-danin-pal, led a revolt in his father's final years, usurping the throne for possibly five years. It took Shalmaneser's younger son, the future king Shamshi-adad IV, two years to dethrone his brother after Shalmaneser's death.[4] Apparently no eponyms were recorded during the brothers' struggle for the empty throne, or, if so, the victorious Shamshi-adad essentially erased his brother's illegitimate rule by not including any eponyms he appointed. So, that correction moves the reign of Shalmaneser III back to 889-854 BCE, which allows his sixth year to coincide with Ahab's death in Syria[5] at Qarqar/Ramoth-gilead.

Inserting twenty-eight years before the traditional dates for the reign of Tiglath-pileser III (r. 745-727) can be justified by that old standby explanation often used by many chronologists to question the Bible's accuracy, scribal error. In the case of

---

[1] The mention of twelve kings on the Kurkh Monolith has puzzled scholars since only eleven kings are mentioned by name. Your author proposes that the phrase "twelve kings" is a reference to the heads of the twelve tribes of Israel. The combined armies of the kingdoms of Israel and Judah were arrayed against the king of Syria at Ramoth-gilead. If that battle was considered part of or associated with the Battle of Qarqar (Gilead was mentioned as Gilzau on the Kurkh Monolith), the field commanders of the armies of the twelve tribes could well have been mistakenly interpreted by Assyrian scribes as twelve kings.

[2] D. D. Luckenbill, *Ancient Records of Assyria and Babylonia* (The University of Chicago Press: 1926); p. 200-252; language and place names updated by Alan Humm.

[3] From the Black Obelisk, translation by Alan Humm (truncated) at www.jewishchristianlit.com.

[4] H. R. Hall, *The Ancient History of the Near East* (London: Methuen & Co.; 1913; p. 455).

[5] The geographical term "Syria" is used generically in this book to refer to the region generally known as Syria today and denoted in the KJV by the names Damascus, Aram, and Syria.

Chapter Two: A New Kingdoms Chronology

Tiglath-pileser, a scribe making a copy of the Eponym Canon soon after his reign ended simply lost his place and dropped the name of twenty-eight *limmus* between the first and second times that Tiglath-pileser himself served as *limmu*, as follows:

YEAR BCE	DOCUMENT BEING COPIED FROM	
774	AY *Nabu-bela-usur*	
773	1st *Bel-dan*	
772	2nd *Tiglath-pileser III* 1st time	
771	3rd	missing eponym #1
770	4th	missing eponym #2
769	5th	missing eponym #3
768	6th	missing eponym #4
767	7th	missing eponym #5
766	8th	missing eponym #6
765	9th	missing eponym #7
764	10th	missing eponym #8
763	11th	missing eponym #9
762	12th	missing eponym #10
761	13th	missing eponym #11
760	14th	missing eponym #12
759	15th	missing eponym #13
758	16th	missing eponym #14
757	17th	missing eponym #15
756	18th	missing eponym #16
755	19th	missing eponym #17
754	20th	missing eponym #18
753	21st	missing eponym #19
752	22nd	missing eponym #20
751	23rd	missing eponym #21
750	24th	missing eponym #22
749	25th	missing eponym #23
748	26th	missing eponym #24
747	27th	missing eponym #25
746	28th	missing eponym #26
745	29th	missing eponym #27
744	30th	missing eponym #28
743	31st *Tiglath-pileser III* 2nd time	=
742	32nd *Nabu-da'inannil*	=
741	33rd *Bêl-Harran-bêla-usur*	=
740	34th *Nabû-etiranni*	=
739	35th *Sin-taklak*	=
738	36th *Adad-bêla-ka'in*	=
737	37th *Bêl-emuranni*	=
736	38th *Inurta-ilaya*	=
735	39th *Aššur-šallimanni*	=
734	40th *Bêl-dan*	=
733	41st *Aššur-da'inanni*	=
732	42nd *Nabû-bêla-usur*	=
731	43rd *Nergal-uballit*	=
730	44th *Bêl-lu-dari*	=
729	45th *Liphur-ilu*	=
728	46th *Dur-Aššur*	=
727	47th *Bêl-Harran-bêla-usur*	=

The ancient scribe successfully copied the names of the first three limmus from the original document to the copy (as shown by the shaded circles), then the copyist apparently lost his concentration, letting his eyes drift down to focus on the second time Tiglath-pileser was listed as limmu on the original document. After focusing on the second time Tiglath-pileser was listed as limmu, mistaking it for the first mention and the place where he left off transcribing names of limmus, the copyist then continued listing names from that point onward, not realizing that he had skipped over the 28 names of limmus who had served between the two times Tiglath-pileser was limmu. In that way, 28 years were omitted from the Assyrian Eponym List that is used by historians and chronologists to synchronize timelines of most ancient empires today. It is also a possibility that there were no limmus appointed during that twenty-eight-year period because the priests in Assur refused to confirm Tiglath-pileser III as king since they considered him to be illegitimate.

COPY

AY *Nabu-bela-usur*
1st *Bel-dan*
2nd *Tiglath-pileser III* 1st time
3rd *Nabu-da'inannil*
4th *Bêl-Harran-bêla-usur*
5th *Nabû-etiranni*
6th *Sin-taklak*
7th *Adad-bêla-ka'in*
8th *Bêl-emuranni*
9th *Inurta-ilaya*
10th *Aššur-šallimanni*
11th *Bêl-dan*
12th *Aššur-da'inanni*
13th *Nabû-bêla-usur*
14th *Nergal-uballit*
15th *Bêl-lu-dari*
16th *Liphur-ilu*
17th *Dur-Aššur*
18th *Bêl-Harran-bêla-usur*

At least one scholar claims that Rawlinson's 763 BCE date is "unambiguously" verified by a Babylonian eclipse in the first year of king Mukin-zeri, saying:

"Therefore it may be helpful to present independent astronomical evidence for the dating of Assyrian kings and thereby of the Eponym List ... In a collection of Babylonian lunar eclipses, an eclipse in Month 1, Year 1 of king Mukin-zeri is mentioned. By the structure of the text, the date of this eclipse (not visible in Babylon but calculated in advance) may unambiguously be established as April 9, 731 B.C. However, it is known that Mukin-zeri fought against Tiglath-pileser III and that his first regnal year coincided with the 14th year of the Assyrian king. This evidence is provided from the Babylonian Chronicle. Thus, the 14th year of Tiglath-pileser III is identified as 731/730 B.C."[1]

The description of the Mukin-zeri eclipse is detailed on a cuneiform tablet [BM 35769 (= LBAT 1414)] that says: *Year 1 Ukin-zer, month I, [lunar eclipse] which passes (sa DIB). (Began) at 1,0 (i.e., 60) degrees after sunrise.*[2] On that tablet, the Babylonian astronomers predicted a lunar eclipse on April 9, 731 BCE, an eclipse that would "pass," which was their way of saying that it would not be observable in Babylon. NASA records confirm that a partial lunar eclipse did occur over the Pacific Ocean on that date. If that eclipse was the eclipse predicted for Mukin-zeri's first year, the one equated with Tiglath-pileser III's fourteenth year, then it does, by validating that the first year of Mukin-zeri and the fourteenth year of Tiglath-pileser III occurred in 731 BCE, confirm the traditional chronology that has the reign of Tiglath-pileser beginning in 745 BCE. However, the Babylonian eclipse from 731 BCE does not provide any information at all about the year when the man Bûr-Saggilê was *limmu* in Assyria, and thus it does not prove the accuracy of Rawlinson's widely-accepted 763 BCE date for Bûr-Saggilê eclipse, nor does it invalidate in any way this chapter's main chronological proposition that the year for the eclipse was 791 BCE. And, it does not invalidate the biblically-supported assumption that Tiglath-pileser ruled Assyria south of the Tigris using the name Pul starting beginning in 773 BCE. Therefore, in this book, 791 BCE is the year used for the Bûr-Saggilê eclipse and the dates for the Assyrian kings have been adjusted as described to align them the more accurate Hebrew kingdoms chronology.

---

[1] Dr. Hermann Hunger, "About the Dating of the Neo-Assyrian Eponym List" (*Altorientalische Forschungen*, volume 35; 2008); p. 323-325; excerpt condensed from English translation.
[2] F. Richard Stephenson, *Historical Eclipses and Earth's Rotation* (Cambridge University Press, 1997); p. 122.

What about Shishak?

The most significant cross-references between the pharaohs of Egypt and the Hebrew kings are the biblical references that connect Shishak, king of Egypt, and Rehoboam, king of the southern kingdom of Judah. The Bible recounts in 1 Kings, chapter 14, verse 25, and 2 Chronicles, chapter 12, verse 2, that Shishak went to Jerusalem, took the Temple treasures and looted the king's palace, then apparently returned to Egypt, all of those events happening in the fifth year of Rehoboam. In 1828, Jean-François Champollion identified the person called Shishak in the Bible as the pharaoh known to history as Shoshenq I, that identification being based on his interpretation of reliefs he viewed on a wall at Karnak (see page 5). Interestingly, the Karnak inscriptions interpreted by Champollion do not mention Rehoboam and barely mention cities in Judah, and the city of Jerusalem is not mentioned at all,[1] but they do recount in detail the conquest of dozens of cities in the northern kingdom of Israel. Thus, the biblical account of the exploits of Shishak, which focus exclusively on conquests in Judah, and the Karnak accounts of the triumphs of Shoshenq I, which focus mainly on conquests in the northern kingdom of Israel, simply do not seem to be in agreement. That inconsistency raises the question: Is Shoshenq I really Shishak, as Champollion said, or is there a better explanation of his identity?

It is worthwhile to review what we know for certain about Shishak and Shoshenq I before tackling the identity question. Shishak, according to the Bible, gave refuge to the rebel Jeroboam during the last years of Solomon's reign. He moved against Jerusalem in the fifth year of Rehoboam, taking the treasures of the Temple and the palace. All of that information is found in 1 Kings, chapters 11-14, and 2 Chronicles, chapter 12. From the tidbits of data given in those chapters, it is obvious that Shishak and Jeroboam had a close relationship over a long period of time. The Septuagint records that Shishak gave his wife's sister, Ano, to Jeroboam in marriage (3 Kings 12:24; LXX).

Shoshenq I is not mentioned in the Bible. Everything we know about him comes from secular sources. Of primary interest for our purpose are the reliefs at Karnak, which tell us about Shoshenq's military foray into the land of Canaan. Egyptologists have dated that campaign to 925 BCE, based on identifying the

---

[1] Some scholars speculate that mention of the cities of Judah and Jerusalem was originally included at Karnak but is now missing due to deterioration of the inscriptions.

years 945-924 BCE for the reign of Shoshenq I, and that date aligns with the fifth year of Rehoboam in the chronology of the kings as calculated using Rawlinson's year for the Bûr-Saggilê eclipse. But, as previously stated, the inscriptions at Karnak reveal that Shoshenq's army fought battles predominantly in the northern kingdom of Israel and along the territory bordering Syria, with dozens of northern cities mentioned in the list of conquered locations. Only a few of the fortified cities in Judah[1] are mentioned, the ones that would be encountered if skirting Judah to go into Israel, and no information is given about any sacking and looting of Solomon's Temple and the king's palace in Jerusalem.

Geopolitically speaking, Shishak's Egypt and Jeroboam's kingdom of Israel should have been close allies, with Egypt depending on Jeroboam and his kingdom to serve as a buffer state between Egypt and Syria. On the other hand, the Judah of Rehoboam would probably have been estranged from Egypt because Shishak had so recently given aid and comfort to Jeroboam prior to the division of the kingdom of United Israel into separate kingdoms. Thus, if Shishak was the same person as Shoshenq I, a campaign to conquer cities in the northern kingdom of Israel as detailed at Karnak, instead of a campaign against the southern kingdom of Judah as detailed in the Bible, simply does not make any geopolitical sense.

In the harmonized chronology of the Hebrew kings that is presented on the preceding pages of this book, the invasion of Judah and looting of Jerusalem in the fifth year of Rehoboam is calculated to have occurred in the year 961 BCE, which does not align with the accepted 925 BCE date for the military campaign by Shoshenq I into Canaan described at Karnak. So, the new chronology for the kings offered herein means that Shishak's invasion of Judah and pharaoh Shoshenq's later campaign in Israel were two separate events. According to the adjusted chronology, Shishak invaded in 961 BCE during the reign of Rehoboam and Shoshenq I invaded as pharaoh thirty-six years later in 925 BCE during the reign of Asa of Judah. That scenario aligns with what is known about the history of the pharaohs during that period, which includes the last years of Dynasty 21 and the early years of Dynasty 22. Looking at the events of Egyptian history on either side of 925 BCE, only two invasions in the direction of or into the land of Canaan are documented on Egyptian monuments, the one undertaken by Shoshenq I that is recorded at Karnak, dated to 925 BCE, and a previous campaign into the Levant during the reign of pharaoh Siamun. That earlier event, which is recorded

---

[1] See list of Rehoboam's fortified cities in 2 Chronicles 11:5-10.

on a wall at Tanis,[1] would have occurred in 961 BCE, thirty-six years before Shoshenq's 925 BCE invasion according to this book's kingdoms chronology. The accepted regnal years for Siamun are 978-959 BCE, which makes that possible. It is also probable that Shoshenq, then only a commander in Siamun's army (and not yet a pharaoh), would have led the campaign against Jerusalem. The biblical references to Shishak as "king" could thus be understood as anachronisms.

Can the Karnak invasion by Shoshenq I be aligned with the reign of Asa of Judah? Yes, it can be, through a person the Bible calls Zerah the Ethiopian, who attacked Asa and Judah as recounted in 2 Chronicles, chapter 14, verses 9-12:

"And there came out against them Zerah the Ethiopian with an host of a thousand thousand, and three hundred chariots; and came unto Mareshah. Then Asa went out against him, and they set the battle in array in the valley of Zephathah at Mareshah. And Asa cried unto the Lord his God, and said, Lord, [it is] nothing with thee to help, whether with many, or with them that have no power: help us, O Lord our God; for we rest on thee, and in thy name we go against this multitude. O Lord, thou [art] our God; let not man prevail against thee. So the Lord smote the Ethiopians before Asa, and before Judah; and the Ethiopians fled" (KJV).

The Bible explains in 2 Chronicles, chapter 16, verse 1, that, after Zerah and his invading army were defeated, Asa and the people of Judah had a victory feast in Jerusalem, Meanwhile, Baasha, king of the northern kingdom of Israel, fortified Ramah and cut off all access to Jerusalem from the north (that action by Baasha may have actually been concurrent with Zerah's attack). That meant that Jerusalem was hemmed in on all sides, since the Egyptians were encamped on Judah's southern border. The reference to Baasha's fortification of Ramah happening in the thirty-sixth year[2] identifies Zerah's invasion as occurring late in the year 926 BCE or possibly in early 925 BCE. When Asa appealed to Damascus for help, Benhadad I attacked Baasha from the north. That is when Baasha's ally in Egypt, Shoshenq I, marshaled his troops and invaded Israel to defend him.

---

[1] K.A. Kitchen, *The Third Intermediate Period in Egypt 1100-650 BC* (Oxford: Aris & Phillips, an imprint of Oxbow Books, 2004); p. 280-281.

[2] Baasha died in Asa's twenty-fifth year, so he could not have moved against Judah in Asa's thirty-sixth regnal year. The phrase "thirty-sixth year" refers to the thirty-sixth year after the division of the kingdoms; see the regnal chronology displayed on pages 22-23.

A close look at the evidence from the Bible and from Karnak indicates that the events of 926/925 BCE probably took place in four stages, as follows (the stage numbers below match the numbers on Map 2.4 on the opposite page):

Stage ❶: Zerah the Ethiopian[1] launched his invasion of Judah by attacking Hebron[2] from the south, overcoming the defenders at that important fortified city. Zerah then attacked the fortified city of Mareshah, or possibly Hebron was not attacked and the fortified city of Mareshah was the point of first attack. In either case, Zerah and his task force were badly defeated by Asa and his Judean army at Mareshah, then were chased south as far as Gerar near Gaza. In the battle, Asa and his Judean forces took much spoil from Zerah and afterwards celebrated their victory in Jerusalem with a feast of thanksgiving, taking an oath to be loyal to God (2 Chronicles 14:9-15).

Stage ❷: Baasha, king of the northern kingdom of Israel and ally of Egypt, had previously negotiated a non-aggression pact with Benhadad I of Damascus. He was thus free to move against Judah, and did so by fortifying the border town of Ramah to cut off access to Jerusalem from the north, possibly doing so simultaneously as Zerah was attacking Judah from the south.

Stage ❸: Asa, fearing invasion by Baasha, sent gold and other treasures to Damascus, asking Benhadad to renounce his non-aggression pact with Baasha and attack Israel on its northern border with Syria. Benhadad agreed and sent troops south to fight Baasha, in that way relieving the military threat to Judah as Baasha withdrew his troops from Ramah to defend his northernmost territories.

Stage ❹: Baasha, now under attack from Damascus in the north, sent to Egypt for help from Shoshenq I, who was still aggrieved at the earlier defeat of his army under Zerah (from Karnak: "Now, My [Maj]esty found that ... [they] were killing ... [my soldiers?, and] my army leaders. His majesty was troubled about them").[3] Not wanting to have Syria overrun the northern kingdom and control all of Canaan, Shoshenq mustered his army and moved to confront Benhadad in northern Israel, skirting the cities of Judah (except Ajalon) before moving northward into Israel to begin his main campaign to protect the northern kingdom. Shoshenq proceeded to neutralize the threat to Israel by Benhadad, then returned to Egypt.

---

[1] Zerah is never referred to in the Bible as "pharaoh" or "king" and was probably a general in pharaoh Shoshenq's Egyptian army. Use of Libyan and Ethiopian mercenaries in the army of Egypt during that period is well documented.

[2] Hebron was denoted by its ancient name "Rubuti" on the Karnak inscription.

[3] Kitchen, *The Third Intermediate Period in Egypt 1100-650 BC*, p. 294.

Chapter Two: A New Kingdoms Chronology

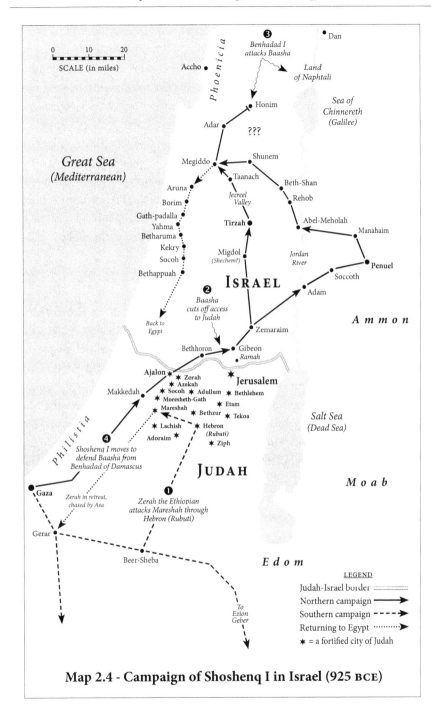

Map 2.4 - Campaign of Shoshenq I in Israel (925 BCE)

Admittedly, an invasion of Canaan by Shoshenq I during the reign of Asa as proposed above is speculative, but less so than the traditional explanations that associate the Karnak reliefs with the reign of Rehoboam. The advantage of the Shoshenq-Asa scenario is that it fits both the Karnak inscriptions and the Bible. Also, its chronology agrees with the harmonized chronology of the Hebrew kings, whereas hypothesizing that Shoshenq I moved against Judah as "king of Egypt" in the fifth year of Rehoboam does not match the facts. Based on the new kingdoms chronology in this book, Shishak's invasion of Judah happened during the reign of Siamun (r. 978-959), when Shoshenq (Shishak) apparently commanded Siamun's army but was not yet a pharaoh. As stated earlier, the biblical references to Shishak as "king of Egypt" are anachronisms. Siamun's general Shoshenq had become the pharaoh Shoshenq I by the time his invasions were recorded in the Bible.

Which Way is Better?

Ultimately, there are two ways to establish a chronology of the Hebrew kings. The traditional way starts with a secular date—usually Rawlinson's 763 BCE date for the Bûr-Saggilê eclipse—and uses it to align chronological details gleaned from inscriptions on the stone stele and clay tablets of ancient Assyria, and from the stone monuments and papyrus fragments of ancient Egypt. Scholars have done a remarkable job of assembling a coherent timeline from the often sparse and usually incomplete records of both civilizations. In recent years, Bible scholars have accepted the resulting timeline of secular scholars as preeminent, arranging the chronology of the Hebrew kings to fit it. Almost all modern Bible commentaries, study Bibles, and religious publications use the kingdoms chronology resulting from that secular-based approach. However, this chapter has shown that there is a better way to establish a chronology of the Hebrew kings. The better way starts by accepting what the Bible says about the reigns as accurate. It then uses a Bible-based anchor date and the chronological data and crosschecks in the biblical text to achieve harmonization of the reigns. Once a Bible-only timeline has been achieved, and only then, is it useful to compare the secular chronologies of major contemporaneous civilizations, specifically those of Egypt and Assyria, with the chronology of the Hebrew kings. If they differ, then the secular timeline must be made to conform to the more accurate Bible-only timeline, not the other way around. That better way has been used to establish the new chronology of the Hebrew kings presented in this book.

CHAPTER THREE

KINGS OF UNITED ISRAEL
1,086-961 BCE

The chronology of the kingdom of United Israel can be calculated from the date that the united kingdom separated into the kingdoms of Israel and Judah. The year 964 BCE was identified as the year that the united kingdom was rent from Rehoboam, using the allegorical prophecy in Daniel, chapter 4, to identify the exact year (see page 14). From that date, and from the chronological clues given in the Bible, the time of Solomon's death can then be pinpointed as occurring between the 1st of Tishri in the year 967 BCE and the 1st of Tishri in the year 966 BCE.[1] Since Saul, David, and Solomon are stipulated by the biblical text to have each reigned for forty years, counting back one hundred and twenty civil New-Year Days (one hundred and twenty 1st of Tishris; see Table 3.1 on next page) reveals the beginning year for the reign of Saul as the year 1,086 BCE.

Saul of Israel
1,086-1,046 BCE

After the Children of Israel entered and took possession of the promised land of Canaan in 1,402 BCE, they lived in a theocracy in which God ruled directly through the Law, the priests, judges, and prophets raised up from time to time as needed to administer God's pronouncements to the people. During the time of the prophet Samuel, though, the people demanded a king, so as to be more like the surrounding nations, and God granted their wish. In 1,086 BCE, Saul, the son of Kish of the tribe of Benjamin, was anointed by Samuel as the first king of Israel. The story of Saul's anointing and troubled reign is recounted in 1 Samuel, chapters 9-31. Saul reigned for forty years (meaning that he was on the throne for forty 1st of Tishris), according to the Book of Acts, chapter 13, verse 21, although the length of his reign is not mentioned in the Hebrew Scriptures.[2] Consequently, arbitrary

---

[1] The years in the reigns of the kings in the kingdom of United Israel were apparently numbered from the start of the civil New Year, which began on the 1st of Tishri, although that time for the start of a new year is not specified in Scripture.

[2] Many biblical scholars have questioned the forty-year reign attributed to Saul in Acts, considering it merely an artificial literary device to make it identical with the forty-year reigns attributed to David and Solomon, and thus easy to remember and recall.

Table 3.1 - How to Identify the First Regnal Year of Saul
by counting back 120 New-Year Days from Solomon's last New-Year Day; T = New-Year Day (1st of Tishri)

SOLOMON - The 40 New-Year Days that fell within Solomon's Reign (967-1,006 BCE)							
T1 - 967 BCE	T2 - 968 BCE	T3 - 969 BCE	T4 - 970 BCE	T5 - 971 BCE	T6 - 972 BCE	T7 - 973 BCE	T8 - 974 BCE
T9 - 975 BCE	T10 - 976 BCE	T11 - 977 BCE	T12 - 978 BCE	T13 - 979 BCE	T14 - 980 BCE	T15 - 981 BCE	T16 - 982 BCE
T17 - 983 BCE	T18 - 984 BCE	T19 - 985 BCE	T20 - 986 BCE	T21 - 987 BCE	T22 - 988 BCE	T23 - 989 BCE	T24 - 990 BCE
T25 - 991 BCE	T26 - 992 BCE	T27 - 993 BCE	T28 - 994 BCE	T29 - 995 BCE	T30 - 996 BCE	T31 - 997 BCE	T32 - 998 BCE
T33 - 999 BCE	T34 - 1000 BCE	T35 - 1001 BCE	T36 - 1002 BCE	T37 - 1003 BCE	T38 - 1004 BCE	T39 - 1005 BCE	T40 - 1006 BCE
DAVID - The 40 New-Year Days that fell within David's Reign (1,006-1,046 BCE)							
T1 - 1007 BCE	T2 - 1008 BCE	T3 - 1009 BCE	T4 - 1010 BCE	T5 - 1011 BCE	T6 - 1012 BCE	T7 - 1013 BCE	T8 - 1014 BCE
T9 - 1015 BCE	T10 - 1016 BCE	T11 - 1017 BCE	T12 - 1018 BCE	T13 - 1019 BCE	T14 - 1020 BCE	T15 - 1021 BCE	T16 - 1022 BCE
T17 - 1023 BCE	T18 - 1024 BCE	T19 - 1025 BCE	T20 - 1026 BCE	T21 - 1027 BCE	T22 - 1028 BCE	T23 - 1029 BCE	T24 - 1030 BCE
T25 - 1031 BCE	T26 - 1032 BCE	T27 - 1033 BCE	T28 - 1034 BCE	T29 - 1035 BCE	T30 - 1036 BCE	T31 - 1037 BCE	T32 - 1038 BCE
T33 - 1039 BCE	T34 - 1040 BCE	T35 - 1041 BCE	T36 - 1042 BCE	T37 - 1043 BCE	T38 - 1044 BCE	T39 - 1045 BCE	T40 - 1046 BCE
SAUL - The 40 New-Year Days that fell within Saul's Reign (1,046-1,086 BCE)							
T1 - 1047 BCE	T2 - 1048 BCE	T3 - 1049 BCE	T4 - 1050 BCE	T5 - 1051 BCE	T6 - 1052 BCE	T7 - 1053 BCE	T8 - 1054 BCE
T9 - 1055 BCE	T10 - 1056 BCE	T11 - 1057 BCE	T12 - 1058 BCE	T13 - 1059 BCE	T14 - 1060 BCE	T15 - 1061 BCE	T16 - 1062 BCE
T17 - 1063 BCE	T18 - 1064 BCE	T19 - 1065 BCE	T20 - 1066 BCE	T21 - 1067 BCE	T22 - 1068 BCE	T23 - 1069 BCE	T24 - 1070 BCE
T25 - 1071 BCE	T26 - 1072 BCE	T27 - 1073 BCE	T28 - 1074 BCE	T29 - 1075 BCE	T30 - 1076 BCE	T31 - 1077 BCE	T32 - 1078 BCE
T33 - 1079 BCE	T34 - 1080 BCE	T35 - 1081 BCE	T36 - 1082 BCE	T37 - 1083 BCE	T38 - 1084 BCE	T39 - 1085 BCE	T40 - 1086 BCE

lengths for Saul's reign are assigned by various expositors, with the *Seder Olam* calculating a reign as short as three years, that figure based on assuming a one-year coreign with Samuel and a two-year reign after Samuel's death. Lacking any contradictory chronological evidence based on the Hebrew text, the forty-year reign for Saul designated in Acts is accepted by your author as valid until definitive Bible-based evidence showing otherwise is produced.

The Bible devotes twenty-three chapters to describing the reign of Saul, but does not provide much chronologically specific data about him in the text. The only chrono-specific event mentioned during his reign is the one in 1 Samuel, chapter 13, verses 1-2, that describes Saul choosing men to serve in the first royal army of United Israel. The King James translation reads, *"Saul reigned one year; and when he had reigned two years over Israel, Saul chose him three thousand [men] of Israel."* By assuming that Saul chose his army after he had observed his second 1st of Tishri as king, that assumption being based on the way reigns were counted in Israel, the time that he formed his army can be dated to the year that fell between the 1st of Tishri in 1,085 BCE and the 1st of Tishri in 1,084 BCE (see Table 3.1 on the opposite page). According to verse 2, Saul kept two-thirds of the army with him at Micmash and the remaining third he put under the command of his son Jonathan at Gibeah. Since Jonathan would have had to be at least twenty years old—the required age for going to war in Israel was twenty years old according to Numbers, chapter 1, verse 3: *"From twenty years old and upward, all that are able to go forth to war in Israel: thou and Aaron shall number them by their armies"* (KJV)—Saul would have been at least thirty-five to forty years old when he was selected as king in order to have a son who was the mandatory twenty years of age for going to war. Yet, the account of Saul's selection in 1 Samuel, chapter 9, verse 2, seems to indicate that he was a much younger man, perhaps in his late teens or early twenties. Still, the age of Jonathan at the time Saul became king (or about a year later at the most) simply does not allow so young an age for the newly-crowned king.

Saul was a contemporary of Ramesses XI (r. 1,098-1,070), the last pharaoh in Dynasty 20, and Smendes I (r. 1,069-1,043), first pharaoh in Dynasty 21. Both pharaohs were preoccupied with dynastic conflicts at home, and with the struggle for control that raged between the power centers in upper and lower Egypt. Both regions were eventually pacified somewhat and united by Smendes. That preoccupation with domestic turmoil on the part of the pharaohs probably accounts for their lack of interest in the emergence of a new kingdom on their northern border during the reign of Saul. To the north of Israel, the kings of the early Neo-Assyrian Empire were also similarly preoccupied with consolidating their domestic power base during Saul's reign, forming an alliance with Babylon to counter the rising power of the Syrians but showing little interest in the emergence of the kingdom of Israel further south. On the other hand, the Philistines, who occupied the coastal plain to the west of Israel, were a constant threat, and the Bible indicates continuous warfare between Saul and the Philistine kings.

The reign of Saul came to a tragic end. He killed himself by falling on his sword to avoid capture by the Philistines after his army lost a battle at Mount Gilboa, an event calculated to have happened sometime in the year 1,046 BCE. Saul is estimated to have been approaching eighty years old when he died, that total being calculated by assuming that he was probably close to forty years old when he became king, and then by adding the forty years that he reigned as king over the twelve tribes that comprised the kingdom of United Israel.

David of Judah and Israel
1,046-1,006 BCE

The death of King Saul in battle at Mount Gilboa, along with the death of his logical heir, Jonathan, and two of Saul's other sons, left the throne of Israel empty. Saul had derived his authority to rule Israel from an anointing by the prophet Samuel at the instruction of God, and that same granting of authority by Samuel had been extended to the shepherd boy David before Saul's death. David was the God-chosen successor to Saul. However, the court of Saul, under the influence of Saul's army commander, Abner, did not respect God's will and set up Saul's only surviving son, Ishbosheth, as king ruling from the city of Mahanaim in Gilead. Meanwhile, David and his troops were instructed by the Lord to retire to Hebron in Judah, whereupon the men of Judah recognized David as their king.

The chronology of that early period in the reigns of David and Ishbosheth is subject to interpretation. All that is stated directly is that Ishbosheth reigned for two years in Mahanaim (2 Samuel 2:10) and that David reigned for six years and six months in Hebron (2 Samuel 2:11). It can be assumed from the order of the text that David's reign began soon after Saul's death, which means that his reign over the tribe of Judah began before the 1st of Tishri in the year 1,046 BCE. From the biblical text, it is uncertain exactly where the reign of Ishbosheth fits into the years of David's reign over Judah. It seems to have happened in the first two years after Saul's death, followed by a long period of conflict between the house of David and the house of Saul led by Abner (2 Samuel 3:1). All that can be said with chronological certainty is that there was instability in Israel for the six-plus years while David was ruling Judah from Hebron. After seven years, during which time Ishbosheth was murdered, the twelve tribes of Israel recognized David as king over all of Israel, not just Judah (2 Samuel 5:1-3). He reigned for seven 1st of Tishris over Judah, then for thirty-three 1st of Tishris over Israel, for a total reign that included forty 1st of Tishris (1 Kings 2:11).

By making logical assumptions, the various events in David's life that are recounted in the biblical text can be used to construct a hypothetical chronology for the life of David, but a definitive chronology for his life is not possible. The text states that David was a young boy when he was anointed king by Samuel. He had to be less than twenty years old, since later (a few years?) he was only allowed to visit, not join, his older brothers who were serving on the front lines fighting against the Philistines in the army of Saul. It seems reasonable to assume that

David had reached *bar mitzvah* age before his anointing, which would mean that he was at least thirteen years old. Since the text reveals that David was thirty years old when he became king of Judah (2 Samuel 5:4), and assuming that his becoming king of Judah happened on or before the 1st of Tishri in 1,046 BCE, within a few months after Saul's death at Mount Gilboa, that reveals that David was born *circa* 1,076 BCE, and that he was anointed by Samuel *circa* 1,063 BCE, about twenty-three years after Saul had been anointed as Israel's first king.

It is impossible to know David's exact age when he fought and killed the giant Goliath, so once again logical assumptions have to be made based on what is indicated in the biblical text. As stated before, David was not old enough to be a soldier in the army, so that means he had to be somewhere between thirteen, the assumed lowest age at his anointing, and twenty years old, the age at which he would have been a soldier and not just a younger brother visiting his older brothers at the front lines, as was the case according to the text. It is known that David was the youngest of eight brothers, with the three eldest brothers fighting in Saul's army (1 Samuel 17: 13-14), so it can be assumed that there were four brothers older than David but also too young to be in Saul's army. Subtracting four years (to allow for the birth of David's four older brothers) from twenty years old, the age of military service, reveals that David was about fifteen or sixteen years old when he slew Goliath, and that seems to fit the description of David for that event that is given in the biblical text. At that age, David would have been given some adult responsibilities (tending the flocks alone), but nevertheless would still not have been considered a man. If the assumptions are correct, then David would have slain Goliath around the year 1,060 BCE.

David began ruling as king of Judah in the year 1,046 BCE, when he was thirty years old. His seven-year reign over Judah coincided with the last three years of the reign of pharaoh Smendes I (*r.* 1,069-1,043), first pharaoh in Dynasty 21 in Egypt, and the short four-year reign of pharaoh Amenemnisu (*r.* 1,043-1,039), also of Dynasty 21. Neither pharaoh left any record of interaction with Judah or Israel. David seems to have established Jerusalem as his capital in the first year of his reign as king over United Israel in 1,039 BCE. His thirty-three year reign from Jerusalem began that year, the same year that saw the beginning of the reign of pharaoh Psusennes I (*r.* 1,039-991), whose long reign in Tanis extended to the early years of the reign of David's son, Solomon. It can be assumed that David's kingdom enjoyed peaceful relations with Egypt during the reign of Psusennes I, since no record of belligerency against Israel has been found in the Egyptian artifacts describing the pharaoh's reign, and the biblical text has no mention of aggression against Egypt by David. The fact that Solomon was given a daughter of pharaoh as a wife so soon after David's death testifies to the emergence of David's kingdom as a regional power with which it was of benefit to form an alliance, and to the decades of apparent good relations between the court of Psusennes I and the house of David that laid the groundwork for such a union advantageous to both parties. Having a friendly Egyptian ally on his southern border gave David the freedom to expand his kingdom to the east across the Jordan and northeast toward the Euphrates, which is what he did, defeating in turn the Moabites, Edomites, Ammonites and Syrians (Arameans) during the course of his reign. To the northwest of Israel, David formed an alliance with Hiram I, king of the Phoenician city of Tyre, and they apparently became close personal friends as well (1 Kings 5:1). To the southwest, the Philistines continued to be aggressive, but were repeatedly defeated by David, who had served for a "full year and four months" in the Philistine army under king Achish of Gath before he himself became king of Judah (1 Samuel 27:7). Later, as king of United Israel, David captured Philistine cities and territory, neutralized their threat to the southern tribes of Israel, and eventually even incorporated Philistine mercenaries into his own army. After the reign of David, the Philistines never again threatened Israel and they gradually faded from history as a distinct people.

David had many sons and daughters during his reign, but his relationship with Solomon is the one that is most chronologically significant, mainly because any reconstruction of Bible chronology that goes back in time beyond the reign of David depends on understanding the chronology of Solomon. David captured Jerusalem in 1,039 BCE, and it had to be later than that date when he seduced Bathsheba, the mother of Solomon, after seeing her bathing on a Jerusalem rooftop. The biblical text does not say how long after the capture of Jerusalem that David married Bathsheba, but it is logical to assume that several years passed before their union. After the marriage, Bathsheba lost their first child, so at least three years passed before the birth of Solomon, an event that could not have happened earlier than 1,035 BCE. That would have made Solomon about twenty-eight years old when he was chosen to be heir to the throne. However, David, when he recognized Solomon as the heir to the throne just before his death in the year 1,006 BCE, referred to Solomon as "young and tender" (1 Chronicles 29:1), which can be interpreted as meaning he was too young to serve in the army, making him less than twenty years old. The *Seder Olam* says that Solomon was between seven and twelve years old when he became king, arriving at that conclusion by making numerous assumptions, not all based on the biblical text. From the chronological information preserved in the Books of Kings and Chronicles, it is impossible to definitively determine Solomon's exact age when he became king, but discovering his age at his coronation is unimportant compared to establishing the actual year that he became king.

Solomon of Israel
1,006-966 BCE

The Bible does not give the year that Solomon became king over Israel after the death of David, at least not explicitly, but that year can be calculated from Daniel, chapter 4, which reveals the year that the kingdom of Israel was rent from Solomon's son, Rehoboam. That year is revealed as the year 964 BCE. By knowing the year for the rending of the kingdom, Rehoboam's first 1st of Tishri can be calculated to have occurred in 966 BCE (see Timeline 2.1 on page 17). That means that Solomon's final 1st of Tishri as king of Israel occurred in 967 BCE. Counting forty 1st of Tishris back from that final 1st of Tishri in Solomon's forty-year reign reveals that Solomon's began his reign as sole ruler of Israel sometime before the 1st of Tishri in the year 1,006 BCE (see Table 3.1 on page 42). Jewish tradition says that David died on the Day of Pentecost, so Solomon would have had about a four-month accession year from that date until the next 1st of Tishri, which means that the first year of his reign began on the 1st of Tishri in the year 1,006 BCE (see Timeline 3.2 on page 49).

Once the first numbered year of Solomon's reign has been identified, the all-important fourth regnal year can be calculated. It is from that fourth year, the year when the Bible says that he began construction on the Temple, that pre-Solomonic biblical chronology can be anchored. His fourth regnal year turns out to be the Jewish year that ran from the 1st of Tishri in 1,003 BCE to the 1st of Tishri in 1,002 BCE. That year is one of the most significant chronological anchor points in all of sacred chronology. For instance, from that anchor point the year of the Exodus can be determined, and from the year of the Exodus the dates of the patriarchs can be determined. The start of construction on Solomon's Temple occurred in the second month of the fourth year of Solomon's reign, in the year 1,002 BCE, keeping in mind that months were numbered from the first month Nisan, which occurred in spring, whereas regnal years began on the 1st of Tishri, the seventh month, which occurred in the fall. Thus, the second month would have occurred in spring of the year 1,002 BCE, a month after Passover.

As stated before, Solomon was young when he became king. While offering sacrifices at Gibeon during his first regnal year, the Lord appeared to him in a dream. Solomon confessed to the Lord in 1 Kings, chapter 3, verse 7 that he was *"[... but] a little child: I know not [how] to go out or come in"* (KJV), essentially invoking the request Moses had made to God in Numbers, chapter 27, verse 17, *"Let the Lord, the God of the spirits of all flesh, set a man over the congregation, Which may go out before them, and which may go in before them, and which may lead them out, and which may bring them in; that the congregation of the Lord be not as sheep which have no shepherd"* (KJV). It was at that time that God granted Solomon wisdom to rule his people Israel. During the next three years, Solomon established the authority of his kingship over both secular and sacred realms, sentencing his enemies Adonijah, Joab, and Shimei to death and appointing the trustworthy Benaiah son of Jehoiada to take Joab's place as commander of the army and Zadok the priest to take Abiathar's place as high priest.

The chronology of the early years of Solomon's reign are dominated by two events, his marriage to a pharaoh's daughter and the construction of the Temple. In 1 Kings, chapter 3, verse 1, it is stated that Solomon *"made affinity with Pharaoh king of Egypt, and took Pharaoh's daughter, and brought her into the city of David"* (KJV). From the order given in the biblical text, that alliance of marriage took place very early in the reign of Solomon, probably in his first full regnal year, 1,005 BCE. That would identify the pharaoh with whom Solomon made such an alliance as Psusennes I (r. 1,039-991 BCE) of Dynasty 21. Only one daughter of Psusennes, named Istemkheb C by Egyptologists, is known from inscriptions, and she is thought by Professor Ken Kitchen to have married the Egyptian high priest Menkheperre at Thebes, so the daughter of pharaoh who married Solomon remains unnamed. The biblical text does reveal in 1 Kings, chapter 9, verse 16,

---

[1] Going back four-hundred and forty years from the fourth year of Solomon's reign yields the year 1,442 BCE (1,002 BCE + 440 years back in time) as the year of the Exodus. Subtracting the forty years that the Children of Israel wandered in the wilderness reveals the year 1,402 bce as the year when Joshua and the Children of Israel crossed the Jordan River, entered the promised land, and began the conquest of Canaan. After seven years of conquest, the land was at peace and each of the twelve tribes received its allotment in the year that saw the observance of the forty-ninth Passover after the Exodus (see Timeline A on page 137 and the "Sabbath and Jubilee Years" table for years bce on page 131' also, see full explanation for using 440 years in "Date of the Exodus" on page 135).

Chapter Three: Kings of United Israel (1,086-961 BCE)

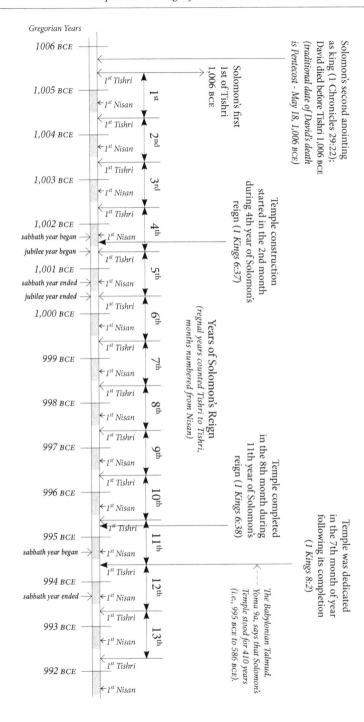

that *"Pharaoh king of Egypt had gone up, and taken Gezer, and burnt it with fire, and slain the Canaanites that dwelt in the city, and given it for a portion unto his daughter, Solomon's wife"* (KJV). Solomon then rebuilt the walls of Gezer.[1]

The greatest achievement of Solomon was that of creating the Temple as a center of worship that required the twelve tribes to look to Jerusalem for their spiritual sustenance. The construction of the Temple began in the second month of his fourth regnal year, 1,002 BCE, which was a sabbath year when no sowing or harvesting could be done, thus freeing manpower for gathering materials and building the structure. Construction of the Temple continued for seven years and was completed in the eighth month of Solomon's eleventh regnal year, in 996 BCE. He waited until the next 10th of Tishri, the Day of Atonement, for the Temple's dedication, a major spiritual event that was accomplished during the sabbath year that began in 995 BCE. A diagram showing the events of Solomon's reign with respect to the Temple is provided on the previous page.[2]

Solomon reigned for forty years over a prosperous and peaceful United Israel (1 Kings 11:42). The later years of his long reign coincided with the reigns of three pharaohs, Amenemope (r. 993-984), Osochor (r. 984-978), and Siamun (r. 978-959). Solomon died in late 967 BCE or possibly early in 966 BCE.

Rehoboam of Israel
966-961 BCE

The Bible records that Rehoboam, Solomon's son and David's grandson, was recognized in Jerusalem as king when his father died, and indicates indirectly that he reigned as king of United Israel for four-plus years. It also records that his rule was never fully established over the northern ten tribes, which perhaps had factions still harboring resentment against Judah that had roots going back to the schism between the houses of Saul and David decades before. The chronology of the reigns of the kings after the death of Solomon and during the period of the divided monarchies is discussed in the next chapter.

---

[1] At Tel Gezer in modern Israel, archaeologists have uncovered the remains of a large, six-chambered gate, which is almost identical to gates found in excavations at Hazor and Megiddo, all three mentioned in the biblical text as being built by Solomon (1 Kings 9:15).

[2] The *Babylonian Talmud (Tractate Yoma 9a)* says that Solomon's Temple operated for 410 years. Since it was destroyed in 586 BCE, counting back 410 Passovers (counting Passovers being the ancient scribal way of marking the passage of years) confirms 995 BCE as the year of its dedication.

CHAPTER FOUR

KINGS OF ISRAEL AND JUDAH
961-721 BCE

Solomon died knowing that the kingdom of United Israel would be rent from his son and successor, Rehoboam (1 Kings 11:11-12). Solomon's death occurred after the 1st of Tishri in 967 BCE and before Passover in 966 BCE. Rehoboam then claimed the throne, taking up residence in the king's palace and consolidating rule in Jerusalem. Sometime before Passover on the 15th of Nisan in 966 BCE, Rehoboam, who had been recognized only by the southern tribe of Judah at that point, traveled to Shechem to be confirmed as king by the ten northern tribes. Jeroboam, his rival for power who had taken refuge from Solomon by fleeing to the court of pharaoh Siamun during Solomon's last years and had recently returned from Egypt, acted as spokesperson for the northern tribes, laying out conditions for giving their allegiance to Rehoboam. Those conditions centered on securing a reduction in the share of the annual tax levied to pay for Temple construction. The levy would have been especially burdensome that year, the second year in which no crops were harvested following the sabbath year that bagan in 967 BCE and was ending on 1st of Nisan in 966 BCE. Rehoboam eventually refused to lessen the levy, so the ten northern tribes rejected his kingship during Passover week in 964 BCE, fulfilling the prophecy about God's judgement against Solomon for his idolatry and unfaithfulness in keeping the commandments. The northern tribes coalesced under the leadership of Jeroboam, who then led a rebellion against Rehoboam.

For the next three years, Rehoboam tried to reassert his dominion over the rebellious tribes in the north, relying on the people's need to worship in Jerusalem three times a year to remind them of his authority. Jeroboam, realizing that the Temple continually focused the people's spiritual life toward Jerusalem, and thus seeing it as the greatest threat to his authority, established an alternative temple system in the north, with golden calves, non-Levite priests, and two altars for offering sacrifices located in Bethel and Dan. The turn to idolatry caused the Levites and priests to migrate south to Judah over the next few years (2 Chronicles 11:13-17), whereupon Jeroboam apparently reacted to the weakening of his kingdom by asking for help from his Egyptian ally Siamun and his relative-by-marriage, Shishak (the future Sheshenq I), who led Siamun's army against Jerusalem in the fifth year of Rehoboam (the fifth year after he had succeeded Solomon as king of Israel). Shishak took the holy things and treasures from tJerusalem in an attempt to diminish the allure of the Temple and the claim to supreme authority by its priesthood. It was at that time that Rehoboam was apparently reduced to being king of Judah only, and that the separate kingdoms of Israel and Judah were made permanent. The year that the divided monarchies began was 961 BCE, and it is from that year that the regnal years recorded in 1 and 2 Kings, 2 Chronicles, and the prophets must be counted. On pages 21-29, the reigns of the thirty-eight kings (and one queen) of the kingdoms of Israel and Judah are shown harmonized with one another, using 961 BCE as the starting date for both kingdoms. In the notes that follow, the reign of each king or queen, and the chronological details associated with his or her reign, are discussed in the order in which the reigns began in time.

Jeroboam of Israel
961-940 BCE

Rehoboam of Judah
961-944 BCE

The traditional chronology of the Hebrew kings says that Shishak, pharaoh of Egypt, came against Jerusalem in Rehoboam's fifth regnal year, which is also assumed to be Jeroboam's fifth regnal year. However, that traditional chronology does not accurately reflect the actual sequence of events that took place between the death of Solomon and the point in time when the northern kingdom of Israel was established as a separate kingdom under Jeroboam and Rehoboam was reduced to being king of only the southern kingdom of Judah.

Jeroboam made his first appearance on the stage of history during the reign of Solomon (1 Kings 11:26-41). It is recorded in the Bible that he was a *"mighty man of valour"* (KJV), so much so that Solomon made him ruler over the house of Joseph. Later, after being told by the prophet Ahijah that God would divide the united kingdom and make him ruler over the northern ten tribes, Jeroboam *"lifted up his hand against the king"* (KJV). That treasonous act caused Solomon to seek Jeroboam's life, whereupon he fled to Egypt and was given sanctuary by Shishak, previously identified in this book as Shoshenq, the commander of pharaoh Siamun's army and the future pharaoh Shoshenq I (see page 36). The dates of Siamun's reign (r. 978-959) reveal that Jeroboam fled to Egypt sometime during the final twelve years of Solomon's reign. Interestingly, there is an earlier account of an Egyptian pharaoh giving refuge to another prince of the Levant, Hadad of Edom, who was taken to Egypt as an infant when David defeated the Edomites (1 Kings 11:14-22), probably during the reign of Psusennes I. Hadad was given

Chapter Four: Kings of Israel and Judah (961-721 BCE)

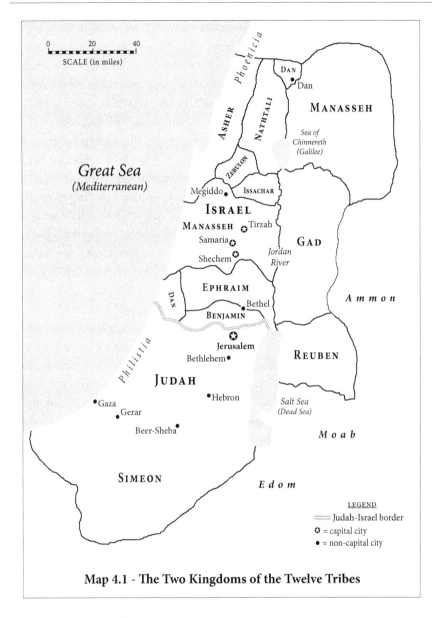

Map 4.1 - The Two Kingdoms of the Twelve Tribes

a house and pharaoh's sister-in-law as his wife, and they had a son named Genubath. When David died, Hadad returned to rule over Edom and proceeded to become an enemy of Solomon. It was during that time, when Hadad of Edom and Rezon of Syria were busy harassing Israel, that Jeroboam rebelled against

Solomon and fled to Egypt, where he received a similar reception to the one that Hadad had received decades earlier, this time from Siamun's court. The Septuagint even records that Shishak (Sheshonq) gave his wife's sister to Jeroboam in marriage. After Solomon died, the people of the north sent for Jeroboam. The Bible does not say how soon thereafter he returned to Israel, but the indication from the biblical text is that it happened while Rehoboam was trying to establish his reign.

Rehoboam was proclaimed king in Jerusalem by the men of Judah at the time of Solomon's death (1 Kings 11:43), a coronation that happened before the 1st of Tishri in the year 966 BCE. His kingship began with an accession year in accordance the scribal custom of Judah. Apparently, the recognition of Rehoboam's kingship that took place in Judah was not universally accepted throughout Israel and a separate recognition ceremony involving the other ten tribes had to take place later, in the north and outside of Jerusalem. That explains why Rehoboam felt the need to travel to Shechem to be recognized as king over all of Israel, as indicated in the biblical text (1 Kings 12:1), and it may indicate that there was still lingering distrust from the animosity that had existed between the house of Saul and the house of David. Since the north began its civil year by observing New-Year Day on the 1st of Nisan (judging from the way the kingdom of Israel later recorded the regnal years of its kings), Rehoboam probably went to Shechem to receive the north's obeisance on the 1st of Nisan. There the people petitioned him to give them relief from the heavy tax burden levied to offset the cost of Temple construction during Solomon's reign.

Although not stated directly in the biblical text, the timing of the people's request to Rehoboam for tax relief is significant, and can best be understood when examined in relation to the seven-year sabbath cycle. The meeting between Rehoboam and the people happened on the 1st of Nisan in the year 966 BCE. That New-Year Day marked the conclusion of a sabbath year that spanned the year 967/966 BCE, which meant that there had been no crops harvested in the spring of 967 BCE, and no crops planted in the winter of that year for harvesting in the spring of 966 BCE. The next harvest would come in the spring of 965 BCE. In essence, the people were facing two taxation periods during which there would be only one harvest from which those taxes could be paid. In ancient Israel, taxes were paid in produce and livestock, either directly or sometimes indirectly as those commodities could be exchanged for gold and silver. Although tradition says that no civil taxes were collected during the sabbath year and in the year following, since no crops were harvested in those years, it is probable that the

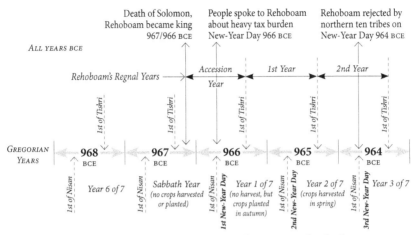

Diagram 4.2 - First Two Years in the Reign of Rehoboam

people were only seeking relief from the extra taxes Solomon had levied to pay for building the Temple and the king's palace, a taxation which the people in the north resented, not only because it was an extra financial burden, but because it benefitted Judah at the expense of the other tribes. As previously stated, the spokesperson who presented the people's grievances and stipulated their conditions for giving allegiance to Rehoboam was Jeroboam, who had returned from Egypt at the request of the people sometime after the death of Solomon.

After hearing the petition for relief from the extra Temple taxes, Rehoboam told the people that he would give them an answer to their petition on the third day (1 Kings 12:12). At first reading, it is easy to conclude that Rehoboam simply wanted a day or two to consult with his advisors to consider the economic ramifications of changing tax policy, but that fails to take into account the sabbath cycle and taxation schedule. When Rehoboam said to return on the "third day," he was saying that he would give his answer on the third New-Year Day from the one on which the request was made. That would be the one in 964 BCE, the first one to occur after the first taxable harvest in the new sabbath cycle. So, Rehoboam was telling the northern tribes that he would return to Shechem and give them his answer to their request for tax relief after twenty-four months, on the third New-Year Day (see Diagram 4.2 above). When the people gathered at Shechem to hear the king's answer on that appointed New-Year Day, Rehoboam harshly rejected their demands, causing the northern ten tribes to reject his kingship sometime during

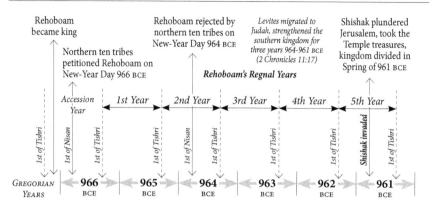

Diagram 4.3 - First Five Years in the Reign of Rehoboam

the week of Passover in 964 BCE. The kingdom was thus rent from Rehoboam as foretold (1 Kings 12:16).[1] The northern tribes then recognized Jeroboam as their king, probably soon after Passover week in 964 BCE, but his kingdom would not become politically autonomous for several years. Upon being rejected in the north, Rehoboam returned to Jerusalem, where he mustered the army of Judah to invade and subdue Jeroboam and the ten breakaway tribes. The invasion did not happen, though. The prophet Shemaiah, speaking for the Lord, warned Rehoboam against engaging in warfare with his kinsmen (1 Kings 12:21-24). Still, Rehoboam had control of Judah, which included the tribal lands of Simeon, the city of Jerusalem, surrounding lands belonging to Benjamin, and, most important, the Temple. The three annual pilgrimage festivals—Festival of Unleavened Bread (Passover), Festival of Weeks, and Day of Atonement (Festival of Tabernacles)—compelled the people from all twelve tribes to submit to the spiritual authority of the Temple and required them to visit Jerusalem three times a year, seriously enhancing the civil authority of Rehoboam and the spiritual authority of the Levitical priests. Jeroboam responded by establishing his own competing temple system in the north. He made two golden calves, locating them at Bethel and Dan. He also recruited a new priesthood, allowing non-Levites to serve as priests. Rejecting Jeroboam's apostasy and turn to idolatry, the Levites began to exit the northern tribal areas and migrate to Judah over the next three years (2 Chronicles 11:13-17).

---

[1] In Daniel, chapter 4, 964 BCE was identified as the year of the rending; see pages 14-17.

At this point, his authority eroding, Jeroboam appealed to his ally Siamun (and his brother-in-law Shishak, the future Shoshenq I) for help, whereupon Siamun sent his army, under the command of Shishak, against Judah and Jerusalem. The attack took place in Siamun's seventeenth regnal year, which was the fifth year of Rehoboam—that is, in the year after the fifth 1st of Tishri observed by Rehoboam as king of United Israel (see Diagram 4.3 on the opposite page)—which was the year that had its spring in the Gregorian year 961 BCE. In Jerusalem, Siamun's army led by Shishak/Shoshenq proceeded to loot the Temple and the king's palace, taking the Temple treasures, including the golden shields of Solomon (losses mentioned in the biblical text, 1 Kings 14:25; 2 Chronicles 12:2). Seizing the Temple treasures, which seems to have been the main thrust of the invasion, was a deliberate attempt to diminish the authority of the Jerusalem Temple and its priestly system, and, in that way, to enhance the authority of Egypt's ally, Jeroboam, with his alternative temple system and priesthood in the north. The main result of the invasion in 961 BCE was that the kingdom of United Israel was permanently divided into the kingdoms of Israel and Judah, and it was from that date of separation that the regnal years of Jeroboam and Rehoboam began to be numbered by their royal scribes. The permanence of the separation was reflected in the differing systems used to record the reigns thereafter.

Once the kingdom of United Israel had divided into two separate kingdoms, Rehoboam, who was forty-one years old when he became king of Judah, ruled the southern kingdom from Jerusalem for seventeen years, until the year 944 BCE (1 Kings 14:21; 2 Chronicles 12:13). Jeroboam, whose age when he became king is not recorded, ruled the northern kingdom from Shechem for twenty-two years, until 940 BCE (1 Kings 14:20). The reigns of both kings coincided with the last two pharaohs of Dynasty 21, Siamun (r. 978-959) and (Har)-Psusennes II (r. 959-945), and the first pharaoh in Dynasty 22, Shoshenq I (r. 945-924).

Abijah of Judah
944-942 BCE

Abijah, son of Rehoboam, became king of Judah in the eighteenth year of Jeroboam of Israel, and reigned for three years from Jerusalem (1 Kings 15:1-2; 2 Chronicles 13:1-2), meaning that he observed three 1st of Tishris as king. He fought against Jeroboam and the army of Israel, handing them a stinging defeat. During the warfare, Abijah captured the apostate religious center in Bethel and expanded his dominion to the strategically important lands north of Jerusalem belonging to the tribe of Ephraim (2 Chronicles 13:2-20). The reign of Abijah coincided with the reign of Shoshenq I (r. 945-924) in Egypt.

Asa of Judah
942-900 BCE

Asa, son of Abijah, became king of Judah in the twentieth year of Jeroboam of Israel, and reigned for forty-one years in Jerusalem (1 Kings 15: 9-10). In the third year of Asa, Baasha, son of Ahijah of Issachar, murdered Nadab, Jeroboam's successor, and declared himself king in Shechem. The Bible says that a perpetual state of hostility existed between Asa and Baasha (1 Kings 15:16).

Once he was king, Asa began to purify the land, removing the idols of his fathers (Solomon and Rehoboam; 1 Kings 15:12), and he restored the dedicated treasures and vessels to the Temple. That raises the possibility that the treasures of the Temple captured by Shishak during his 961 BCE campaign had been given to Jeroboam, who placed them in his apostate temple in Bethel, where they were then recaptured by Asa's father Abijah. After reconsecration, the treasures would have been returned to the Temple. Asa went so far as to removed his mother as queen for making an idol, but failed to remove all of the high places where the people offered sacrifices to foreign gods. Still, to reward his efforts, God granted Asa's kingdom ten years of peace (2 Chronicles 14:1). Except for those years of peace, the chronology of the early years of Asa is not specified in the biblical text. It can be assumed that the ten years of peace ended with the invasion of Zerah the Ethiopian in 926 BCE, which would mean that the ten years began sometime in 937 BCE. In that case, Asa would have dedicated the first five years of his reign to bringing the spiritual life of Judah into compliance with the Law.

Zerah the Ethiopian was most likely a general in Shoshenq I's army. The attack by Zerah on the cities in southern Judah in 926 BCE (2 Chronicles 14:9-15) can best be understood as the first event in a series of larger events. Why he led an Egyptian army to invade Judah is not revealed in the biblical text, but it made strategic sense for Egypt to control all of Canaan. The northern kingdom of Israel was already allied with Egypt. The capture of Judah would have meant that it could be ruled directly by Egypt or placed under the governance of Baasha of Israel, in either case the result being a unified Egypt-friendly buffer area between Egypt and Syria (see timeline for Zerah's invasion, Asa's repulsion of that invasion, Baasha's blockade of Jerusalem, Benhadad's attack on Baasha, and the followup invasion by Shoshenq to defend Baasha and Israel on page 38).

Zerah's attack on Judah probably started from the south with an assault on Hebron, which was called by its ancient name "Rubuti" in the list of conquered cities on the Karnak inscription that describes the Canaan campaign of Shoshenq. After attacking Hebron, Zerah moved on to the fortified city of Mareshah, where his forces were met in the valley of Zephathah by Asa and his army, or possibly Hebron was skipped and Mareshah was attacked first. At any rate, the Egyptians were routed by the Judeans at Mareshah and driven back beyond Gerar in disarray (2 Chronicles 14:12-15). The relief at Karnak records that Shoshenq was troubled by the defeat, saying "Now, My [Maj]esty found that ... [they] were killing ... [my soldiers?, and] my army leaders. His majesty was troubled about them." [1] After Mareshah, Asa and his forces plundered the remnants of Zerah's army and the cities around Gerar, gathering much loot before returning to Jerusalem, where they held a victory celebration and gave thanks to God for their success. The celebration took place in the third month, Sivan (May/June), in the fifteenth regnal year of Asa, which was in the Gregorian year 926 BCE (2 Chronicles 15:10).

The actions of Baasha while all of the above events were unfolding are difficult to determine precisely. He fortified Ramah, which is located on the main trade route north of Jerusalem, effectively cutting off access to Judah from the north. Whether this happened in conjunction with the raid of Zerah or after the attack cannot be determined. What is known is that the aggressive stance of Baasha alarmed Asa to the point that he sent gold and Temple treasures to Damascus in an attempt to entice Benhadad I to attack Baasha, with whom Benhadad had a non-aggression agreement of some sort. Asa's appeal and bribe worked. Benhadad sent the captains of his army against the kingdom of Israel in the north, attacking and destroying the cities of Ijon, Dan, Abelmaim, and all the store cities of Naphtali. When Baasha learned that his northern border region was under attack, he abandoned his fortifications at Ramah and headed northward to defend his kingdom from being overrun by Benhadad (2 Chronicles 16:3-5).

Baasha also called upon his Egyptian ally, Shoshenq I, for help. The pharaoh quickly assembled his army at Gaza and headed northward to help Baasha. The Egyptian army skirted the fortified cities of Judah, taking only Ajalon on the periphery according to the Karnak inscription, before crossing the border into

---

[1] Kitchen, *The Third Intermediate Period in Egypt 1100-650 BC*, p. 294.

the northern kingdom. The main body of troops bypassed Jerusalem and headed northward from Gibeon to secure the cities in the highlands of Israel, including its capital Tirzah, while another task force headed into the Jordan River valley, crossed the river, and began to reinforce the cities on both sides of the river that were closest to the border. The task forces rejoined at Megiddo and proceeded to secure the area north of that city, including the land of Naphtali that was under attack by the forces of Benhadad. Once the kingdom of Israel and the cities of the north had been secured and the threat from the Syrians had been neutralized, the army of Shoshenq turned south and returned to Egypt. By late 925 BCE, the invasion and defense of the northern kingdom of Israel by Shoshenq I had concluded.

One chronological detail in the King James translation concerning the reign of Asa must be clarified. The KJV translation says that, *"In the twenty and sixth year of Asa king of Judah began Elah the son of Baasha to reign over Israel in Tirzah, two years"* (1 Kings 16:8), and it also says, *"In the six and thirtieth year of the reign of Asa Baasha king of Israel came up against Judah, and built Ramah"* (2 Chronicles 16:1a). Since Elah became king upon Baasha's death in year twenty-six of Asa, how could Baasha come against Judah in the thirty-sixth year of Asa? Obviously, he could not, since he had been dead for ten years. What is actually being stated in 2 Chronicles, chapter 16, verse 1, and what is poorly translated in the KJV, is that *"In the thirty-sixth year after the division of United Israel into the two kingdoms of Israel and Judah, during the reign of Asa king of Judah, Baasha king of Israel came up against Judah and built Ramah"* (Au), and that paraphrase fits the chronology of the kings perfectly (see pages 22-23).

The *Seder Olam* adds an intriguing footnote to the events surrounding the invasion of Canaan by Shoshenq I during the reign of Asa of Judah. It says that Asa himself regained from Zerah the Ethiopian the Temple treasures that had been taken by Shishak thirty-six years earlier during the reign of Rehoboam.[1] There is no biblical evidence to support that story, and it negates the possible recapture of Temple treasures by Abijah when he retook Bethel, but it does raise some interesting questions if true. Did Zerah bring the ark to the battle, hoping to use its power against the Israelites, as the Philistines had done during the period of the judges? Was the ark part of the plunder captured by Asa when his army routed the Egyptians at Mareshah and Gerar? If so, were the Temple treasures retrieved from Zerah the Temple treasures later sent to Benhadad?

---

[1] Guggenheimer, *Seder Olam*, p. 150.

Nadab of Israel
940-939 BCE

Nadab, son of Jeroboam, succeeded his father as king of Israel in the second year of Asa of Judah, and he reigned in Shechem for two years (1 Kings 15:25), but observed only one 1st of Nisan as king, the one in 939 BCE. Later that year he led the army of Israel into battle against the Philistines, laying siege to the city of Gibbethon. While the siege was underway, Baasha conspired against Nadab and eventually killed him, seizing the throne for himself. Nadab's short and uneventful reign coincided with the reign of Shoshenq I (r. 945-924) and the rise of the Neo-Assyrian Empire under its first king, Adad-nirari II (r. 940-919). It can be assumed that Nadab continued the friendly relations with Egypt that characterized his father's reign, but no contact with Assyria is indicated.

Baasha of Israel
939-916 BCE

Baasha, son of Ahijah from the tribe of Issachar, murdered Nadab, son of Jeroboam, while the king was leading the army of Israel in a siege at Gibbethon, a Philistine city. After the regicide in 939 BCE, the third year of Asa, Baasha seized the throne of Israel and reigned from the highland town of Tirzah, which he made the capital of the northern kingdom (1 Kings 15:21, 33). A perpetual state of warfare existed between Baasha and Asa according to the biblical text (1 Kings 15:16), but the Bible does not mention specific hostile events between the two kings until 926 BCE. Prior to that year, Baasha had apparently agreed to some sort of non-aggression pact with Benhadad I of Damascus that gave him the freedom to turn his attention away from his northern border and look to the south, probably as part of a plan to attack Judah that was coordinated with his Egyptian allies who were threatening Judah from the south. In conjunction with a failed Egyptian campaign against Judah led by Zerah the Ethiopian in the thirty-fifth year after the kingdom of United Israel separated into the kingdoms of Israel and Judah, Baasha fortified Ramah and blockaded Judah, preventing access to Jerusalem from the north. At that point, Asa sent treasures from the Temple to Damascus, bribing Benhadad to break his pact with Baasha and attack the northern kingdom on its northern border. Benhadad sent his army southward into the land of Naphtali around the Sea of Chinnereth (Galilee).

Fearing the loss of part of his kingdom, Baasha then appealed to Shoshenq I for help in repelling the invaders. The pharaoh, fearing a united Israel and Judah allied with Syria and the possibility of having hostile troops stationed not far from his capital at Tanis in the Nile Delta, responded by mustering his army and marching northward, bypassing the fortified cities of Judah, except Ajalon, to confront the Syrians in the north of Israel. The campaign to restore Baasha and the kingdom of Israel as an ally of Egypt is described in detail by the inscriptions at Karnak attributed to the reign of Shoshenq I (see pages 35-40). Baasha's twenty-four year reign coincided with the reign of Shoshenq I (r. 945-924) and with the early years in the reign of Osorkon I (r. 924-889) in Egypt, and with the reigns of Adad-nirari II (r. 940-919) and Tikulti-ninurta (r. 919-912) in Assyria.

Elah of Israel
916-914 BCE

Elah, son of Baasha of Israel, became king in Tirzah upon the death of his father late in the year 916 BCE, in the twenty-sixth year of Asa of Judah, and he reigned in Tirzah for two years, but his reign included only one 1st of Nisan (1 Kings 16:8). Other than continuing the "vanities" of Baasha and being killed while in a drunken stupor, no other information about the reign of Elah is provided in the biblical text. The reign of Elah coincided with the reigns of Osorkon I (r. 924889) in Egypt and Tikulti-ninurta (r. 919-912) in Assyria.

Zimri of Israel
914 BCE

Zimri, who was captain over half the king's chariots, murdered Elah in the house of the king's steward while Elah was drunk. Zimri declared himself king of Israel in the year 914 BCE, apparently with the backing of his army faction, and ruled as king from the capital of the northern kingdom, Tirzah, all of that taking place during the twenty-seventh regnal year of Asa (1 Kings 16:9-10, 15a). Zimri did not celebrate a New-Year Day as king, since he occupied the throne for only seven days. The other half of the army was away from Tirzah, surrounding the Philistine city Gibbethon, the same city that had been besieged by Nadab about a quarter-century before, and that portion of the army was led by Omri. When the army at Gibbethon heard that Zimri had killed Elah, they declared allegiance to Omri and made him king over all of Israel. Omri then led his troops to Tirzah and surrounded the city, which quickly surrendered and recognized him as king. Zimri, hearing that Omri had captured the capital, and perhaps realizing that he did could not muster a defense, retreated to the king's palace and committed suicide by burning the palace around him. The brief illegitimate reign of Zimri coincided with the reigns of Osorkon I (*r.* 924-889) in Egypt and Tikulti-ninurta (*r.* 919-912) in Assyria.

Omri of Israel
914-904 BCE

Omri was declared king of Israel on the battlefield at Gibbethon by his army after Zimri murdered Elah back in Tirza in 914 BCE, during the twenty-seventh regnal year of Asa of Judah. Omri was not recognized as king by all of Israel immediately, however. Half of the tribes, with opposition leadership arising from tribal factions loyal to the house of Elah, recognized Tibni, son of Ginath, as king (1 Kings 16:21). The *Seder Olam* says that civil war raged between the two factions for four years until the forces of Tibni were defeated by the forces of Omri in the year 911 BCE, whereupon Omri became sole ruler. According to the biblical text, Omri's reign began in Asa's thirty-first regnal year, with six years as king in Tirzah from the time he was made king by the army, after which he built a new capital, Samaria. He ruled from Samaria for another five or six years, for a total reign of twelve years (1 Kings 16:23). The reign of Omri coincided with the reigns of Osorkon I (*r.* 924-889) in Egypt, and with Tikulti-ninurta (*r.* 919-912) and Adhur-nasir-pal II (*r.* 912-887) in Assyria.

The Mesha Stele, *aka* the Moabite Stone, refers to "Omri, King of Israel," saying that Moab was oppressed by Omri and that Mesha won a great victory against his son.[1] Mesha is mentioned in the Bible, *"And Mesha king of Moab was a sheepmaster, and rendered unto the king of Israel an hundred thousand lambs, and an hundred thousand rams, with the wool. But it came to pass, when Ahab was dead, that the king of Moab rebelled against the king of Israel"* (2 Kings 3:4-5; KJV). Mesha's reign was concurrent with Ahab's reign, but probably not with Omri's, so the defeated "son" was Omri's grandson, Joram (see page 67).

---

[1] W. F. Albright, "Palestinian Inscriptions." (*Ancient Near Eastern Texts*, edited by J. B. Pritchard, 3rd edition; Princeton: Princeton University Press, 1969); p. 320-21.

Ahab of Israel
904-883 BCE

Ahab of Israel is mentioned on the Kurkh Monolith as being one of the kings defeated by Shalmaneser III at the Battle of Qarqar. That mention makes the reign of Ahab one of the most important reigns of any Hebrew king, at least from the standpoint of kingdoms chronology, since it is also known that the Battle of Qarqar took place in Shalmaneser's sixth regnal year. Scholars can thus equate the sixth regnal year of Shalmaneser III, which is traditionally dated to 853 BCE based on Rawlinson's identification of 763 BCE as the year of the Bûr-Saggilê eclipse, to the final regnal year of Ahab, and that connection between the two chronologies makes it possible to count back in time from the last year of Ahab to the first year of Rehoboam of Judah. Using that method, modern scholars have identified the year 931/930 BCE as the first regnal year of Rehoboam and, by extension, the first year of Jeroboam of Israel. Of course, as has been shown by using the Bible-only chronology in Daniel, chapter 4 (see page 17), the kingdoms did not divide in 931/930 BCE, but instead went their separate ways thirty years earlier in the year 961 BCE. Based on that latter date, the years of Ahab's reign can be calculated by subtracting the number of New-Year Days (1st of Nisans) observed as king by Jeroboam, Nadab, Baasha, Elah, Zimri, and Omri from the year 961 BCE to reveal that he began his reign in the year 904 BCE.

Ahab became king upon the death of his father Omri, and he reigned over Israel from Samaria for twenty-two years until he was killed in battle in 883 BCE. The beginning of Ahab's reign coincided with the thirty-eighth year of Asa of Judah (1 Kings 16:29). He married Jezebel, the daughter of Ethbaal of the Zidonians, and went and served Baal, and worshipped him. He also built an altar to Baal in Samaria. He and Jezebel had at least three children, Azariah, Joram (also called Jehoram of Ahab/Israel), and Athaliah, all of whom would eventually govern Israel or Judah or both kingdoms after Ahab's death. The ministry of Elijah was prominent during the reign of Ahab, with the prophet performing great miracles in the name of the God of Israel and thereby engendering the wrath of Jezebel, who, influential with her husband, was devoted to the worship of Baal.

In the realm of foreign affairs, Ahab's reign coincided with the reigns of Osorkon I (r. 924-889), Shoshenq II (ca. 890), and Takeloth I (r. 889-874) in Egypt, and with Ashur-nasir-pal II (r. 914-889) and Shalmaneser III (r. 889-854?) in Assyria. He was able to keep Moab as a tribute-paying vassal, and it was to him that the biblical text refers when it recounts, *"And Mesha king of Moab was a sheepmaster, and rendered unto the king of Israel an hundred thousand lambs, and an hundred thousand rams, with the wool. But it came to pass, when Ahab was dead, that the king of Moab rebelled against the king of Israel"* (KJV; 2 Kings 3:4-5). Ahab was able to resist Benhadad II when he besieged Samaria, and to defeat him when Benhadad returned in the following year with thirty-two kings to battle Ahab at Aphek east of the Jordan. Ahab's army surprised a drunken Benhadad in camp, captured him as he was fleeing, and made him beg for his life. Benhadad was then forced to make a covenant with Ahab, promising non-aggression and returning cities belonging to Israel that were taken in an earlier campaign, all of those events probably taking place in the years 887-886 BCE (1 Kings 20:1-34).

Closer to home, Ahab apparently had good relations with the neighboring kingdom of Judah throughout his reign. Jehoshaphat's son, Jehoram, was given Athaliah, the daughter of Ahab, in marriage, so a close relationship is indicated. That close relationship is further confirmed by the willingness of Jehoshaphat to go into battle with Ahab in his attempt to retake Ramoth-gilead from Damascus. That misadventure, during which Ahab maneuvered to put Jehoshaphat in danger of being killed in his place, resulted instead in the wounding and eventual death of Ahab (2 Chronicles 18:1-34). Some scholars have puzzled that the Battle of Qarqar is not mentioned by that name in the Bible if Ahab was present at that battle, but Ramoth-gilead is mentioned instead. Some have also pointed to the improbability that Ahab would have participated in a military coalition with Israel's enemy, Benhadad, but the Bible indicates that they would not have been enemies at that time because the covenant of non-aggression was in effect.

From the words on the Kurkh Monolith and the Black Obelisk that describe the Battle of Qarqar (see page 33), the first of which claims that Shalmaneser III defeated Ahab of Israel and the second of which claims that it happened in the sixth year of Shalmaneser, 883 BCE (the year of Ahab's death as determined by the sacred chronology in this book), it seems probable that the campaign to retake Ramoth-gilead was at the least tangentially associated with Qarqar, if not in fact part of it. Or, even more likely based on the biblical text, Ahab saw an opportunity to seize territory from Syria while Benhadad was preoccupied with the Assyrian threat to his north. In both cases, it is not unreasonable to propose that the admittedly less-than-diligent Assyrian scribe who composed the Kurkh Monolith simply lumped all of the military actions during that year together and used them to enhance the description of Shalmaneser's victory at Qarqar.

Jehoshaphat of Judah
900-875 BCE

Jehoshaphat began to reign over Judah when his father, Asa of Judah, died in the fourth regnal year of Ahab of Israel. He was thirty-five years old when he became king, and reigned in Jerusalem for twenty-five years (1 Kings 22:41-42). Immediately, he began to restore his kingdom to spiritual purity and to fortify the cities of Judah and Ephraim against aggression. In his third regnal year, the sabbath year 897 BCE, *"he sent to his princes, [even] to Benhail, and to Obadiah, and to Zechariah, and to Nethaneel, and to Michaiah, to teach in the cities of Judah. And with them [he sent] Levites, [even] Shemaiah, and Nethaniah, and Zebadiah, and Asahel, and Shemiramoth, and Jehonathan, and Adonijah, and Tobijah, and Tobadonijah, Levites; and with them Elishama and Jehoram, priests. And they taught in Judah, and [had] the book of the law of the Lord with them, and went about throughout all the cities of Judah, and taught the people"* (KJV; 2 Chronicles 17:7-9). Jehoshaphat married his son Jehoram (later known as Jehoram of Judah) to Athaliah, daughter of Ahab, and they had a son named Ahaziah. Since Ahaziah was twenty-two years old when he succeeded his father as king of Judah in 868 BCE, the marriage had to take place prior to 891 BCE.

During Jehoshaphat's reign, Benhadad II of Damascus besieged Samaria, and the following year he battled Ahab's army at Aphek, where Ahab defeated him and forced him to make a non-aggression covenant. As a result, there was peace between Syria and the kingdom of Israel for three years. In the third year of that period of peace, which was probably the year 884 BCE (a year before the Battle of Qarqar), Jehoshaphat visited Ahab in Samaria and was entertained and feted lavishly. It was during that visit that Ahab persuaded Jehoshaphat to join him in a campaign against Syria to recover Ramoth-gilead and its surrounding territories, lands which had formerly belonged to Israel. Jehoshaphat responded affirmatively, and the following year, in 883 BCE, the combined armies of Israel and Judah battled against Benhadad and his Syrian troops.[1] At the beginning of the battle, Ahab apparently used Jehoshaphat as a decoy, letting the Syrians assume that he was the king of Israel, but the Syrians soon caught on to the

---

[1] The *Seder Olam* says that a three-year famine began in Ahab's thirteenth year (891-889 BCE), followed by two-plus years of war with Benhadad II (888-887 BCE), followed by three years of peace (886-884 BCE), followed by the war against Ramoth-gilead (883 BCE).

deception and went after Ahab instead. Ahab was fatally wounded as he fled the battlefield and died soon thereafter. He was succeeded by his son, Ahaziah, who began to reign as king in Samaria in the seventeenth year of Jehoshaphat.

Jehoshaphat's reign was a prosperous time for Judah. Commerce thrived and the surrounding nations paid homage to the king and sent tribute to Judah (2 Chronicles 17:10-13). In the last years of his reign, the Moabites came against Jehoshaphat, perhaps sensing his vulnerability after the losses at Ramoth-gilead, but they were beaten back by a coalition of the three kings of Judah, Israel, and Edom. Jehoshaphat's reign coincided with the reigns of Osorkon I (r. 924-889), Shoshenq II (ca. 890), and Takeloth I (r. 889-874) in Egypt, and with Ashur-nasir-pal II (r. 914-889) and Shalmaneser III (r. 889-854?) in Assyria.

Ahaziah of Israel
883-882 BCE

Ahaziah, the eldest son of Ahab and Jezebel, became king of Israel upon the death of his father in the seventeenth year of Jehoshaphat of Judah, and he reigned in Samaria for two years (1 Kings 22:51). He celebrated only one New-Year Day as king, on the 1st of Nisan in 882 BCE. The biblical text records only two events during his reign, a failed joint venture in shipbuilding and foreign trade with Jehoshaphat, and his falling through a lattice in his palace, suffering injuries that soon led to his death. Ahaziah's brief reign coincided with the reigns of Takeloth I (r. 889-874) in Egypt and Shalmaneser III (r. 889-854?) in Assyria.

Joram of Israel | Jehoram of Judah
882/879-867 BCE | 875-868 BCE

The reigns of Joram of Israel and Jehoram of Judah are intertwined in the biblical text, as were the relationships of the various individuals in the house of Ahab and the house of Jehoshaphat with one another. The patriarch of the northern kingdom, Ahab of Israel, had at least three children with his wife Jezebel—the eldest a son named Ahaziah, a daughter named Athaliah, and a younger son named Joram, all three of whom eventually ruled Israel or Judah, or, in one case, both. Athaliah married Jehoram of Judah, son of Jehoshaphat of Judah, and they had a son, Ahaziah (named after his uncle Ahaziah, son of Ahab and a king of Israel) who became king of Judah. To complicate matters, Joram of

Israel is sometimes called Jehoram the son of Ahab in the text, and Jehoram of Judah is sometimes called Joram.

Two verses are key to understanding the chronology of the reigns of Joram of Israel and Jehoram of Judah: *"So he [Ahaziah] died according to the word of the Lord which Elijah had spoken. And Jehoram reigned in his stead in the second year of Jehoram the son of Jehoshaphat king of Judah; because he had no son."* (KJV; 2 Kings 1:17) and *"And in the fifth year of Joram the son of Ahab king of Israel, Jehoshaphat [being] then king of Judah, Jehoram the son of Jehoshaphat king of Judah began to reign"* (KJV; 2 Kings 8:16). Verse 1:17 says that Joram of Israel began his reign in the second year of Jehoram of Judah. Verse 8:16 says that Jehoram of Judah began his reign in the fifth year of Joram of Israel. Taken at face value, the two verses seemingly contradict each other, so a meaning apart from the obvious must be discerned. Based on the biblical context, specifically that suggested by verse 1:17, the following sequence of events is proposed:

891 BCE	Athaliah, daughter of Ahab of Israel, married prince Jehoram, son of Jehoshaphat of Judah (2 Kings 8:18), and bore a son, Ahaziah of Judah.
883 BCE	Ahab of Israel was killed at Ramoth-gilead (Qarqar); his eldest son Ahaziah of Israel became king of Israel in the seventeenth year of Jehoshaphat of Judah and reigned for two years (1 Kings 22:51).
882 BCE	Ahaziah of Israel died, leaving no heir; his younger brother Joram of Israel became king, but was too young to rule so his sister Athaliah's husband, Jehoram of Judah, served as regent and ruled Israel for two years (regency and two-year rule of Jehoram implied by 2 Kings1:17).
879 BCE	Joram of Israel came of age and assumed office of king in Israel in the eighteenth year of Jehoshaphat, reigned for twelve years (2 Kings 3:1).
875 BCE	Jehoshaphat died, was succeeded by Jehoram of Judah as king of Judah in the fifth year of Joram of Israel, reigned for eight years (2 Kings 8:16).
868 BCE	Jehoram of Judah died, was succeeded by his son Ahaziah of Judah who reigned for less than one year (2 Kings 8:25-26).
867 BCE	Jehu killed Joram of Israel and Ahaziah of Judah (2 Kings 9:24-27).

The above scenario, which has Jehoram of Judah ruling Israel as regent for two years (together with his wife, Ahab's daughter and Joram's sister Athaliah at his side as regent-queen) until the underage king of Israel, Joram, can reach his majority and be installed as sole ruler, fits the chronological requirements of the biblical texts. In addition, there is indirect support for that chronology in the inscription on the Mesha Stele (the "Moabite Stone"), which says:

> "I am Mesha, son of Kemosh[-yatti], the king of Moab, the Dibonite. My father was king over Moab for thirty years, and I became king after my father. And I made this high-place for Kemosh in Qarcho ... Omri was the king of Israel, and he oppressed Moab for many days, for Kemosh was angry with his land. And his son reigned in his place; and he also said, "I will oppress Moab!" In my days he said so. But I looked down on him and on his house, and Israel has been defeated; it has been defeated forever! And Omri took possession of the whole land of Medeba, and he lived there in his days and half the days of his son: forty years." [1]

Note that the inscription says that the house of Omri held sovereignty over Moab for forty years. Omri reigned over Israel for only twelve years, so his reign and those of his son and grandson were needed to produce that forty-year total. If Omri reasserted authority over Moab at the time he began his reign, in the year 914 BCE, subtracting forty years gives the year 874 BCE, which is exactly the midpoint year in the reign of Joram of Israel. So, the inscription is actually referring to the mid-point year of the twelve-year reign of Omri's grandson Joram, not to his son Ahab, with the sixth year ("half his days") occurring in 874 BCE (see page 24).

The houses of Israel and Judah constituted essentially one kingdom during those years. Unfortunately, the close relationship with the wicked house of Ahab caused Jehoram to lead Judah astray. Because of their unfaithfulness, the biblical text says that God began to reduce both kingdoms. During the reigns of Joram and Jehoram, Moab, Edom and Libnah gained independence. God also stirred up the Philistines and Arabs, who looted Jerusalem and even the palace of Jehoram of Judah, carrying away his wives and sons, all except his youngest son Ahaziah. Jehoram of Judah was himself afflicted with an intestinal disease for two years leading to his death in 868 BCE (2 Chronicles 21:4-20). Joram of Israel would battle Hazael in his last years, and would be killed less than a year after Jehoram's death by Jehu, an Israelite probably allied with Assyria. The reigns of Joram and Jehoram coincided with the reigns of Takeloth I (*r.* 889-874) and Osorkon II (*r.* 874-850) in Egypt, and with Shalmaneser III (*r.* 889-854?) in Assyria.

---

[1] Translation by K. C. Hanson, (www.kchanson.com), adapted from Albright, "Palestinian Inscriptions," p. 320-21.

Ahaziah of Judah
868-867 BCE

Ahaziah, son of Jehoram of Judah and his wife Athaliah, daughter of Ahab, became king upon the death of his father in the year 868 BCE. He reigned only one year in Jerusalem (2 Chronicles 22:2), a reign apparently lasting less than twelve months and including no more than one 1st of Tishri. He joined with Joram of Israel to fight Hazael of Damascus at Ramoth-gilead (2 Chronicles 22:5). After Joram was wounded in battle at Ramah and had retreated to Jezreel to heal, Ahaziah went to visit him. It was at Jezreel that Jehu, who had been anointed king in Ramoth-gilead by a prophet of God and commissioned to slay all of the men of the house of Ahab, killed Joram. Ahaziah fled to Samaria, where he was captured and executed. The reign of Ahaziah of Judah coincided with the reigns of Osorkon II (r. 874-850) in Egypt and Shalmaneser III (r. 889-854?) in Assyria.

Of apologetic interest, a seeming chronological discrepancy about the reign of Ahaziah of Judah is present in two verses of the biblical text, as follows: "*In the **twelfth year** of Joram the son of Ahab king of Israel did Ahaziah the son of Jehoram king of Judah begin to reign*" (2 Kings 8:25) and "*... in the **eleventh year** of Joram the son of Ahab began Ahaziah to reign over Judah*" (2 Kings 9:29). The discrepancy can be easily explained by remembering that Israel used the non-accession year system, while Judah used the accession-year system. In other words, Ahaziah began to reign in Joram's twelfth year using Israel's non-accession year counting, and in the eleventh year using Judah's accession-year counting (see page 23).

Jehu of Israel
867-840 BCE

The earliest mention of Jehu of Israel in history is not found in the Bible, but instead on the Black Obelisk of Shalmaneser III. That inscription says in part: "The tribute of Jehu, son of Omri: I received from him silver, gold, a golden bowl, a golden vase with pointed bottom, golden tumblers, golden buckets, tin, a staff for a king [and] spears."[1] The year of Jehu's payment of tribute has been identified as occurring in Shalmaneser's eighteenth year,[2] which is traditionally dated to

---

[1] Alan Millard, *Discoveries from Bible Times* (Oxford: Lion Hudson plc; 1997); p. 121.
[2] D. D. Luckenbill, *The Ancient Records of Assyria and Babylonia* (Chicago: 1927; vol. I); p. 243.

841 BCE, but is dated to 871 BCE by the chronology for the kings of Assyria used in this book. That means that Jehu paid tribute to Assyria three to four years before he became king of the northern kingdom of Israel in 867 BCE (see page 23), and, significantly, Jehu is not called a king in the Assyrian account. The army of Israel, ruled by Joram and commanded in the field by Jehu, had been engaged in a fight with Hazeal of Damascus for several years. In 871 BCE, Shalmaneser defeated Hazael and threatened Israel. It is not unreasonable to assume that Joram of Israel sent tribute to Shalmaneser by way of his general Jehu, as a hedge against invasion and to make an alliance with Assyria, although payment of tribute by Joram (or Jehu) is not mentioned in the Bible. Three years later, in 868 BCE, in the Assyrian king's twenty-first year, Shalmaneser again waged war against Hazael and captured four of his cities. That was undoubtedly the reason that Joram and Jehu were in Ramoth-gilead, as recorded in the biblical text, to attack Hazael from the south as their ally Shalmaneser was attacking from the north However, during the fighting against Hazael in 868 BCE, several transformative events transpired. Joram was wounded and had to retire from the battlefield. At the same time, Jehu was anointed as king of Israel and Hazael was recognized as the legitimate king of Syria by a prophet sent from Elisha, and it seems that an alliance between the two was the result.

After his anointing by the prophet, Jehu began to conspire against Joram of Israel, who had been wounded by the Syrians in the fighting at Ramoth-gilead and had retreated to Jezreel to allow his wounds to heal. Jehu, who had the backing of the army, and of Hazael, took a chariot and drove from Ramoth-gilead to Jezreel, where he sought out and killed Joram and his kinsmen from the house of Ahab (2 Kings 9:14). Ahaziah of Judah, Joram's ally at Ramoth-gilead against Hazael, traveled from Jerusalem to visit Joram in Jezreel, but fled when he heard that Joram had been killed by Jehu, who had proclaimed himself king of Israel in Joram's place. Ahaziah took refuge in Samaria, but was captured and killed there by Jehu, bringing an end to the dynasties originating from the house of Ahab. The reign of Jehu of Israel coincided with the reigns of Osorkon II (r. 874-850) and Takeloth II (r. 850-825) in Egypt, and with Shalmaneser III (r. 889-854?), Ashur-danin-pal (r. 854?-852), and Shamshi-adad V (r. 852-839) in Assyria.

The Tel Dan Stele, discovered in northern Israel in the early 1990s, mirrors the biblical account of the slaying of Joram and Ahaziah, saying in part:

"Now the king of Israel entered formerly in the land of my father's land; [*but*] Hadad made me myself king, ... and I slew seve[*nty ki*]ngs, who harnessed thou[*sands of cha*]riots and thousands of horsemen. [*And I killed Jo*]ram, son of A[*hab*] king of Israel, and [*I*] killed [*Ahazi*]yahu, son of [*Joram, kin*]g of the house of David."[1]

The Tel Dan inscription quoted above does not exactly match the biblical account of the deaths of Joram and Ahaziah, but it is strikingly similar. Ancient ownership of the stele is currently attributed to Hazael of Syria (or by some scholars to his son Benhadad III), but there is sufficient uncertainty about the identity of the king who had it placed at Tel Dan to allow a future explanation that will bring it into exact accord with the biblical account that credits Jehu with killing Joram and Ahaziah. One possibility, the one accepted by your author, is that the biblical account is correct, and that Hazael, who was under attack by Shalmaneser III at the time, reached some kind of peaceful accommodation with Jehu as the *de facto* king of Israel after both Jehu and Hazael had been anointed as kings of their respective realms by a prophet sent from Elisha, who in turn was acting on the instructions given earlier to the prophet Elijah by God (1 Kings 19:15-16). While Hazael was preoccupied with the Assyrians in the north, Jehu turned south to Jezreel to pursue and kill Joram and Ahaziah, exactly as the biblical text asserts. Hazael then did what kings often did back then. He took credit for someone else's accomplishments on his stele at Tel Dan.

Athaliah of Judah
867-861 BCE

Athaliah was the daughter of Ahab of Israel, the wife of Jehoram of Judah, and the mother of Ahaziah of Judah. She was the only female to rule over a Hebrew kingdom before the time of the Babylonian exile. After her son Ahaziah of Judah was killed by Jehu of Israel in 867 BCE, she became queen-ruler by having all of the seed royal of Judah killed, that is, except for the infant Joash who was hidden in the Temple by her sister-in-law. She then usurped the throne, reigning in Jerusalem for six years (2 Chronicles 22:12), her years being counted and recorded using the non-accession-year system of the kingdom of Israel from whence she had originated as Ahab's daughter. The reign of Athaliah coincided with the reigns of Osorkon II (*r.* 874-850) in Egypt and Shalmaneser III (*r.* 889-854?) in Assyria.

---

[1] William M. Schniedewind, "Tel Dan Stele: New Light on Aramaic and Jehu's Revolt" (*Bulletin of the American Schools of Oriental Research* 302; 1996): p. 75-90; missing text in italics.

Joash of Judah
861-822 BCE

Joash, son of Ahaziah of Judah through Zibiah of Beersheba, was seven years old when he became king of Judah, and he reigned in Jerusalem for forty years (2 Kings 12:1-2). As an infant, he escaped being killed by Athaliah when her son Ahaziah was killed by Jehu. Athaliah had the rest of the seed royal murdered and usurped the throne of Judah for herself, but Joash's aunt, Jehosheba, the sister of Ahaziah and daughter of Jehoram of Judah, hid Joash and his nursemaid in the Temple, and he stayed there sequestered and protected by the priests for six years while Athaliah ruled as queen. In the seventh year, the high priest Jehoiada, Joash's uncle by marriage to Jehosheba, brought him forth to be received as king by the assembled nobles and captains of the army, who Jehoiada had called together sometime after the sabbath year that concluded on the 1st of Nisan in 861 BCE (2 Kings 11:9) and before the 1st of Tishri that same year, and they hailed Joash as king. Jehoiada then dispatched soldiers to kill the usurper-queen, Athaliah, and they did so. Once confirmed as king, Joash of Judah, a boy-king under the influence of his uncle Jehoiada, the high priest, proceeded to restore the kingdom of Judah to spiritual purity. He had the Jerusalem temple of Baal built by Athaliah destroyed, and later ordered the first major restoration of the neglected Temple of Solomon, a restoration that was finished in the king's twenty-third regnal year (2 Kings 12:6), which was the Jewish year beginning in 840 BCE (see page 24).

The *Seder Olam* says that the restoration of the Temple in the twenty-third year of Joash of Judah occurred one-hundred and fifty-five years after Solomon had completed building the first Temple in Jerusalem. It also says that the Temple restoration by Joash occurred two-hundred and eighteen years before the second major restoration, the one undertaken during the eighteenth year of Josiah of Judah, which was the Jewish year that ended in 622 BCE (see page 29).[1] Counting back 218 Passovers (years) from 622 BCE yields the year 840 BCE for the twenty-third regnal year of Joash. Counting back an additional 155 Passovers (years) after the Passover in 840 BCE yields the year 996 BCE as the year Solomon completed the Temple. It began its operation as the spiritual center of the Hebrew nation in the following year, when it was dedicated in the seventh month Tishri, in the year 995 BCE (see page 49).

---

[1] Guggenheimer, *Seder Olam,* p. 161, 210.

In the realm of foreign affairs, the only event recorded in the biblical text during the reign of Joash was the threatened invasion by Hazael, king of Syria, an event that happened sometime after the death of Jehoiada the priest in a time of increasing apostasy in Jerusalem. Joash averted invasion of Judah by sending tribute to Hazael, but weakened his position with the people. He was murdered by his servants in late 822 BCE, bringing his reign to an abrupt and inglorious end (2 Kings 12:17-21). The reign of Joash of Judah coincided with the reigns of Osorkon II (r. 874-850), Takeloth II (r. 850-825), and Shoshenq III (r. 825-773) in Egypt, and with Shalmaneser III (r. 889-854?), Ashur-danin-pal (r. 854?-852), Shamshi-adad V (r. 852-839), and Adad-nirari III (r. 839-811) in Assyria.

Jehoahaz of Israel | Jehoash of Israel
840-824 BCE | 825/824-808 BCE

Jehoahaz, the son of Jehu, became king of Israel in the twenty-third regnal year of Joash of Judah (the same year that Joash restored the Temple), and he ruled as king in Samaria for seventeen years (2 Kings 13:1). During most of the reign of Jehoahaz, Hazael of Syria and his son and successor Benhadad III extended the oppression of Israel begun in the latter days of the reign of Jehu, leaving Israel with a token force of fifty horsemen, ten chariots, and ten-thousands foot soldiers (2 Kings 13:7), just enough to maintain civil order but not enough to threaten Syria with invasion. The Bible records that a "saviour" was given who delivered Israel from Syria during the last years of the reign of Jehoahaz, but does not identify the deliverer. More than likely, the "saviour" of Israel was Adad-nirari III of Assyria, who resumed his western campaign against Syria (Aram) in 827 BCE, or perhaps the biblical text is referring to Jehoahaz's son, Jehoash, who recovered cities from Benhadad III, who had succeeded his father Hazael (2 Kings 13:24).

According to the *Seder Olam*,[1] Jehoash coreigned with Jehoahaz for at least the last two years of his father's reign, from 825-824 BCE, during which time he apparently led the army of Israel against Benhadad. That coreign coincided with the pressure on Syria that resulted when Adad-nirari III of Assyria attacked Damascus in 827 BCE. The power of Benhadad was neutralized by the Assyrians, allowing Jehoash, as commander of the army of Israel, to free the northern kingdom from Syrian control by 824 BCE, that year coinciding with Adad-nirari's

---

[1] Guggenheimer, *Seder Olam*, p. 164.

campaign against Manṣuate (*aka* Massyas in Strabo's *Geography* 16:2, 18) in the valley of Lebanon. Adad-nirari also attacked Damascus that year and defeated the Syrian armies, exacting a heavy tribute from Benhadad III. That payment of tribute has been verified by an inscription on the Tel-al-Rimah Stele, discovered in 1967, which records payment of tribute to Adad-nirari III by the king of Damascus and Jehoash of Israel soon after the Assyrian king's western campaign, which coincided with Jehoash's first year as sole ruler in Israel.

Jehoash became sole ruler in Israel upon the death of his father Jehoahaz in the year 824 BCE, and his sixteen-year reign is counted from that year, although he actually began to coreign as king and army commander in 825 BCE, in the thirty-seventh year of Joash of Judah (see page 24). Later in his reign, Jehoash, who had only recently gained Israel's independence from Syria, was apparently challenged militarily by Amaziah, who was fresh off a great military success against the Edomites. The two met to negotiate their differences at a town in Judah, whereupon Jehoash's troops sent the army of Judah into disarray, took Amaziah hostage, marched to Jerusalem, tore down its wall, and looted the Temple and king's palace of their treasures. The Bible does not clarify the long-term relationship between the two kings after Amaziah was taken hostage and Jerusalem was plundered except to say that Jehoash was outlived by Amaziah by fifteen years (2 Kings 14:17). The reigns of Jehoahaz and Jehoash of Israel coincided with the reigns of Takeloth II (*r.* 850-825), Shoshenq III (*r.* 825-773), and Pedubast (*r.* 818-793) in Egypt, and with Shamshi-adad V (*r.* 852-839), Adad-nirari III (*r.* 839-811), and Shalmaneser IV (*r.* 811-801) in Assyria.

Amaziah of Judah
822-794 BCE

The reign of Amaziah of Judah began when his father Joash was murdered in the year 822 BCE. He was twenty-five years old when he began to reign, and he remained recognized as king in Jerusalem for twenty-nine years, although the chronological data given in the biblical text indicates that he was sole ruler in Jerusalem for only sixteen years before being supplanted by his son Uzziah in 805 BCE. In contrast to the disruption experienced in his last years, Amaziah began his reign deliberately by avenging the murder of his father and doing what was right in the eyes of the Lord (2 Kings 14:1-3). He then recruited an army of mercenaries to attack Edom, but was commanded by a prophet of God to send them home before the battle, whereupon the mercenaries began plundering the towns of Judah instead. In the meantime, Amaziah led a successful military expedition against the Edomites, an event the *Seder Olam* says happened in his twelfth year,[1] which would have been in the Jewish year spanning 811/810 BCE.

After his victory over Edom, Amaziah turned his attention to the northern kingdom, challenging Jehoash of Israel to a face-to-face confrontation on the field of battle. Jehoash led his army south to meet Amaziah at Bethshemesh in Judah, with disastrous results for Amaziah. The Israelites routed the Judeans, capturing Amaziah and holding him hostage as they moved against Jerusalem. Jehoash's troops quickly overran the city, demolished a major section of the wall that defended the city from the north, and plundered the Temple and the king's palace. The biblical text does not say so specifically, but it can be inferred that Amaziah was left in Jerusalem as a vassal to Jehoash and the northern kingdom, and most likely had to pay tribute. After the defeat of Amaziah by Jehoash at Bethshemesh, the leadership in Jerusalem began to conspire against the king, eventually deposing him in favor of his sixteen-year-old son, Uzziah, that act occurring in the year 805 BCE. According to the biblical text and the *Seder Olam*, Amaziah fled south to Lachish, where ten years later in 794 BCE he was slain (2 Chronicles 25:27). The reign of Amaziah of Judah coincided with the reign of Shoshenq III (r. 825-773) in Egypt, and with the reigns of Adad-nirari III (r. 839-811) and Shalmaneser IV (r. 811-801) in Assyria.

Jeroboam II of Israel
808-768 BCE

Jeroboam II, the son of Jehoash of Israel, became king of the northern kingdom of Israel in the fifteenth regnal year of Amaziah of Judah, and he reigned in Samaria for forty-one years (2 Kings 14:23).[2] During the reign of Jeroboam II, the kingdom of Israel regained almost all of the territory that had been lost since the death of Solomon, with the exception of the territory controlled by Judah. The expansion came at the expense of Syria. The biblical text records that

---

[1] Guggenheimer, *Seder Olam*, p. 165.
[2] Jeroboam II is mentioned in the biblical text in the following references: 2 Kings 13:13; 14:16, 23, 27-29; 15:1, 8; 1 Chronicles 5:17; Hosea 1:1; and Amos 1:1; 7:9-11. All other biblical references to the name Jeroboam are referring to Jeroboam, son of Nebat, who was the first king of the northern kingdom of Israel after United Israel divided in 961 BCE.

Jeroboam captured the city of Damascus and extended the northern border of Israel to its former limits, including the region from Hamath to the coastal plain, roughly equivalent to the part of modern Syria that borders on the Mediterranean (2 Kings 14:25-28). A reference to a census of the sons of Gad in Bashan that was taken in the days of Jotham of Judah has been used by some expositors to make the reigns of Jotham and Jeroboam II concurrent, since both kings are mentioned in connection with the census (1 Chronicles 5:17). However, Jotham became king of Judah in 756 BCE, twelve years after the death of Jeroboam II, so there must have been two censuses, one during Jeroboam's reign, probably after he had recaptured Damascus, and a later census during the reign of Jotham, perhaps in preparation for his warfare against Syria.

The long reign of Jeroboam saw great prosperity in the northern kingdom, mainly from trade in olive oil, wine, and other agricultural products, with the rivals Egypt and Assyria both being customers for Israel's bounty. Four prophets, Hosea, Joel, Jonah, and Amos urged national rejection of the excesses of materialism and idolatry and preached a return to living by the commandments of the living God, but their warnings went unheeded by the king and the people during the reign of Jeroboam. The reign of Jeroboam II coincided with the reigns of Shoshenq III (r. 825-773), Pedubast (r. 818-793), Iuput (r. 804-783), Shoshenq IV (r. 783-777), Akara (r. 780-760), Osorkon III (r. 777-749), and Pimay (r. 773-767) in Egypt, and Shalmaneser IV (r. 811-801), Ashur-dan III (r. 801-783), Ashur-nirari V (r. 783-773), and Tiglath-pileser III (also called Pul in the Bible; r. 773-727) in Assyria.

Uzziah of Judah
805/794-754 BCE

Uzziah (*aka* Azariah), son of Amaziah, became king of Judah at the age of sixteen when the leaders of Judah lost confidence in his father Amaziah. They placed Uzziah on the throne in his place, and he reigned for fifty-two years. *"And all the people of Judah took Azariah, which was sixteen years old, and made him king instead of his father Amaziah"* (2 Chronicles 26:3; KJV). The *Seder Olam* says that when Uzziah was recognized as king, Amaziah fled to Lachish, staying there until his death in 794 BCE. Apparently, Uzziah ruled Judah for nine years or so from Jerusalem while Amaziah held separate court in Lachish. Scripture says, *"In the twenty and seventh year of Jeroboam king of Israel began Azariah son of Amaziah king of Judah to reign"* (1 Kings 15:1; KJV), which is chronologically impossible (see page 25). That verse was mistranslated by the KJV translators, or perhaps the text was poorly transmitted through the centuries. Whatever happened, the text does preserve all of the important chronological elements intact—Uzziah began to reign while Jeroboam II was king of Israel and a period of twenty-seven years was involved—but it can be more accurately paraphrased as, *"When he was twenty-seven years old, while Jeroboam II was king of Israel, Uzziah son of Amaziah began to reign as king of Judah"* (Au). That paraphrase is supported by Jewish tradition, which says that Jeroboam II and Uzziah began to reign at about the same time, and the kingdoms chronology in this book shows that they did, in 808 BCE and 805 BCE respectively. It also agrees with the precedent of recording an event in Uzziah's life by referencing the event to his age at the time (see 2 Chronicles 26:3 quoted on the previous page).

In the early part of his reign, Uzziah *"did that which was right in the sight of the Lord"* (2 Kings 15:3; KJV), and his kingdom prospered. Uzziah was a vigorous military leader, fortifying Jerusalem's walls and gates, building towers in the desert, and equipping an army of three-hundred thousand soldiers with weaponry. To secure his borders, he conducted successful campaigns against the Philistines, the Arabians, the Mehunims, broke down the walls of Gath, Jabneh, and Ashdod, and built fortified cities in the region around Ashdod and among the Philistines. Scripture records that the Ammonites paid tribute and that *"his name spread far abroad"* (2 Chronicles 26:6-15; KJV).

In his forty-ninth regnal year, though, Uzziah overstepped his authority. In the year 757 BCE, at the start of a jubilee year (see page 26), probably on the Day of Atonement, he tried to offer incense on the Temple altar. The Jewish historian Josephus describes the events of Uzziah's downfall as follows.

> "Accordingly, when a remarkable day was come, and a general festival was to be celebrated, he put on the holy garment, and went into the temple to offer incense to God upon the golden altar, which he was prohibited to do by Azariah the high priest, who had fourscore priests with him, and who told him that it was not lawful for him to offer sacrifice, and that 'none besides the posterity of Aaron were permitted so to do.' And when they cried out that he must go out of the temple, and not transgress against God, he was wroth at them, and threatened to kill them, unless they would hold their peace. In the mean time a great earthquake shook the ground and a rent was made in the temple, and the bright rays of the sun shone through it, and fell upon the king's face, insomuch that the leprosy seized upon him immediately ... Now, as soon as the priests saw that the king's face was infected with the leprosy, they told him of the

calamity he was under, and commanded that he should go out of the city as a polluted person. Hereupon he was so confounded at the sad distemper, and sensible that he was not at liberty to contradict, that he did as he was commanded, and underwent this miserable and terrible punishment for an intention beyond what befitted a man to have, and for that impiety against God which was implied therein. So he abode out of the city for some time, and lived a private life, while his son Jotham took the government; after which he died with grief and anxiety at what had happened to him, when he had lived sixty-eight years, and reigned of them fifty-two; and was buried by himself in his own gardens." ... *Antiquities 9.10.4* (Whiston translation).

As Josephus indicated above, an earthquake occurred in conjunction with Uzziah's unlawful acts in the Temple in his forty-ninth regnal year. However, the prophet Amos indicates that the earthquake occurred in the early years of Uzziah's reign, when Jeroboam II was king of Israel, two years after the start of Amos' own ministry according to Amos 1:1. By examining dates when Uzziah and Jeroboam II reigned at the same time (see page 25), the earliest that both were reigning concurrently was the year 794 BCE. Assuming that Amos began his prophetic ministry that year—the same year that Uzziah became sole ruler in Judah—the earthquake would have occurred two years later in 792 BCE.[1] On the other hand, if the wording in the first verse of Amos can be interpreted so that it does not require Uzziah and Jeroboam II to have been occupying their respective thrones at the same time, then the earthquake could have happened in 757 BCE, Uzziah's forty-ninth year when he acted unlawfully in the Temple, just as Josephus recorded. The year of the earthquake is important to archaeologists, since many ancient sites contain a rubble layer that can be attributed to it. The year 760 BCE ± 35 years is the traditional date scholars use for the earthquake.

The reign of Uzziah coincided with the reigns of Shoshenq III (r. 825-773), Pedubast (r. 818-793), Iuput (r. 804-783), Shoshenq IV (r. 783-777), Akara (r. 780-760), Osorkon III (r. 777-749), Pimay (r. 773-767), Shoshenq V (r. 767-730), and Kashta/Maatre (ca. 760-747) in Egypt, and Shalmaneser IV (r. 811-801), Ashur-dan III (r. 801-783), , Ashur-nirari V (r. 783-773), and Tiglath-pileser III (also called Pul in the Bible; r. 773-727) in Assyria.

---

[1] The year 792 BCE was the eighth year of Ashur-dan III in Assyria. A major regional earthquake occurring in his eighth year would explain why no military campaign was undertaken by Ashur-dan that year, something highly unusual for an Assyrian king. It could also explain the revolt in that took place in Libbi-āli the following year (the year of the Bûr-Saggilê eclipse).

Zachariah of Israel
768 BCE

Shallum of Israel
767 BCE

Zachariah, son of Jeroboam II, became king of Israel in the thirty-eighth year of Uzziah of Judah. Six months later, he was murdered by Shallum, son of Jabesh, who then took the throne of Israel (2 Kings 15:8-10). Shallum reigned as king of Israel for one month before Menahem killed him and usurped the throne for himself in the thirty-ninth year of Uzziah (2 Kings 15: 13-14). Zachariah's reign included one 1st of Nisan, and he had an accession year in his regnal count before year one of his reign, the first king of the northern kingdom to have his reign recorded with an accession year. Zachariah's death brought the dynasty of Jehu to an end in its fourth generation, as had been prophesied (2 Kings 15:12). Shallum's reign did not include a 1st of Nisan, so he had only an accession year in his regnal count. The reigns of Zachariah and Shallum coincided with the reigns of Akara (r. 780-760), Osorkon III (r. 777-749), and Pimay (r. 773-767) in Egypt, and Tiglath-pileser III (also called Pul in the Bible; r. 773-727) in Assyria.

Menahem of Israel
767-757 BCE

Menahem, son of Gadi and a general in the army of Israel according to Josephus (*Antiquities* 9.11.1), became king of Israel in the thirty-ninth year of Uzziah of Judah. He usurped the throne after he murdered Shallum, and ruled from Samaria for ten years (2 Kings 15:14, 17). The biblical text records his reign as one of extreme cruelty, saying, *"Then Menahem smote Tiphsah, and all that were therein, and the coasts thereof from Tirzah: because they opened not to him, therefore he smote it; and all the women therein that were with child he ripped up"* (2 Kings 15:16, KJV). The prophet Hosea condemns the king for his apostasy, reporting that the northern kingdom's allegiance wavered between Egypt and Assyria (Hosea 7:1-15). The first Assyrian incursion into the territory of Israel occurred during Menahem's reign. To retain his throne, Menahem paid tribute of a thousand talents of silver to Pul, king of Assyria (2 Kings 15:19), who scholars have equated with Tiglath-pileser III (1 Chronicles 5:26). The reign of Menahem coincided with the reigns of Akara (r. 780-760), Osorkon III (r. 777-749), Pimay (r. 773-767), and Shoshenq V (r. 767-730) in Egypt, and Tiglath-pileser III (also called Pul in the Bible; r. 773-727) in Assyria.

Pekah of Israel
758/757-738 BCE

Pekahiah of Israel
757-755 BCE

Pekah, the son of Remaliah, a captain in the army of Israel under the command of the king's son, Pekahiah, broke away from the king and his son and set up a rival kingdom in Gilead. That breakaway kingdom, possibly called Ephraim by the prophet Hosea (Hosea 5:5), was established in the year 758 BCE, about a year before Menahem's death. After Menahem died, Pekahiah became king of Israel in the fiftieth year of Uzziah of Judah, 757 BCE, and reigned from Samaria for two years. In Pekahiah's second regnal year, 755 BCE, Pekah killed Pekahiah in the fifty-second year of Uzziah and established himself as sole ruler over Israel. Pekah reigned for twenty years, which are counted from the time he set himself up as king in Gilead (2 Kings 15:23-25). The biblical text records that Pekah allied Israel with Rezin of Damascus to move against Ahaz of Judah, probably in late 739 BCE. Ahaz appealed to Tiglath-pileser III, who responded by invading Israel in 738 BCE, capturing many cities and deporting thousands of Israelites to various parts of the empire (2 Kings 15:29; KJV). Pekah was killed by Hoshea in his twentieth year. The reigns of Pekah and Pekahiah coincided with the reigns of Osorkon III (*r.* 777-749), Shoshenq V (*r.* 767-730), Kashta/Maatre (*ca.* 760-747), Takeloth III (*r.* 754-734), and Piankhy/Piyi/Sneferre (*r.* 747-716) in Egypt, and Tiglath-pileser III (also called Pul in the Bible; *r.* 773-727) in Assyria.

Jotham of Judah
757/754-738 BCE

Ahaz of Judah
742-727 BCE

Jotham, son of Uzziah, began a coreign with his father in 757 BCE, in the second regnal year of Pekah (that is, the second year after Pekah set himself up as a breakaway king of Israel in Gilead). Uzziah, who became leprous after trying to burn incense in the Temple on the Day of Atonement that year, retired from the palace and Jotham judged Israel in the king's place for about four years until his father's death. The duration of Jotham's reign is recorded as sixteen years (2 Kings 15:32-33), during which he fought against Rezin of Damascus and the Ammonites, the latter paying him tribute (2 Kings 27:5). Hoshea killed Pekah in Jotham's twentieth year, which must include the four years of coreign with Uzziah to make chronological sense. Jotham yielded rule to his son Ahaz beginning in his sixteenth regnal year and the seventeenth regnal year of Pekah. It appears that Jotham lived for four years after Ahaz replaced him as king (see page 28). Scripture does not say what happened to Jotham, but some have speculated that he was deposed by Ahaz, who was supported by a pro-Assyrian faction, in the year 742 BCE. Some even speculate that Jotham was taken hostage to Assyria. At any rate, Jotham died and Ahaz became sole ruler of Judah in early 738 BCE. That year Pekah and Rezin attacked Judah and Ahaz appealed to Assyria for help, resulting in an Assyrian invasion of Israel that same year. The reigns of Jotham and Ahaz coincided with the reigns of Osorkon III (r. 777-749), Shoshenq V (r. 767-730), Kashta/Maatre (ca. 760-747), Takeloth III (r. 754-734), Piankhy/Piyi/Sneferre (r. 747-716), Rudamon (r. 734-731), Iuput II (r. 731-720), Osorkon IV (r. 730-715), and Tefnakht (r. 727-720) in Egypt, and in Assyria Tiglath-pileser III (also called Pul in the Bible; r. 773-727).

[The northern kingdom was a province of Assyria with no king from 738-731 BCE.]

Hoshea of Israel
731-721 BCE

In 731 BCE, at the end of the period of eight years when there had been no king in the northern kingdom, the Assyrian king Tiglath-pileser III, during his western campaign that coincided with the twelfth regnal year of Ahaz of Judah, installed Hoshea, who had probably been serving as provincial governor in Gilead, as king of Israel (2 Kings 17:1). Hoshea ruled as king in Samaria for nine years. When Tiglath-pileser died in 727 BCE, Hoshea, encouraged by the support of an Egyptian king (named So in the Bible and identified by some scholars as Osorkon IV of Dynasty 22), refused to pay the annual tribute to the new king of Assyria, Shalmaneser V, who responded by besieging Samaria and imprisoning Hoshea in 724 BCE. The siege lasted for three years, during which time Shalmaneser died and was succeeded by Sargon II. After Samaria fell to Sargon in early 721 BCE, the people of the kingdom of Israel were deported to various cities and lands beyond the Euphrates River, bringing the northern kingdom of Israel to an end (2 Kings 17:6). The eventual fate of Hoshea is unknown. The reign of Hoshea coincided with the reigns of Piankhy/Piyi/Sneferre (r. 747-716), Iuput II (r. 731-720), Osorkon IV (r. 730-715), and Tefnakht (r. 727-720) in Egypt, and with Tiglath-pileser III (also called Pul in the Bible; r. 773-727), Shalmaneser V (r. 727-722), and Sargon II (r. 722-705) in Assyria.

CHAPTER FIVE

KINGS OF JUDAH
727-560 BCE

After the fall of Samaria and deportation of the northern tribes to various parts of Assyria in 721 BCE, the kingdom of Judah continued to exist as a political entity and Jerusalem continued as Judaism's spiritual center for 135 years, with Judah's kings continuing the royal house established by David in 1,046 BCE.

Hezekiah of Judah
727-698 BCE

Hezekiah succeeded his father Ahaz as king of Judah in the year 727 BCE and reigned in Jerusalem for twenty-nine years (2 Kings 18:1-2). The Bible describes the chronological details of his reign in the Books of 2 Kings, chapters 18-20; 2 Chronicles, chapters 29-32; and Isaiah, chapters 36-39. The reign of Hezekiah is displayed diagrammatically as a timeline on pages 27-28. The fifteen extra years that the Bible says were added to the life of Hezekiah, in which the Lord says in Isaiah, chapter 26, verse 6a: *"And I will add unto thy days fifteen years"* (KJV), are included on the diagram's timeline. Traditional interpretations of the reign of Hezekiah often assume that the biblical details about his reign, and specifically the part about the God-given extra fifteen years, are chronologically flawed, and many scholars outright dismiss that part as myth that should not be included in any serious chronological discussion. This exposition takes the opposite approach. It demonstrates that the details of Hezekiah's reign can be understood chronologically ***only*** if those fifteen extra years are included.

Since the invasion of Judah by Sennacherib in the fourteenth year of Hezekiah's reign can be pinpointed to 701 BCE, Hezekiah seemingly had to begin his reign in the year 715 BCE according to the traditional interpretation. However, the Bible states in 2 Kings, chapter 18, verse 1, that Hezekiah began his reign in the third regnal year of Hoshea of Israel (r. 731-721 BCE), which can be identified by the harmonized chronology of the Hebrew kings in this book as occurring in the year 727 BCE (see page 27 showing the relationship between the reigns of Hoshea of Israel and Hezekiah of Judah). Obviously, that contradiction involving the beginning of the reign of Hezekiah means that something is wrong with the traditional interpretation, but that is not the only problem.

In addition to the extra fifteen years given to Hezekiah, the king is promised a sign about the deliverance of Jerusalem from the king of Assyria. That sign is described in Isaiah, chapter 37, verse 30, as follows: *"And this shall be a sign unto thee, Ye shall eat this year such as groweth of itself; and the second year that which springeth of the same: and in the third year sow ye, and reap, and plant vineyards, and eat the fruit thereof"* (KJV). The traditional interpretation assumes that the two years without crops were a sabbath year followed by a jubilee year during which no crops could be planted or harvested, followed by a third year in which crops were planted and harvested. It is also assumes that the observance of that sabbath-jubilee cycle coincided with the invasion of Judah by Sennacherib in 701 BCE.

Fortunately, having a correct understanding of how planting and harvesting were done in sabbath and jubilee years can help to sort out the chronology of Hezekiah's reign. No harvesting could be done for two years in either a sabbath-only year or a sabbath-jubilee year combination (see diagram on page 128). The sabbath-jubilee tables show that the year of Sennacherib's invasion, 701 BCE, was a sabbath-only year, with no jubilee (see "Sabbath and Jubilee Years" on page 127). So, the assumption of a sabbath-jubilee year combination required by the traditional interpretation is not necessary as an explanation for the two years without crops.

Since the year 701 BCE saw the start of a sabbath-only year, which began in the twenty-sixth regnal year of Hezekiah (see diagram on opposite page), that year must be considered as the first year in the two-year period when no crops were harvested. Soon thereafter, Sennacherib invaded and devastated the cities of Judah and began his siege of Jerusalem. The account of his campaign is given in the Scriptures and a secular account is recorded on the Taylor Prism (also called Sennacherib's Prism, discovered *circa* 691 BCE).

From the diagram on the opposite page, it is obvious that the sabbath year, plus the disruption caused by Sennacherib's invasion of Judah in the spring of the year 701 BCE, prevented planting of barley and wheat from being done in the fall and winter of 701 BCE, making those crops unavailable for harvest in the spring of 700 BCE. That means both planting and harvesting would not have been carried out normally in Hezekiah's twenty-seventh regnal year, the second year with no crops. The Bible records that Sennacherib's army was later devastated by an angel of death that overnight killed 185,000 Assyrians, requiring Sennacherib to withdraw back to Assyria, all of that taking place during Passover week in the year 700 BCE according to Jewish records. So, after two seasons with no crops harvested, the land was at peace again in the third year, late in 700 BCE, and barley

Chapter Five: Kings of Judah (727-560 BCE)

Hezekiah's Regnal Years and 3rd-Year Sign

(years shown in left column are proleptic Gregorian years, with sabbath years shown in bold type; A = accession or partial year; sabbath and jubilee observances shown below are not mentioned in the Bible)

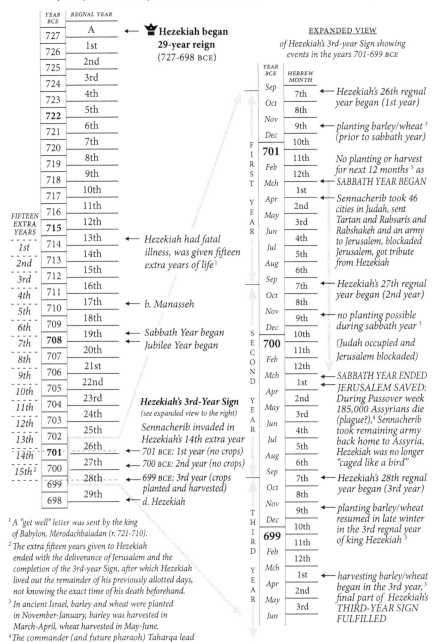

[1] A "get well" letter was sent by the king of Babylon, Merodachbaladan (r. 721-710).
[2] The extra fifteen years given to Hezekiah ended with the deliverance of Jerusalem and the completion of the 3rd-year Sign, after which Hezekiah lived out the remainder of his previously allotted days, not knowing the exact time of his death beforehand.
[3] In ancient Israel, barley and wheat were planted in November-January, barley was harvested in March-April, wheat harvested in May-June.
[4] The commander (and future pharaoh) Taharqa lead Shebitku's army out of Egypt to oppose Sennecherib.

and wheat were planted that fall and harvested the following spring in the year 699 BCE. Thus, the "3-year sign" given by God to Hezekiah through the prophet Isaiah was fulfilled exactly as foretold. No crops could be planted or harvested in Hezekiah's twenty-sixth and twenty-seventh regnal years (the first and second years in the prophecy). In his twenty-eighth regnal year (the third year), crops were planted and harvested.

That timeline reveals another chronological paradox, though. If Hezekiah began his reign in the year 727 BCE and was invaded by Sennacherib in 701 BCE, how could the invasion have taken place in the fourteenth year of Hezekiah, as stated in 2 Kings, chapter 18, verse 13, and Isaiah, chapter 36, verse 1? That apparent inconsistency is actually quite easy to explain. The Hebrew text does not say fourteenth year of reign. It says only that Sennacherib invaded Judah in Hezekiah's fourteenth year. Since God had extended Hezekiah's life by fifteen years, the invasion was referenced to the extended-years period. Sennacherib invaded in the fourteenth year of the fifteen-year extension, not in the fourteenth year of Hezekiah's total reign of twenty-nine years. That the deliverance of Jerusalem would signal the end of the extra fifteen years is indicated in 2 Kings, chapter 20, verse 6, which says: *"And I will add unto thy days fifteen years; and [at the end of the years] I will deliver thee and this city out of the hand of the king of Assyria; and I will defend this city for mine own sake, and for my servant David's sake"* (KJV). The extra fifteen years given to Hezekiah ended with the deliverance of Jerusalem, after which Hezekiah lived out the remainder of his previously allotted days, not knowing the exact time of his death beforehand.

The chronology of Hezekiah's reign is admittedly complicated, but, as shown above, it can be reconciled to incorporate all of the details given in the biblical text, specifically: a reign beginning in the third regnal year of Hoshea of Israel, no long co-regency with Ahaz (as proposed by Edwin Thiele *et al* without biblical support), a siege of Samaria beginning in Hezekiah's fourth regnal year, God giving Hezekiah fifteen extra years of life, the fall of Samaria occurring in Hezekiah's sixth regnal year, and the end of the extra fifteen years and fulfillment of the 3-year sign both signified by the deliverance of Jerusalem. All of those details fit together perfectly without having to assume scribal emendation, as Thiele did concerning the text of 2 Kings, chapters 17 and 18, or myth-making on the part of the ancient Hebrew scribes as many modern expositors assume.

The reign of Hezekiah coincided with the reigns of Piankhy/Piyi/Sneferre (*r.* 747-716), Iuput II (*r.* 731-720), Osorkon IV (*r.* 730-715), Tefnakht (*r.* 727-720),

Bakenranef (r. 7720-715), Shoshenq VI (r. 720-715), Shabako (r. 716-702), and Shebitku (r. 702-690) in Egypt, and Tiglath-pileser III (r. 773-727), Shalmaneser V (r. 727-722), Sargon II (r. 722-705), and Sennacherib (r. 705-681) in Assyria.

Manasseh of Judah
698-643 BCE

Manasseh, son of Hezekiah through Hephzibah, became king of Judah in the year 698 BCE, when his father Hezekiah died. He was twelve years old when he became king, and he ruled from Jerusalem for fifty-five years (2 Kings 21:1). The biblical text recounts the wickedness and idolatry of Manasseh, how he filled Jerusalem with blood[1] and caused the people of Judah to commit offenses against God that were greater than those committed by the nations that had inhabited the land of Canaan before the Children of Israel took possession. The Bible says that God's patience finally ran out during the reign of Manasseh, and his judgement against Jerusalem and Judah was decreed:

> *"Because Manasseh king of Judah hath done these abominations, and hath done wickedly above all that the Amorites did, which were before him, and hath made Judah also to sin with his idols. Therefore thus saith the Lord God of Israel, Behold, I am bringing such evil upon Jerusalem and Judah, that whosoever heareth of it, both his ears shall tingle. And I will stretch over Jerusalem the line of Samaria, and the plummet of the house of Ahab: and I will wipe Jerusalem as a man wipeth a dish, wiping it, and turning it upside down. And I will forsake the remnant of mine inheritance, and deliver them into the hand of their enemies; and they shall become a prey and a spoil to all their enemies"* (2 Kings 21:11-14; KJV).

Manasseh is mentioned in the records of two Assyrian kings, Esarhaddon, who succeeded Sennacherib, and Ashurbanipal, who succeeded him. According to the biblical text, Manasseh was taken to Babylon in chains and fetters by the captains of Esarhaddon. The biblical text describes the events of Manasseh's captivity without giving a chronological reference point, as follows:

---

[1] The *Jerusalem Talmud* (Sanhedrin 10) says that Isaiah, fearing Manasseh, hid himself in a cedar-tree, but his presence was betrayed by the fringes of his garment, and the king ordered that the tree be sawn in half. That story is recounted in several Jewish sources.

> "Wherefore the Lord brought upon them the captains of the host of the king of Assyria, which took Manasseh among the thorns, and bound him with fetters, and carried him to Babylon. And when he was in affliction, he besought the Lord his God, and humbled himself greatly before the God of his fathers, And prayed unto him: and he was intreated of him, and heard his supplication, and brought him again to Jerusalem into his kingdom. Then Manasseh knew that the Lord he was God" (2 Chronicles 33:11-13a).

According to the *Seder Olam*, the deportation of Manasseh to Babylon took place in his twenty-third regnal year, in the year 677 BCE. Assyrian archives do not mention the captivity, but Manasseh is listed as one of twenty-two kings who provided materials for the building projects of Esarhaddon, and Ashurbanipal's annals say that Manasseh assisted his Egyptian campaign in 667 BCE.[1]

Manasseh was apparently a reformed man when he returned to Jerusalem from Babylon. The biblical text records numerous good deeds done by the king:

> "Now after this he built a wall without the city of David, on the west side of Gihon, in the valley, even to the entering in at the fish gate, and compassed about Ophel, and raised it up a very great height, and put captains of war in all the fenced cities of Judah. And he took away the strange gods, and the idol out of the house of the Lord, and all the altars that he had built in the mount of the house of the Lord, and in Jerusalem, and cast [them] out of the city. And he repaired the altar of the Lord, and sacrificed thereon peace offerings and thank offerings, and commanded Judah to serve the Lord God of Israel" (2 Chronicles 33:14-16; KJV).

The repentance of Manasseh mentioned in 2 Chronicles is not mentioned in 2 Kings, which focuses on the sins of the king and people and the judgements against them—destruction of Jerusalem, removal from Judah, and captivity in a foreign land. Events ending with those judgements would begin happening in 609 BCE, after the death of Josiah. The reign of Manasseh coincided with the reigns of Shebitku (*r.* 702-690), Taharqa (*r.* 690-664), Tanutamani (*r.* 664-656), and Psammetichus I (*r.* 664-610) in Egypt, and with Sennacherib (*r.* 705-681), Esarhaddon (*r.* 681-669), and Ashurbanipal (*ca.* 669-631) in Assyria.

---

[1] James B. Pritchard, *Ancient Near Eastern Texts Relating to the Old Testament* (Princeton University Press; 3rd edition, with supplement; 1969); p. 291, 294.

Chapter Five: Kings of Judah (727-560 BCE)

Amon of Judah
643-641 BCE

Amon, son of Manasseh, became king of Judah in 643 BCE, and ruled from Jerusalem for two years (2 Kings 21:19). Amon continued the wickedness that had characterized his father's early reign, but did not follow his father in repentance as the Bible credits Manasseh with doing. The *Babylonian Talmud* (Sanhedrin 103b) says that Amon's most egregious sin was that of ordering all copies of the Torah to be burned. Considering that there was only one surviving copy of the Law two decades later during his son Josiah's reign, that story has credibility. It also seems to have provoked the condemnation of the prophet Zephaniah, who said that Jerusalem's *"prophets are light and treacherous persons: her priests have polluted the sanctuary, they have done violence to the law"* (Zephaniah 3:4). The reign of Amon was cut short when his servants assassinated him in the palace, *"And the servants of Amon conspired against him, and slew the king in his own house. And the people of the land slew all them that had conspired against king Amon; and the people of the land made Josiah his son king in his stead"* (2 Kings 21:23-24). The chronology of the Hebrew kings in this book shows that Amon must have been slain sometime prior to the 1st of Tishri in the year 641 BCE (see page 29). The reign of Amon coincided with the reigns of Psammetichus I (r. 664-610) in Egypt and Ashurbanipal (ca. 669-631) in Assyria.

Josiah of Judah
640-609 BCE

Josiah, son of Amon, became king of Judah in the year 640 BCE, which was his accession year.[1] He was an eight-year old boy when his father was assassinated. The biblical text indicates that a period of turmoil followed as the assassins were being dispatched by the people, saying *"But the people of the land slew all them that had conspired against king Amon; and the people of the land made Josiah his*

---

[1] Josiah was anointed king of Judah sometime ***after*** the 1st of Tishri in the year 641 BCE. Since his father had been assassinated by his servants sometime ***before*** the 1st of Tishri in 641 BCE, the throne of Judah was vacant on the 1st of Tishri in 641 BCE while his father's assassins were hunted down by supporters of the boy king and the throne was made secure for him. So, Josiah's first regnal year did not begin until he celebrated his first 1st of Tishri as king, which was the 1st of Tishri that occurred in 640 BCE (see page 29).

son king in his stead" (2 Chronicles 33:25). Josiah reigned in Jerusalem for thirty-one years (2 Kings 22:1). His reign was completely different from that of his wicked father, probably because of the influence of his mother Jedidah and her advisors who had control of the boy before and after he was made king.

In his eighteenth regnal year, which began in 623 BCE, the Bible records that Josiah determined that the Temple was in need of repair, saying:

"And it came to pass in the eighteenth year of king Josiah, that the king sent Shaphan the son of Azaliah, the son of Meshullam, the scribe, to the house of the Lord, saying, Go up to Hilkiah the high priest, that he may sum the silver which is brought into the house of the Lord, which the keepers of the door have gathered of the people: And let them deliver it into the hand of the doers of the work, that have the oversight of the house of the Lord: and let them give it to the doers of the work which is in the house of the Lord, to repair the breaches of the house, Unto carpenters, and builders, and masons, and to buy timber and hewn stone to repair the house" (2Kings 22:3-6; KJV).[1]

As the repairs were being done, the high priest Hilkiah discovered a copy of the Law, perhaps the last remaining copy, one that had been hidden by a priest to keep it from being destroyed during the reign of Amon. He shared his discovery with Shaphan the scribe, who took it to the palace and read it to the king. When Josiah heard the words of the Law and understood the apostasy and rebelliousness of Judah, he rent his clothes and despaired. The king then sent Hilkiah and others to inquire of Huldah the prophetess about what should be done. Huldah sent the following word back to Josiah:

"Tell the man that sent you to me, Thus saith the Lord, Behold, I will bring evil upon this place, and upon the inhabitants thereof, even all the words of the book which the king of Judah hath read: Because they have forsaken me, and have burned incense unto other gods, that they might provoke me to anger

---

[1] The *Seder Olam* records that Josiah finished refurbishing the Temple in his eighteenth regnal year, 622 BCE, 218 years after Joash had begun refurbishing the Temple in his twenty-third regnal year, 840 BCE, and that Joash's refurbishing was 155 years after the Temple was completed, confirming the year of completion as 996 BCE and dedication in 995 BCE. The *Babylonian Talmud (Tractate Yoma 9a)* says that Solomon's Temple operated for 410 years. Since it was destroyed in 586 BCE, counting back in time 410 Passovers as a crosscheck confirms 995 BCE as the year of its dedication.

with all the works of their hands; therefore my wrath shall be kindled against this place, and shall not be quenched. But to the king of Judah which sent you to enquire of the Lord, thus shall ye say to him ... As touching the words which thou hast heard; Because thine heart was tender, and thou hast humbled thyself before the Lord, when thou heardest what I spake against this place, and against the inhabitants thereof, that they should become a desolation and a curse, and hast rent thy clothes, and wept before me; I also have heard thee, saith the Lord. Behold therefore, I will gather thee unto thy fathers, and thou shalt be gathered into thy grave in peace; and thine eyes shall not see all the evil which I will bring upon this place" (2 Kings 22:15-20; KJV).

Josiah immediately set out to restore the nation to compliance with the Law. He gathered all of the leaders of Judah and read the Book of the Law in their hearing, afterwards making a covenant requiring the nation to be faithful to the commandments. He then removed all pagan influences from the kingdom. On the 15th of Nisan in 622 BCE, the king presided over the greatest Passover observed since the Children of Israel entered the land (2 Kings 23:22; 2 Chronicles 35). However, the countdown to the promised wrath of God against the people was only delayed until the death of Josiah. In the spring of 609 BCE, Necho II, pharaoh of Egypt, moved northward through Judah to aid his ally Assyria against an attack on Harran by the Babylonians. Josiah, who was in some way allied with Babylon, marshaled his army to confront Necho in the Jezreel Valley and was fatally wounded at Megiddo (2 Chronicles 35:22-25). The reign of Josiah coincided with the reigns of Psammetichus I (*r.* 664-610) and Necho II (*r.* 610-595) in Egypt, and Ashurbanipal (*ca.* 669-631), Ashur-etil-ilani (*ca.* 631-627), Sin-sar-ishkun (*ca.* 627-612), Sin-shumu-lishir (*ca.* 626), and Ashur-uballit II (*ca.* 612-609) in Assyria.

The final days of the kingdom of Judah were presided over by three of Josiah's sons and one of his grandsons. In order of birth, the sons were Johanan the firstborn (who did not reign as king), Eliakim, Mattanyahu, and Shallum. Surprisingly, the youngest son, Shallum, was the first one to succeed Josiah as king of Judah, reigning under the name Jehoahaz. Shallum was succeeded by Eliakim, who reigned under the name Jehoiakim. He was succeeded by his son Jeconiah (Coniah), who reigned under the name Jehoiachin. Then Jeconiah was succeeded on the throne by his uncle Mattanyahu, who reigned under the name Zedekiah. Zedekiah was the last king of Judah, reigning until Jerusalem was conquered by Nebuchadnezzar II in 586 BCE.

Jehoahaz of Judah
609 BCE

Jehoiakim of Judah
609-598 BCE

Jehoahaz became king of Judah upon the death of his father Josiah in the summer of 609 BCE, and reigned for three months, including one 1st of Tishri, before being deposed and sent into exile in Egypt by Necho II, who established his older brother, Jehoiakim, as king. Under Jehoiakim, who reigned in Jerusalem for eleven years, Judah was a vassal to Egypt, paying heavy tribute. After Egypt was defeated by the Babylonians at Carchemish in 605 BCE, Jehoiakim switched sides and became a vassal to Nebuchadnezzar II of Babylon. Around 602 BCE, Jehoiakim changed his loyalties again, siding with Egypt. That change resulted in an invasion and siege of Jerusalem by Nebuchadnezzar beginning in 598 BCE, during which time Jehoiakim died and was succeeded by his son Jehoiachin.

Jehoiachin of Judah
598-597 BCE

Jehoiachin became king of Judah in December of 598 BCE, after the 1st of Tishri, while Jerusalem was besieged by Nebuchadnezzar II. He reigned for three months and ten days, until March of 597 BCE, having only an accession year. When the city surrendered, Jehoiachin and the royal family were taken to Babylon, where he remained in prison until being released by Evil-Merodach in early 560 BCE.

Zedekiah of Judah
597-586 BCE

Zedekiah was appointed king of Judah by Nebuchadnezzar II after Jerusalem surrendered in 597 BCE. He reigned for eleven years. The prophet Jeremiah was prominent during his reign, advising the king to continue submission to Babylon. Zedekiah eventually rejected the prophet's advice and entered into an alliance with Apries, pharaoh of Egypt. Nebuchadnezzar then came against Jerusalem in January of 588 BCE and laid siege to the city. After thirty months of increasing deprivation, the city fell in July, 586 BCE, and the Temple was destroyed a month later. Zedekiah attempted to escape, but was captured and blinded after being made to watch his young sons being executed. Soon after that, the people of Jerusalem and Judah were exiled to Babylon, bringing the era of the Hebrew kings to its end.

CHAPTER SIX

PHARAOHS OF EGYPT
AND THE HEBREW KINGS

In this chapter, the regnal years of the pharaohs in Dynasties 20-26 of Egypt (1,086-586 BCE) are synchronized with the regnal years of the Hebrew kings and displayed in side-by-side timeline tables for easy comparison. Dates for the reigns of the pharaohs are based on those established by professor Kenneth A. Kitchen in the 2004 edition his book *The Third Intermediate Period in Egypt (1100-650 BC)*. Dates for the Hebrew kings are those shown in the kingdoms chronology displayed in the table on pages 21-29 and on page 42. The names of the Neo-Assyrian kings are also shown at the point where each king's reign begins, but the individual years of their reigns are not displayed.

The major point of synchronization between the chronologies of ancient Egypt and those of the kingdoms of Israel and Judah occurred in the reign of pharaoh Shoshenq I, who invaded Canaan in his twentieth regnal year, 925 BCE.[1] Traditional interpretation dating from the early 1800s CE, based on the work of Jean-François Champollion, equated Shoshenq I with the biblical pharaoh Shishak, who the Bible says went to Jerusalem in the fifth year of Rehoboam of Judah, seized the Temple treasures, plundered the king's palace, and absconded with the golden shields of Solomon (1 Kings 14:25-26; 2 Chronicles 12:9).

However, the new kingdoms chronology presented in this book places the fifth year of Rehoboam in the year 961 BCE, and it shows the invasion of Canaan by Shoshenq I as occurring thirty-six years later in history during the reign of Asa of Judah, not in the reign of Rehoboam. That means that the pharaoh who opposed Rehoboam was Siamun, not Shoshenq I. Based on the alignment of the reigns of the pharaohs with the new kingdoms chronology of the Hebrew kings presented in this book, the following associations are revealed:

1) Psusennes I (r. 1,039-991 BCE) was pharaoh during all of David's reign over United Israel and during the earliest years of Solomon's reign. He is the pharaoh who gave refuge and his sister-in-law in marriage to Hadad of Edom (1 Kings 11:17-20), and was also the pharaoh who later gave his daughter in marriage to Solomon. Only one daughter of Psusennes, named Istemkheb C, is known from inscriptions, and she is thought by Professor Kitchen to have married

---

[1] Kitchen, *The Third Intermediate Period in Egypt 1100-650 BC*, p. 74.

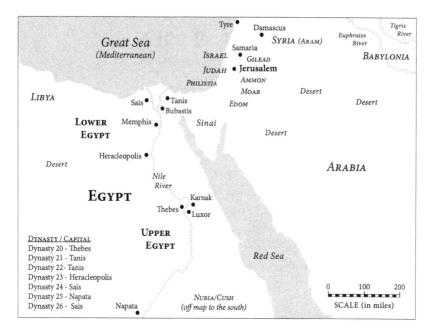

Map 6.1 - Ancient Egypt (Dynasties 20-26)

a Theban high priest, so the daughter of pharaoh who married Solomon remains unnamed.[1] Psusennes I captured Gezer, burned it to the ground, and gave it to Solomon and his daughter as a wedding gift. Solomon then rebuilt the walls of Gezer, adding a massive six-chambered gate matching the design of the gates he had built at Hazor and Megiddo. Archaeologists have dated the destruction of Gezer to *circa* 1,050 BCE; the actual date was probably 1,006-1,004 BCE.

2) Shishak (the future Shoshenq I, but at this time only commander of the army of Siamun, *r.* 978-959) came against Judah and Jerusalem during the fifth year in the reign of Rehoboam in 961 BCE and took the Temple treasures. A fragmentary relief about Siamun on a temple wall at Tanis has been interpreted buy Professor Kenneth Kitchen as describing an invasion of the Levant.[2]

3) Shoshenq I (*r.* 945-924) was the pharaoh who invaded Canaan in 925 BCE during the reign of Asa (see explanation of the invasion starting on page 35).

---

[1] Kitchen, *The Third Intermediate Period in Egypt 1100-650 BC*, p. 264-265.
[2] Kitchen, *The Third Intermediate Period in Egypt 1100-650 BC*, p. 280-281.

Chapter Six: Pharaohs of Egypt and the Hebrew Kings

Pharaohs of Egypt and Kings of United Israel, 1,086-1,051 BCE
(years shown in left column are proleptic Gregorian years; all years BCE, A = accession or partial year)

YEAR BCE	EGYPTIAN DYNASTIES 20, 21 *(regnal years began in Spring)*		UNITED ISRAEL *(regnal years Tishri to Tishri)*
			... begins 1,086 BCE
	10th	← ▲ **Ramesses XI** (1,098-1,070)	A
1086	11th	*Dynasty 20 (Thebes)* ← - - - - - - - - - ♛ **Saul** (1,086-1,046)	1st
1085	12th	*King of United Israel*	2nd
1084	13th		3rd
1083	14th		4th
1082	15th		5th
1081	16th		6th
1080	17th	← - - **Smendes rules in Northern Egypt**	7th
1079	18th	(1,080-1,069)	8th
1078	19th	*[years of reign not shown]*	9th
1077	20th		10th
1076	21st		11th
1075	22nd		12th
1074	23rd		13th
1073	24th		14th
1072	25th		15th
1071	26th		16th
1070	27th		17th
1069	28th/A	← ▲ **Smendes I** (1,069-1,043)	18th
1068	1st	*Dynasty 21 (Tanis)*	19th
1067	2nd		20th
1066	3rd		21st
1065	4th		22nd
1064	5th		23rd
1063	6th		24th
1062	7th		25th
1061	8th		26th
1060	9th		27th
1059	10th		28th
1058	11th		29th
1057	12th		30th
1056	13th		31st
1055	14th		32nd
1054	15th		33rd
1053	16th		34th
1052	17th		35th
1051	18th		36th

Sacred Chronology of the Hebrew Kings

Pharaohs of Egypt and Kings of United Israel, 1,050-1,015 BCE
(years shown in left column are proleptic Gregorian years; all years BCE, A = accession or partial year)

EGYPTIAN DYNASTY 21 **UNITED ISRAEL**
(regnal years began in Spring) *(regnal years Tishri to Tishri)*

YEAR BCE	Smendes (cont.)			Saul (cont.)
1050	17th			37th
1049	18th			38th
1048	19th			39th
1047	20th			40th/A
1046	21st	← — — — — — — — — — — — — —	♛ David (1,046-1,039) King of Judah	1st
1045	22nd			2nd
1044	23rd			3rd
1043	24th			4th
1042	25th/A	← ▲ Amenemnisu (1,043-1,039) *Dynasty 21 (Tanis)*		5th
1041	1st			6th
1040	2nd			7th
1039	3rd/A	← ▲ Psusennes I (1,039-991) *Dynasty 21 (Tanis)*	← — — — — ♛ David (1,039-1,006) King of United Israel	8th
1038	1st			9th
1037	2nd			10th
1036	3rd			11th
1035	4th			12th
1034	5th			13th
1033	6th			14th
1032	7th			15th
1031	8th			16th
1030	9th			17th
1029	10th			18th
1028	11th			19th
1027	12th			20th
1026	13th			21st
1025	14th			22nd
1024	15th			23rd
1023	16th			24th
1022	17th			25th
1021	18th			26th
1020	19th			27th
1019	20th			28th
1018	21st			29th
1017	22nd			30th
1016	23rd			31st
1015	24th			32nd

Pharaohs of Egypt and Kings of United Israel, 1,014-979 BCE
(years shown in left column are proleptic Gregorian years; all years BCE, A = accession or partial year)

	EGYPTIAN DYNASTY 21	**UNITED ISRAEL**
	(regnal years began in Spring)	*(regnal years Tishri to Tishri)*
	Psusennes I (cont.)	David (cont.)

YEAR BCE		
1014	25th	33rd
1013	26th	34th
1012	27th	35th
1011	28th	36th
1010	29th	37th
1009	30th	38th
1008	31st	39th
1007	32nd	40th/A
1006	33rd ←------------------------------ ♛ Solomon (1,006-966)	1st
1005	34th *King of United Israel*	2nd
1004	35th	3rd
1003	36th	4th
1002	37th	5th
1001	38th	6th
1000	39th	7th
999	40th	8th
998	41st	9th
997	42nd	10th
996	43rd	11th
995	44th	12th
994	45th	13th
993	46th/(1st) ◄── ▲ **Amenemope** (993-984)	14th
992	47th/(2nd) *Dynasty 21 (Tanis)*	15th
991	48th/(3rd)	16th
990	4th	17th
989	5th	18th
988	6th	19th
987	7th	20th
986	8th	21st
985	9th	22nd
984	10th/A ◄── ▲ **Osochor (Osorkon the Elder)** (984-978)	23rd
983	1st *Dynasty 21 (Tanis)*	24th
982	2nd	25th
981	3rd	26th
980	4th	27th
979	5th	28th

Pharaohs of Egypt and Kings of United Israel, Israel, and Judah, 978-943 BCE

(years shown in left column are proleptic Gregorian years; all years BCE, A = accession or partial year)

YEAR BCE	EGYPTIAN DYNASTIES 21, 22 (regnal years began in Spring)			UNITED ISRAEL (regnal years Tishri to Tishri)
	Osochor (cont.)			*Solomon (cont.)*
978	--6th/A-- ← ▲ **Siamun** (978-959) *Dynasty 21 (Tanis)*			29th
977	1st			30th
976	2nd			31st
975	3rd			32nd
974	4th			33rd
973	5th			34th
972	6th			35th
971	7th			36th
970	8th			37th
969	9th			38th
968	10th			39th
967	11th			40th/A
966	12th ←------------------------		♛ **Rehoboam** (966-961) *King of United Israel*	1st
965	13th			2nd
			Kingdom of	
964	14th	*Shishak (future pharaoh*	**Kingdom of**	**Kingdom of**
			ISRAEL	**JUDAH**
963	15th	*Shoshenq I) leads Siamun's*	*(regnal years counted*	*(regnal years counted*
962	16th	*army against Rehoboam,*	*Nisan to Nisan)*	*Tishri to Tishri)*
961	17th	←---*takes Temple treasures* ---	♛ **Jeroboam** 1st	♛ **Rehoboam** 1st
960	18th		(961-940) 2nd	(961-944) 2nd
959	19th		*King of Israel* 3rd	*King of Judah* 3rd
958	20th/A ← ▲ **Psusennes II** (959-945) *Dynasty 21 (Tanis)*		4th	4th
957	1st		5th	5th
956	2nd		6th	6th
955	3rd		7th	7th
954	4th		8th	8th
953	5th		9th	9th
952	6th		10th	10th
951	7th		11th	11th
950	8th		12th	12th
949	9th		13th	13th
948	10th		14th	14th
947	11th		15th	15th
946	12th		16th	16th
945	13th		17th	17th/A
944	14th/A ← ▲ **Shoshenq I** (945-924) *Dynasty 22 (Tanis)* ←--------------		18th	♛ **Abijah** (944-942) 1st
943	1st		19th	2nd

- 98 -

Chapter Six: *Pharaohs of Egypt and the Hebrew Kings*

Pharaohs of Egypt and Kings of Israel and Judah, 942-907 BCE

(years shown in left column are proleptic Gregorian years; all years BCE, A = accession or partial year)

YEAR BCE	EGYPTIAN DYNASTY 22 (regnal years began in Spring)	NEO-ASSYRIAN KINGS (this column)	ISRAEL (regnal years Nisan to Nisan)	JUDAH (regnal years Tishri to Tishri)
	Shoshenq I (cont.)		Jeroboam (cont.)	Abijah (cont.)
942	2nd	← Adad-nirari II (942-921)	20th	♛ Asa (942-900) 3rd/A
941	3rd		21st	1st
940	4th	←	♛ Nadab (940-939) 22nd/1st	2nd
939	5th	←	♛ Baasha (939-916) 2nd/1st	3rd
938	6th		2nd	4th
937	7th		3rd	5th
936	8th		4th	6th
935	9th		5th	7th
934	10th		6th	8th
933	11th		7th	9th
932	12th		8th	10th
931	13th		9th	11th
930	14th		10th	12th
929	15th		11th	13th
928	16th		12th	14th
927	17th		13th	15th
926	18th	*Zerah attacks Judah, defeated by Asa,*	14th	16th
925	19th	←--- *Shoshenq ampaigns to defend Israel*	15th	17th
924	20th		16th	18th
923	21st/A	← ▲ Osorkon I (924-889) *Dynasty 22 (Tanis)*	17th	19th
922	1st		18th	20th
921	2nd	← Tikulti-ninurta (921-914)	19th	21st
920	3rd		20th	22nd
919	4th		21st	23rd
918	5th		22nd	24th
917	6th		23rd	25th
916	7th	←	♛ Elah (916-914) 24th/1st	26th
915	8th		2nd/A/1st	27th
914	9th	← ♛ Ashur-nasir-pal II (914-889)	♛ Zimri (914) *for 7 days* 2nd ♛ Omri (914-904)	28th
913	10th		3rd	29th
912	11th		4th	30th
911	12th		5th	31st
910	13th		6th	32nd
909	14th		7th	33rd
908	15th		8th	34th
907	16th		9th	35th

Pharaohs of Egypt and Kings of Israel and Judah, 906-871 BCE

(years shown in left column are proleptic Gregorian years; all years BCE, A = accession or partial year)

YEAR BCE	EGYPTIAN DYNASTY 22 (regnal years began in Spring)		ISRAEL (regnal years Nisan to Nisan)	JUDAH (regnal years Tishri to Tishri)
	Osorkon I (cont.)	NEO-ASSYRIAN KINGS (this column)	Omri (cont.)	Asa (cont.)
906	17th		10th	36th
905	18th		11th	37th
904	19th	←------------------	12th/1st ♛ Ahab (904-883)	38th
903	20th		2nd	39th
902	21st		3rd	40th
901	22nd		4th	41st/A
900	23rd	←------------------	5th --- ♛ Jehoshaphat (900-875)	1st
899	24th		6th	2nd
898	25th		7th	3rd
897	26th		8th	4th
896	27th		9th	5th
895	28th		10th	6th
894	29th		11th	7th
893	30th		12th	8th
892	31st		13th	9th
891	32nd		14th	10th
890	33rd	← ▲ **Shoshenq II** (ca. 890) Dynasty 22 (Tanis)	15th	11th
889	34th/A	▲ **Takeloth I** ♛ **Shalmaneser III**	16th	12th
888	1st	(889-874) (889-854?)	17th	13th
887	2nd	Dynasty 22 (Tanis)	18th	14th
886	3rd		19th	15th
885	4th		20th	16th
884	5th		21st	17th
883	6th	←--- Battle of Qarqar -------- ♛ Ahaziah (883-882)	22nd/1st	18th
882	7th	←------------------ ♛ Joram (882/879-867)	2nd/R = regent	19th
881	8th	♛ Jehoram of Judah	R	20th
880	9th	regent for Joram	R	21st
879	10th	for about 2 years	1st	22nd
878	11th	from 882-879	2nd	23rd
877	12th		3rd	24th/
876	13th		4th	25th/A
875	14th	←------------------	5th --- ♛ Jehoram (875-868)	1st
874	15th/A	← ▲ **Osorkon II** (874-850)	6th	2nd
873	1st	Dynasty 22 (Tanis)	7th	3rd
872	2nd		8th	4th
871	3rd		9th	5th

Pharaohs of Egypt and Kings of Israel and Judah, 870-835 BCE

(years shown in left column are proleptic Gregorian years; all years BCE, A = accession or partial year)

YEAR BCE	EGYPTIAN DYNASTY 22 (regnal years began in Spring)	NEO-ASSYRIAN KINGS (this column)	ISRAEL (regnal years Nisan to Nisan)	JUDAH (regnal years Tishri to Tishri)
	Osorkon II (cont.)		Joram (cont.)	Jehoram (cont.)
870	4th	← Harsiese rules in Thebes	10th	6th
869	5th	(ca. 870-860)	11th	7th
868	6th	[years not shown]	12th	♛ Ahaziah (868-867) 8th/A/(1st)
867	7th	←	♛ Jehu (867-840) 1st	♛ Athaliah (2nd)
866	8th		2nd	usurped throne (3rd)
865	9th		3rd	for 6-plus years (4th)
864	10th		4th	from 867-861 (5th)
863	11th		5th	(6th)
862	12th		6th	(7th)/1st
861	13th	←	7th	♛ Joash (861-822) 2nd
860	14th		8th	3rd
859	15th		9th	4th
858	16th		10th	5th
857	17th		11th	6th
856	18th		12th	7th
855	19th		13th	8th
854	20th		14th	9th
853	21st		15th	10th
852	22nd	← ♛ Shamshi-adad V (852-839)	16th	11th
851	23rd		17th	12th
850	24th		18th	13th
849	25th/A	← ▲ Takeloth II (850-825) Dynasty 22 (Tanis)	19th	14th
848	1st		20th	15th
847	2nd		21st	16th
846	3rd		22nd	17th
845	4th		23rd	18th
844	5th		24th	19th
843	6th		25th	20th
842	7th		26th	21st
841	8th		27th	22nd
840	9th		28th/1st	23rd
839	10th	← ♛ Jehoahaz (840-824)	2nd	24th
838	11th	← ♛ Adad-nirari III (839-811)	3rd	25th
837	12th		4th	26th
836	13th		5th	27th
835	14th		6th	28th

Sacred Chronology of the Hebrew Kings

Pharaohs of Egypt and Kings of Israel and Judah, 834-799 BCE
(years shown in left column are proleptic Gregorian years; all years BCE, A = accession or partial year)

YEAR BCE	EGYPTIAN DYNASTIES 22, 23 *(regnal years began in Spring)*	NEO-ASSYRIAN KINGS *(this column)*	ISRAEL *(regnal years Nisan to Nisan)*	JUDAH *(regnal years Tishri to Tishri)*
	Takeloth II (cont.)		Jehoahaz (cont.)	Joash (cont.)
834	15th		7th	29th
833	16th		8th	30th
832	17th		9th	31st
831	18th		10th	32nd
830	19th		11th	33rd
829	20th		12th	34th
828	21st		13th	35th
827	22nd		14th	36th
826	23rd		♛ Jehoash (825/824-808) 15th	37th
825	24th	←------- coreigns for 2 years ---→	16th/(1st)	38th
824	25th/A ←	▲ Shoshenq III (825-773) *Dynasty 22 (Tanis)*	17th(2nd) Jehoash sole ruler in 824 BCE ---→	39th
823	1st		1st	40th/A
822	2nd ←	-------------------------------	2nd --- ♛ Amaziah (822-794)	1st
821	3rd		3rd	2nd
820	4th		4th	3rd
819	5th		5th	4th
818	6th ←	▲ Pedubast (818-793) *Dynasty 23 (Leontopolis)* [years not shown]	6th	5th
817	7th		7th	6th
816	8th		8th	7th
815	9th		9th	8th
814	10th		10th	9th
813	11th		11th	10th
812	12th		12th	11th
811	13th ←	------- ♛ Shalmaneser IV (811-801)	13th	12th
810	14th		14th	13th
809	15th		15th	14th
808	16th		16th/1st	15th
807	17th	← ------- ♛ Jeroboam II (808-768)	2nd	16th
806	18th		3rd	Uzziah made king (17th)/1st
805	19th ←	---------------------------	4th	in 805 BCE ---→ (18th)/2nd
804	20th ←	▲ Iuput (804-803 CR) *Dynasty 23 (Leontopolis)* [years not shown]	5th	(19th)/3rd
803	21st		6th	(20th)/4th
802	22nd		7th	(21st)/5th
801	23rd ←	------- ♛ Ashur-dan III (801-783)	8th	(22nd)/6th
800	24th		9th	(23rd)/7th
799	25th		10th	(24th)/8th

- 102 -

Chapter Six: Pharaohs of Egypt and the Hebrew Kings

Pharaohs of Egypt and Kings of Israel and Judah, 798-763 BCE
(years shown in left column are proleptic Gregorian years; all years BCE, A = accession or partial year)

YEAR BCE	EGYPTIAN DYNASTY 22, 23 (regnal years began in Spring)	NEO-ASSYRIAN KINGS (this column)	ISRAEL (regnal years Nisan to Nisan)	JUDAH (regnal years Tishri to Tishri)
	Shoshenq III, Iuput (cont.)		Jeroboam II (cont.)	Uzziah/Amaziah (cont.)
798	26th		11th	(25th)/9th
797	27th		12th	(26th)/10th
796	28th		13th	(27th)/11th
795	29th		14th	(28th)/12th
794	30th		15th	(29th)/13th
793	31st		16th	♛Uzziah as sole ruler (794-754) 14th
792	32nd	◄— ▲ Shoshenq IV (793-787) Dynasty 23 (Leontopolis) [years not shown]	17th	15th
791	33rd	◄--- Earthquake in 792 BCE; Bûr-Saggilê solar eclipse on June 24, 791 BCE; see discussion on page 31	18th	16th
790	34th		19th	17th
789	35th		20th	18th
788	36th		21st	19th
787	37th	◄— ▲ Osorkon III (787-759) Dynasty 23 (Leontopolis) [years not shown]	22nd	20th
786	38th		23rd	21st
785	39th		24th	22nd
784	40th		25th	23rd
783	41st	◄-------- ♛Ashur-nirari V (783-773)	26th	24th
782	42nd		27th	25th
781	43rd		28th	26th
780	44th	◄— ▲ Akara (ca. 780-760) Dynasty 25 (Nubian/Kushite) [years not shown]	29th	27th
779	45th		30th	28th
778	46th		31st	29th
777	47th		32nd	30th
776	48th		33rd	31st
775	49th		34th	32nd
774	50th		35th	33rd
773	51st		36th	34th
772	52nd/A	▲ Pimay (773-767) Dynasty 22 (Tanis) ♛Tiglath-pileser III aka Pul (773-745)[1]	37th	35th
771	1st		38th	36th
770	2nd	[1] Pul is mentioned in the Bible but is not listed on the Assyrian King List; biblical scholars assume Pul was Tiglath-pileser III (1 Chr. 5:26).	39th	37th
769	3rd		40th	38th
768	4th	◄-------- ♛Zachariah (768)	41st/A	39th
767	5th	◄-------- ♛Shallum (767) for 1 month	1st/A/A	40th
766	6th/A	▲ Shoshenq V (767-729) Dynasty 22 (Tanis) ♛Menahem (767-757)	1st	41st
765	1st		2nd	42nd
764	2nd		3rd	43rd
763	3rd		4th	44th

– 103 –

Sacred Chronology of the Hebrew Kings

Pharaohs of Egypt and Kings of Israel and Judah, 762-727 BCE
(years shown in left column are proleptic Gregorian years; all years BCE, A = accession or partial year)

YEAR BCE	EGYPTIAN DYNASTIES 22, 24, 25 (regnal years began in Spring)		ISRAEL (regnal years Nisan to Nisan)		JUDAH (regnal years Tishri to Tishri)	
	Pimay, Shoshenq V (cont.)	Neo-Assyrian Kings (this column)	Menahem (cont.)		Uzziah (cont.)	
762	4th	◄— ▲ Takeloth III (763CR/758-757)	5th		45th	
761	5th	Dynasty 23 (Leontopolis) [years not shown]	6th		46th	
760	6th	◄— ▲ Kashta/Maatre (ca. 760-747)	7th		47th	
759	7th	Dynasty 25 (Nubian/Kushite) [years not shown]	8th		48th	
758	8th		9th/(1st)		(49th)/1st	
757	9th	◄— ▲ Rudamon (757-754)	10th/A/2nd	♛ Pekahiah (757-755)	(50th)/2nd	
756	10th	Dynasty 23 (Leontopolis) [years not shown]	1st/(3rd)	♛ Jotham (757/754-738)	(51st)/3rd	
755	11th		♛ Pekah (758/757-738) 2nd/(4th)		(52nd)/4th	
754	12th	◄— ▲ Iuput II (754-720/715?)	5th		5th	
753	13th	Dynasty 23 (Leontopolis) [years not shown]	6th		6th	
752	14th		7th		7th	
751	15th		8th		8th	
750	16th		9th		9th	
749	17th		10th		10th	
748	18th		11th		11th	
747	19th/1st	◄— ▲ Piankhy/Piyi/Sneferre (747-716)	12th		12th	
746	20th/2nd	Dynasty 25 (Nubian/Kushite)	13th		13th	
745	21st/3rd	◄— ♛ Tiglath-pileser III (745?-727)	14th		14th	
744	22nd/4th		15th		15th	
743	23rd/5th		16th		(16th)/1st	
742	24th/6th		17th	♛ Ahaz (742-727)	(17th)/2nd	
741	25th/7th	◄— — — — — — —	18th	coreigns for 4-plus years	(18th)/3rd	
740	26th/8th		19th		(19th)/4th	
739	27th/9th		20th/?		(20th)/5th	
738	28th/10th		?		6th	
737	29th/11th		?		7th	
736	30th/12th	No king in Israel 738-731 BCE. The *Seder Olam* says that Hoshea was king of Gilead (and the lands across the Jordan under Assyrian control) for about eight years before becoming king of Israel in Samaria in 731 BCE.	?		8th	
735	31st/13th		?		9th	
734	32nd/14th		?		10th	
733	33rd/15th		?		11th	
732	34th/16th		?		12th	
731	35th/17th	◄— ♛ Hoshea (731-721)	?/A		13th	
730	36th/18th		1st		14th	
729	37th/A/19th	◄— ▲ Osorkon IV (729-712)	2nd		15th	
728	1st/20th	Dynasty 22 (Tanis)	3rd		16th/A	
727	2nd/21st	◄— ▲ Tefnakht (728-720) Dynasty 24 (Sais) [years not shown]	4th	♛ Hezekiah (727-698)	1st	

Chapter Six: *Pharaohs of Egypt and the Hebrew Kings*

Pharaohs of Egypt and Kings of Israel and Judah, 726-691 BCE
(years shown in left column are proleptic Gregorian years; all years BCE, A = accession or partial year)

YEAR BCE	EGYPTIAN DYNASTIES 24, 25 *(regnal years began in Spring)*	ISRAEL *(regnal years Nisan to Nisan)*	JUDAH *(regnal years Tishri to Tishri)*
	Osorkon IV, Tefnakht (cont.)	*Hoshea (cont.)*	*Hezekiah (cont.)*
726	3rd/22nd	♛ Shalmaneser V (727-722) ⟵ — — — 5th	2nd
725	4th/23rd	NEO-ASSYRIAN KINGS (this column) — 6th	3rd
724	5th/24th	Siege of Samaria ---> 7th	4th
723	6th/25th	8th	5th
722	7th/26th	♛ Sargon II (722-705) ⟵ — — — 9th	6th
721	8th/27th	Fall of Samaria ---> ...	7th
720	9th/28th	KINGDOM OF ISRAEL	8th
719	10th/29th · ▲ **Bakenranef** (720-714) *Dynasty 24 (Sais)*	ENDS IN 721 BCE	9th
718	11th/30th		10th
717	12th/31st · ▲ **Shoshenq VI** (720-715) *Dynasty 23 (Leontopolis) - existence doubted* [years not shown]		11th
716	13th/32nd		12th
715	14th/33rd/A · ▲ **Shabako** (716-702) *Dynasty 25 (Nubian/Kushite)*		13th
714	1st		14th
713	2nd		15th
712	3rd		16th
711	4th		17th
710	5th		18th
709	6th		19th
708	7th		20th
707	8th		21st
706	9th		22nd
705	10th	♛ Sennacherib (705-681) ⟵ — — —	23rd
704	11th		24th
703	12th		25th
702	13th/A · ▲ **Shebitku** (702-691) *Dynasty 25 (Nubian/Kushite)*		26th
701	1st	⟵--- *Sennacherib campaigned in Judah against Jerusalem; future pharaoh Taharqa leads Shebitku's army out of Egypt to oppose him*	27th
700	2nd		28th
699	3rd		29th/A
698	4th	♛ **Manasseh** (698-643) ⟵ — — —	1st
697	5th		2nd
696	6th		3rd
695	7th		4th
694	8th		5th
693	9th		6th
692	10th		7th
691	11th		8th

— 105 —

Pharaohs of Egypt and Kings of Judah, 690-655 BCE

(years shown in left column are proleptic Gregorian years; all years BCE, A = accession or partial year)

	EGYPTIAN DYNASTIES 25, 26		JUDAH
	(regnal years began in Spring)		*(regnal years Tishri to Tishri)*
YEAR BCE	Shebitku (cont.)	NEO-ASSYRIAN KINGS *(this column)*	Manasseh (cont.)
690	--12th/A-- ← ▲ Taharqa (691-664) *Dynasty 25 (Nubian/Kushite)*		9th
689	1st		10th
688	2nd		11th
687	3rd		12th
686	4th		13th
685	5th		14th
684	6th		15th
683	7th		16th
682	8th		17th
681	9th		18th
680	10th ←---------- ♛ Esarhaddon (681-669)		19th
679	11th		20th
678	12th		21st
677	13th		22nd
676	14th		23rd
675	15th		24th
674	16th		25th
673	17th		26th
672	18th		27th
671	19th		28th
670	20th		29th
669	21st		30th
668	22nd ←---------- ♛ Ashurbanipal (*ca.* 669-631)		31st
667	23rd		32nd
666	24th		33rd
665	25th		34th
664	26th/A/A ← ▲ Tanutamani (664-656) ... Thebes sacked by Ashurbanipal *Dynasty 25 (Nubian/Kushite)*		35th
663	1st/1st		36th
662	2nd/2nd ▲ Psammetichus I (664-610) *Dynasty 26 (Saite)*		37th
661	3rd/3rd		38th
660	4th/4th		39th
659	5th/5th		40th
658	6th/6th		41st
657	7th/7th		42nd
656	8th/8th		43rd
655	---/9th		44th

Chapter Six: Pharaohs of Egypt and the Hebrew Kings

Pharaohs of Egypt and Kings of Judah, 654-619 BCE
(years shown in left column are proleptic Gregorian years; all years BCE, A = accession or partial year)

YEAR BCE	EGYPTIAN DYNASTY 26 *(regnal years began in Spring)* Psamtik I *(cont.)*	NEO-ASSYRIAN KINGS *(this column)*	JUDAH *(regnal years Tishri to Tishri)* Manasseh *(cont.)*	
654	10th			45th
653	11th			46th
652	12th			47th
651	13th			48th
650	14th			49th
649	15th			50th
648	16th			51st
647	17th			52nd
646	18th			53rd
645	19th			54th
644	20th			55th/A
643	21st	←--------------------------	♛ Amon (643-641)	1st
642	22nd			2nd/ ?
641	23rd			A
640	24th	←--------------------------	♛ Josiah (640-609)	1st
639	25th			2nd
638	26th			3rd
637	27th			4th
636	28th			5th
635	29th			6th
634	30th			7th
633	31st			8th
632	32nd			9th
631	33rd	←--------- ♛ Ashur-etil-ilani *(ca. 631-627)*		10th
630	34th			11th
629	35th			12th
628	36th			13th
627	37th	←--------- ♛ Sin-sar-ishkun *(ca. 627-612)*		14th
626	38th	♛ Sin-shumu-lishir *(ca. 626)*		15th
625	39th			16th
624	40th			17th
623	41st			18th
622	42nd			19th
621	43rd			20th
620	44th			21st
619	45th			22nd

Pharaohs of Egypt and Kings of Judah, 618-586 BCE
(years shown in left column are proleptic Gregorian years; all years BCE, A = accession or partial year)

EGYPTIAN DYNASTY 26
(regnal years began in Spring)

JUDAH
(regnal years Tishri to Tishri)

YEAR BCE	Psamtik I (cont.)	Neo-Assyrian Kings (this column)	Josiah (cont.)
618	46th		23rd
617	47th		24th
616	48th		25th
615	49th		26th
614	50th		27th
613	51st		28th
612	52nd	← Ashur-uballit II (612-609)	29th
611	53rd	Fall of Nineveh on May, 612 BCE	30th
610	54th/A ←	▲ Necho II (610-595)	31st/A
609	1st ←	Dynasty 26 (Saite)	♛ Jehoahaz (609) for 3 months — 1st/A
608	2nd	Neo-Assyrian Empire Ends	♛ Jehoiakim — 1st
607	3rd		(609-598) — 2nd
606	4th		3rd
605	5th		4th
604	6th		5th
603	7th		6th
602	8th		7th
601	9th		8th
600	10th		9th
599	11th		10th
598	12th		11th/A/A
597	13th ←		♛ Jehoiachin (598-597) — 1st
596	14th ←		♛ Zedekiah — 2nd
595	15th/A ←	▲ Psammetichus II (595-589)	(597-586) — 3rd
594	1st	Dynasty 26 (Saite)	4th
593	2nd		5th
592	3rd		6th
591	4th		7th
590	5th		8th
589	6th/A ←	▲ Apries (589-570)	9th
588	1st ←	Dynasty 26 (Saite) — Siege of Jerusalem →	10th
587	2nd		11th
586	3rd ←	— Fall of Jerusalem →	---

KINGDOM OF JUDAH ENDS
After the fall of Jerusalem, the kingdom of Judah ended with the exile of the people to Babylon and other locales in the Neo-Babylonian Empire.

CHAPTER SEVEN

KINGS OF ASSYRIA
AND THE HEBREW KINGS

In this chapter, the regnal years of the kings in the Neo-Assyrian Empire (942-609 BCE) are synchronized with the regnal years of the Hebrew kings and displayed in side-by-side timeline tables for easy comparison. Dates for the reigns of the Assyrian kings have been modified from the traditional dates generally accepted by scholars and published by historian Jona Lendering on his website Livius.org (www.livius.org), which source-credits Professor Jean-Jacques Glassner (Director of Research for Archaeological Sciences of Antiquity at the French National Centre for Scientific Research) and his book *Chroniques Mésopotamiennes*, 1993 edition.

The Assyrian regnal dates have been modified from the traditional dates in two ways: (1) by adding twenty-eight years to the dates of kings who reigned prior to Tiglath-pileser III, this modification based on identification of the Bûr-Saggilê eclipse as occurring in the year 791 BCE instead of 763 BCE,[1] and (2) by moving the reigns of Shalmaneser III and all prior kings back in time an additional two years to account for the disputed rule of Shalmaneser's eldest son, Ashur-danin-pal, after Shalmaneser's death. Dates for the Hebrew kings are those shown in the harmonized chronology displayed in the tables on pages 21-29 and on page 42.

The major point of synchronization between the chronologies of ancient Assyria and those of the kingdoms of Israel and Judah is the Battle of Qarqar, which occurred during the sixth year of Shalmaneser III. Traditional interpretations dating from the late 1800s, based on the work of Sir Henry Rawlinson, have dated Shalmaneser's sixth regnal year to 853 BCE, but the new kingdoms chronology presented in this book requires that the sixth year be recognized as occurring thirty years earlier in the year 883 BCE. That year is equated with the final regnal year of Ahab of Israel, and in that manner the synchronization of the Assyrian and Hebrew chronologies is accomplished (see explanation on page 30).

A second major point of synchronization is mentioned on the Black Obelisk and in the annals of Shalmaneser III, which records that "Jehu, son of Omri" paid tribute. The tribute was paid in Shalmaneser's eighteenth regnal year, which is traditionally identified as the year 841 BCE. However, the adjusted Assyrian and Hebrew kings chronology in this book shows that Shalmaneser's eighteenth year

---

[1] See reasons for identifying the year of the Bûr-Saggilê eclipse as 791 BCE on page 30.

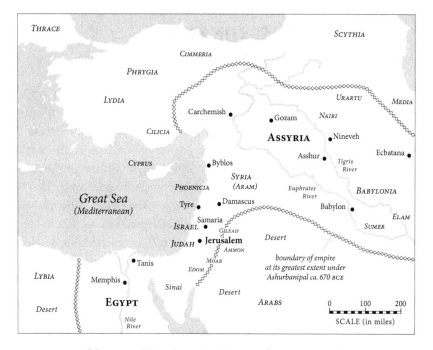

Map 7.1 - Neo-Assyrian Empire (940-609 BCE)

was 871 BCE, which was three to four years before Jehu became king of Israel. One logical explanation is that Joram sent his army captain Jehu as his ambassador to Shalmaneser to pay tribute soon after the Assyrian king had defeated Syria, the tribute being a bribe to keep the Assyrians at bay (see discussion on page 70-72). The payment of tribute by Jehu is not mentioned in the biblical text, since he was not yet king, and Jehu is not called king in the Assyrian records. It is also possible that Jehu was acting independently and subversively.

Additional synchronizations between the Assyrian and Hebrew chronologies are important chronologically as follows:
- 824 BCE - Adad-nirari III defeats Benhadad III of Syria, allowing Jehoash of Israel to deliver Israel from oppression by Damascus (see page 74).
- *ca.* 760 BCE - Tiglath-pileser III exacts tribute from Menahem (see page 80).
- 721 BCE - Sargon II captures Samaria; the kingdom of Israel ends (see page 82).
- 701 BCE - Sennacherib attacks Judah and Jerusalem in his third regnal year, during the fourteenth year of Hezekiah (see pages 83 and 117).

Kings of Assyria, Israel, and Judah, 942-907 BCE

(years shown in left column are proleptic Gregorian years; all years BCE, A = accession or partial year)

YEAR BCE	NEO-ASSYRIAN EMPIRE (regnal years began in Spring)	ISRAEL (regnal years Nisan to Nisan)	JUDAH (regnal years Tishri to Tishri)
		Jeroboam (cont.)	Abijah (cont.)
			2nd
942	A ← 👑 **Adad-nirari II**	20th ←------ 👑 **Asa** (942-900)	3rd/A
941	1st (942-921)	21st	1st
940	2nd ←------	👑 **Nadab** (940-939) 22nd/1st	2nd
939	3rd ←------	👑 **Baasha** (939-916) 2nd/1st	3rd
938	4th	2nd	4th
937	5th	3rd	5th
936	6th	4th	6th
935	7th	5th	7th
934	8th	6th	8th
933	9th	7th	9th
932	10th	8th	10th
931	11th	9th	11th
930	12th	10th	12th
929	13th	11th	13th
928	14th	12th	14th
927	15th	13th	15th
926	16th	14th	16th
925	17th	15th	17th
924	18th	16th	18th
923	19th	17th	19th
922	20th	18th	20th
921	21st/A ← 👑 **Tikulti-ninurta**	19th	21st
920	1st (921-914)	20th	22nd
919	2nd	21st	23rd
918	3rd	22nd	24th
917	4th	23rd	25th
916	5th ←------	👑 **Elah** (916-914) 24th/1st	26th
915	6th	2nd/A/1st	27th
914	7th/A ← 👑 **Ashur-nasir-pal II** ←-- 👑 **Zimri** (914)	2nd	28th
913	1st (914-889) *for 7 days*		29th
912	2nd	👑 **Omri** (914-904) 3rd	30th
911	3rd	4th	31st
910	4th	5th	32nd
909	5th	6th	33rd
908	6th	7th	34th
907	7th ←--- *campaigned in Lebanon, reached the Great Sea*	8th	35th
		9th	

Kings of Assyria, Israel, and Judah, 906-871 BCE

(years shown in left column are proleptic Gregorian years; all years BCE, A = accession or partial year)

YEAR BCE	NEO-ASSYRIAN EMPIRE (regnal years began in Spring)	ISRAEL (regnal years Nisan to Nisan)	JUDAH (regnal years Tishri to Tishri)
	Ashur-nasir-pal II (cont.)	Omri (cont.)	Asa (cont.)
906	8th	10th	36th
905	9th	11th	37th
904	10th ← — — — — — — — — — — — 👑 Ahab (904-883)	12th/1st	38th
903	11th	2nd	39th
902	12th	3rd	40th
901	13th	4th	41st/A
900	14th ← — — — — — — — — — — — — — — — — 5th — — — 👑 Jehoshaphat		1st
			(900-875)
899	15th	6th	2nd
898	16th	7th	3rd
897	17th	8th	4th
896	18th	9th	5th
895	19th	10th	6th
894	20th	11th	7th
893	21st	12th	8th
892	22nd	13th	9th
891	23rd	14th	10th
890	24th	15th	11th
889	25th/A ← 👑 **Shalmaneser III**	16th	12th
888	1st (889-854?)	17th	13th
887	2nd	18th	14th
886	3rd	19th	15th
885	4th	20th	16th
884	5th	21st	17th
883	6th ← - - - *Battle of Qarqar*[1] - - - - 👑 Ahaziah (883-882) 22nd/1st		18th
882	7th ← — — — — — — — — — — 👑 Joram (882/879-867) 2nd/R		19th
881	8th — — — 👑 Jehoram of Judah R		20th
880	9th *regent (R) for Joram* R		21st
879	10th ← - - - *campaigned in Syria* *for two-plus years* R/1st		22nd
		from 882-879	
878	11th	2nd	23rd
877	12th	3rd	24th/
876	13th	4th	25th/A
875	14th ← - - - *campaigned in Syria* ← — — — — — — 5th — — — 👑 Jehoram		1st
			(875-868)
874	15th	6th	2nd
873	16th	7th	3rd
872	17th	8th	4th
871	18th ← - - - *campaigned in Syria,*	9th	5th
	Jehu pays tribute for Joram		

[1] The Battle of Qarqar was fought in the springtime of the year 883 BCE between Shalmaneser III and a coalition of twelve kings; an account of the battle is recorded on the Kurkh Monolith, which mentions Ahab, who the Bible says was fatally wounded at Ramoth-gilead in 883 BCE; for a discussion of the events in the reign of Ahab, see page 62.

Chapter Seven: Kings of Assyria and the Hebrew Kings

Kings of Assyria, Israel, and Judah, 870-835 BCE

(years shown in left column are proleptic Gregorian years; all years BCE, A = accession or partial year)

YEAR BCE	NEO-ASSYRIAN EMPIRE *(regnal years began in Spring)*	ISRAEL *(regnal years Nisan to Nisan)*	JUDAH *(regnal years Tishri to Tishri)*
	Shalmaneser III (cont.)	*Joram (cont.)*	*Jehoram (cont.)*
870	19th	10th	6th
869	20th	11th	7th
868	21st	12th	♛ Ahaziah (868-867) 8th/A/(1st)
867	22nd ←-------------------------	♛ Jehu (867-840)[1] 1st	♛ Athaliah (2nd)
866	23rd	2nd	usurped throne (3rd)
865	24th	3rd	for 6-plus years (4th)
864	25th	4th	from 867-861 (5th)
863	26th	5th	(6th)
862	27th ←--- *campaigned against Syria,*	6th	(7th)/1st
861	28th *siege of Damascus failed*	7th ----	♛ Joash (861-822) 2nd
860	29th	8th	3rd
859	30th	9th	4th
858	31st	10th	5th
857	32nd	11th	6th
856	33rd *Ashur-danin-pal leads a five-year revolt,*	12th	7th
855	34th *reigns for two years after Shalmaneser III*	13th	8th
854	35th/(A) ← *dies in 854 BCE, overthrown by his brother*	14th	9th
853	(1) *Shamsi-Adad V, eponyms missing for the*	15th	10th
852	(2)/A ← *two-year reign of Ashur-danin-pal*	16th	11th
	♛ **Shamshi-adad V**		
851	1st (852-839)	17th	12th
850	2nd	18th	13th
849	3rd [1] According to 2 Kings, 9-10,	19th	14th
848	4th Jehu was anointed as king by a	20th	15th
847	5th young prophet sent from Elisha,	21st	16th
846	6th and was thereafter recognized	22nd	17th
845	7th as king of Israel by the army;	23rd	18th
844	8th Jehu paid tribute to Assyria in	24th	19th
843	9th Shalmaneser III's eighteenth year	25th	20th
842	10th (871 BCE) in order to ally himself	26th	21st
841	11th with the Assyrian king (tribute	27th	22nd
840	12th payment is recorded on the Black	28th/1st	23rd
839	13th/A ← *Obelisk but is not mentioned in* ♛ Jehoahaz (840-824)	2nd	24th
	♛ **Adad-nirari III** *the Bible); then, in 867 BCE, Jehu*		
838	1st (839-811) *returned to Jezreel to kill Joram*	3rd	25th
837	2nd *of Israel and Ahaziah of Judah;*	4th	26th
836	3rd *Jehu's regnal years are counted*	5th	27th
835	4th *from the time he began to reign*	6th	28th
	from Samaria in 867 BCE.		

Kings of Assyria, Israel, and Judah, 834-799 BCE

(years shown in left column are proleptic Gregorian years; all years BCE, A = accession or partial year)

YEAR BCE	NEO-ASSYRIAN EMPIRE (regnal years began in Spring)	ISRAEL (regnal years Nisan to Nisan)	JUDAH (regnal years Tishri to Tishri)
	Adad-nirari III (cont.)	Jehoahaz (cont.)	Joash (cont.)
834	5th	7th	29th
833	6th	8th	30th
832	7th	9th	31st
831	8th	10th	32nd
830	9th	11th	33rd
829	10th	12th	34th
828	11th	13th	35th
827	12th	14th	36th
826	13th	♛ Jehoash (825/824-808) 15th	37th
825	14th	← - - - - coreigns for 2 years - - -→ 16th/(1st)	38th
824	15th	← - Syria subdued by Adad-nirari III, — Jehoash sole ruler 17th(2nd)	39th
823	16th	allowing Israel to gain its freedom; — in 824 BCE - - -→ 1st	40th/A
822	17th	Jehoash pays tribute to Adad-nirari [2] ← - Syrians invade, despoil Jerusalem [3] ← - - - - - 2nd - -	♛ Amaziah (822-794) 1st
821	18th	3rd	2nd
820	19th	[2] Jehoash coreigned with his father for two years, according to the *Seder Olam*. When Adad-nirari III of Assyria resumed his western campaigns in Syria in 827 BCE, the power of Syria was weakened, so Jehoash was able to free Israel from Syriaean control in 824 BCE, coinciding with Adad-nirari's campaign against Manṣuate in the Lebanon valley (*Massyas* according to Strabo 16:2, 18). At that time, the king of Assyria also attacked Damascus, defeated the Syrian armies, and exacted a heavy tribute from Benhadad III, the king of Syria. - adapted from the online article titled "Jehoash" at www.jewishvirtuallibrary.org; also, see 2 Kings 13:5; payment of tribute by Jehoash recorded on the Tel-al-Rimah Stele discovered in 1967. 4th	3rd
819	20th	5th	4th
818	21st	6th	5th
817	22nd	7th	6th
816	23rd	8th	7th
815	24th	9th	8th
814	25th	10th	9th
813	26th	[3] A weakened Syrian army, called *"a small company of men"* (KJV), captured Jerusalem in spring of 822 BCE, taking much plunder (to pay the tribute exacted by Adad-nirari the previous year), and seriously wounded Joash; see 2 Chronicles 24:23-24. 11th	10th
812	27th	12th	11th
811	28th/A ← ♛ Shalmaneser IV (811-801)	13th	12th
810	1st	14th	13th
809	2nd	15th	14th
808	3rd	← - - - - - - - ♛ Jeroboam II 16th/1st	15th
807	4th	(808-769) 2nd	16th
806	5th	3rd	Uzziah made king (17th)/1st
805	6th	← - - - - - - - - - - - - - - - - 4th - -	in 805 BCE - - -→ (18th)/2nd
804	7th	5th	(19th)/3rd
803	8th	6th	(20th)/4th
802	9th	7th	(21st)/5th
801	10th/A ← ♛ Ashur-dan III (801-783)	8th	(22nd)/6th
800	1st	9th	(23rd)/7th
799	2nd	10th	(24th)/8th

— 114 —

Kings of Assyria, Israel, and Judah, 798-763 BCE

(years shown in left column are proleptic Gregorian years; all years BCE, A = accession or partial year)

YEAR BCE	NEO-ASSYRIAN EMPIRE *(regnal years began in Spring)*		ISRAEL *(regnal years Nisan to Nisan)*	JUDAH *(regnal years Tishri to Tishri)*
	Ashur-dan III (cont.)		*Jeroboam II (cont.)*	*Uzziah/Amaziah (cont.)*
798	3rd		11th	(25th)/9th
797	4th		12th	(26th)/10th
796	5th		13th	(27th)/11th
795	6th		14th	(28th)/12th
794	7th	←-------	15th -------	♛ Uzziah (29th)/13th
793	8th		16th	as sole ruler
792	9th		17th	(794-754) 14th
791	10th	←--- Earthquake in 792 BCE; Bûr-Saggilê	18th	15th
790	11th	solar eclipse on June 24, 791 BCE; see	19th	16th
789	12th	discussion on page 31	20th	17th
788	13th		21st	18th
787	14th		22nd	19th
786	15th		23rd	20th
785	16th		24th	21st
784	17th		25th	22nd
783	18th/A	← ♛ **Ashur-nirari V**[1]	26th	23rd
782	1st	(783-773)	27th	24th
781	2nd	[1] The Urartun Empire reached the zenith of its power	28th	25th
780	3rd	during the reigns of Ashur-dan III and Ashur-nirari V, the latter being defeated (and possibly killed in	29th	26th
779	4th	battle in 773 BCE), as recorded on an inscription	30th	27th
778	5th	of the Urartun king Sarduri II. The hypothesis of	31st	28th
777	6th	this book is that the defeat of Ashur-nirari V led to a period of Uratun disruption and domination	32nd	29th
776	7th	of northern Assyria that lasted for twenty-eight	33rd	30th
775	8th	years (773-745 BCE), during which time the future Tiglath-pileser III ruled southen Assyria, gradually	34th	31st
774	9th	regaining dominance over northern Assyria and its	35th	32nd
773	10th/A	rebellious allies in the north and west, so as to be crowned king of a united Assyria in 745 BCE.	36th	33rd
772	1st	← ♛ **Tiglath-pileser III aka Pul** (773-745) [2]	37th	34th
771	2nd	[2] Pul is mentioned in the Bible but is not listed on	38th	35th
770	3rd	the Assyrian King List; biblical scholars assume	39th	36th
769	4th	Pul was Tiglath-pileser III (1 Chr. 5:26).	40th	37th
768	5th	←-------	♛ Zachariah (768) 41st/A	38th
767	6th	←-------	♛ Shallum (767, 1st/A/A	39th
766	7th		for 1 month)	40th
765	8th		♛ Menahem 1st	41st
764	9th		(767-757) 2nd	42nd
763	10th		3rd	43rd
			4th	44th

Sacred Chronology of the Hebrew Kings

Kings of Assyria, Israel, and Judah, 762-727 BCE

(years shown in left column are proleptic Gregorian years; all years BCE, A = accession or partial year)

YEAR BCE	NEO-ASSYRIAN EMPIRE (regnal years began in Spring)	ISRAEL (regnal years Nisan to Nisan)	JUDAH (regnal years Tishri to Tishri)
	Pul (cont.)	Menahem (cont.)	Uzziah (cont.)
762	11th ←--- Syro-Ephraimite War	5th	
761	12th	6th	45th
760	13th ←--- Damascus falls,	7th	46th
759	14th Menahem pays tribute?	8th	47th
758	15th	9th/(1st)	48th
757	16th	10th/A/2nd ♕ Pekahiah	(49th)/1st
756	17th ←-------------------	1st/(3rdd) -♕ Jotham	(50th)/2nd
755	18th	(757-755) ♕ Pekah	(757/754-738) (51st)/3rd
754	19th	2nd/(4th) (758/757-738)	(52nd)/4th
753	20th	5th	5th
752	21st	6th	6th
751	22nd	7th	7th
750	23rd	8th	8th
749	24th	9th	9th
748	25th	10th	10th
747	26th	11th	11th
746	27th	12th	12th
745	28th/A ← ♕ Tiglath-pileser III	13th	13th
744	1st (745-727)	14th	14th
743	2nd	15th	15th
742	3rd ←-------------------------------	-17th-- ♕ Ahaz	(16th)/1st
741	4th	18th	(742-727) (17th)/2nd
740	5th	19th	coreigns for (18th)/3rd
739	6th	20th/?	4-plus years (19th)/4th
738	7th	?	(20th)/5th
737	8th	?	6th
736	9th	No king in Israel 739-731 BCE ?	7th
735	10th	The *Seder Olam* says that Hoshea was ?	8th
734	11th	king of Gilead (and the lands across ?	9th
733	12th	the Jordan under Assyrian control) ?	10th
732	13th	for about eight years before becoming ?	11th
731	14th ←--------------------	king of Israel in Samaria in 731 BCE. ♕ Hoshea (731-721) ?/A	12th
730	15th	1st	13th
729	16th	2nd	14th
728	17th	3rd	15th
727	18th ←---------------------------------	4th ♕ Hezekiah (727-698)	16th/A 1st

Kings of Assyria, Israel, and Judah, 726-691 BCE

(years shown in left column are proleptic Gregorian years; all years BCE, A = accession or partial year)

YEAR BCE	NEO-ASSYRIAN EMPIRE (regnal years began in Spring)	ISRAEL (regnal years Nisan to Nisan)	JUDAH (regnal years Tishri to Tishri)
	Tiglath-pileser III (cont.)	Hoshea (cont.)	Hezekiah (cont.)
726	19th/A ← ♛ **Shalmaneser V**	5th	2nd
725	1st (727-722)	6th	3rd
724	2nd ←-------- Siege of Samaria --→	7th	4th
723	3rd	8th	5th
722	4th ← ♛ **Sargon II**	9th	6th
721	5th/A (722-705) ←------- Fall of Samaria --→	...	7th
720	1st	<u>KINGDOM OF ISRAEL</u>	8th
719	2nd	<u>ENDS IN 721 BCE</u>	9th
718	3rd		10th
717	4th		11th
716	5th		12th
715	6th		13th
714	7th		14th
713	8th		15th
712	9th		16th
711	10th		17th
710	11th		18th
709	12th		19th
708	13th		20th
707	14th		21st
706	15th		22nd
705	16th		23rd
704	17th/A ← ♛ **Sennacherib**		24th
703	1st (705-681)		25th
702	2nd		26th
701	3rd ←--- *Sennacherib campaigned in Judah, besieged*		27th
700	4th *Jerusalem; future pharaoh Taharqa leads*		28th
699	5th *Shebitku's army out of Egypt to oppose him*		29th/A
698	6th ←-----------------------------------	♛ **Manasseh**	1st
697	7th	(698-643)	2nd
696	8th		3rd
695	9th		4th
694	10th		5th
693	11th		6th
692	12th		7th
691	13th		8th

Kings of Assyria, Israel, and Judah, 690-655 BCE

(years shown in left column are proleptic Gregorian years; all years BCE, A = accession or partial year)

YEAR BCE	NEO-ASSYRIAN EMPIRE (regnal years began in Spring)		ISRAEL (no more kings)	JUDAH (regnal years Tishri to Tishri)
	Sennacherib (cont.)			*Manasseh (cont.)*
690	14th			
689	15th			9th
688	16th			10th
687	17th			11th
686	18th			12th
685	19th			13th
684	20th			14th
683	21st			15th
682	22nd			16th
681	23rd			17th
680	24th/A	← ♛ Esarhaddon (681-669)		18th
679	1st			19th
678	2nd			20th
677	3rd			21st
676	4th			22nd
675	5th			23rd
674	6th			24th
673	7th			25th
672	8th			26th
671	9th			27th
670	10th			28th
669	11th			29th
668	12th/A	← ♛ Ashurbanipal		30th
667	1st	(ca. 669-631)		31st
666	2nd			32nd
665	3rd			33rd
664	4th	←--- sacked Thebes		34th
663	5th			35th
662	6th			36th
661	7th			37th
660	8th			38th
659	9th			39th
658	10th			40th
657	11th			41st
656	12th			42nd
655	13th			43rd
				44th

Kings of Assyria, Israel, and Judah, 654-619 BCE

(years shown in left column are proleptic Gregorian years; all years BCE, A = accession or partial year)

YEAR BCE	NEO-ASSYRIAN EMPIRE (regnal years began in Spring)	ISRAEL (no more kings)	JUDAH (regnal years Tishri to Tishri)
	Ashurbanipal (cont.)		*Manasseh (cont.)*
654	14th		45th
653	15th		46th
652	16th		47th
651	17th		48th
650	18th		49th
649	19th		50th
648	20th		51st
647	21st		52nd
646	22nd		53rd
645	23rd		54th
644	24th		55th/A
643	25th	♛ Amon (643-641)	1st
642	26th		2nd/?
641	27th		A
640	28th	♛ Josiah (640-609)	1st
639	29th		2nd
638	30th		3rd
637	31st		4th
636	32nd		5th
635	33rd		6th
634	34th		7th
633	35th		8th
632	36th		9th
631	37th/A	♛ Ashur-etil-ilani (ca. 631-627)	10th
630	1st		11th
629	2nd		12th
628	3rd		13th
627	4th	♛ Sin-sar-ishkun (ca. 627-612)	14th
626	5th/A		15th
625	1st/?	♛ Sin-shumu-lishir (ca. 626)	16th
624	2nd		17th
623	3rd		18th
622	4th		19th
621	5th		20th
620	6th		21st
619	7th		22nd

Sacred Chronology of the Hebrew Kings

Kings of Assyria, Israel, and Judah, 618-612 BCE

(years shown in left column are proleptic Gregorian years; all years BCE, A = accession or partial year)

	NEO-ASSYRIAN EMPIRE *(regnal years began in Spring)*	**ISRAEL** *(no more kings)*	**JUDAH** *(regnal years Tishri to Tishri)*
YEAR BCE	Sin-sar-ishkun (cont.)		Josiah (cont.)
618	8th		23rd
617	9th		24th
616	10th		25th
615	11th		26th
614	12th		27th
613	13th		28th
612	14th	←--- *Fall of Nineveh (May, 612 BCE)*	29th
611	15th	← ♛ Ashur-uballit II (612-609)	30th
610	---		31st
609	---	←------------------- d. Josiah →	---

<u>NEO-ASSYRIAN EMPIRE ENDS</u>

After the fall of Nineveh, the kingdom of Judah increasingly came under the hegemony of the rising Neo-Babylonia Empire.

APPENDICES

APPENDIX ONE

TIMEKEEPING IN ANCIENT ISRAEL

The earliest reference to biblical timekeeping is found in Genesis, chapter 1, verse 14: *"And God said, Let there be lights in the firmament of the heaven to divide the day from the night; and let them be for signs, and for seasons, and for days, and years"* (KJV). As that verse demonstrates, timekeeping was related to astronomy from the very beginning of biblical history. Unfortunately, the Bible does not describe the actual calendar system used by the ancients, so we can only guess about its structure, astronomical associations, and accuracy.

The first calendar component with a numerical notation is found in the Book of Exodus, when God commanded that the Passover be observed in the first month, called Abib. The early books of the Bible mention only four months by name: Abib, the first month (Exodus 12:2, 13:4); Zif, the second month (1 Kings 6:1); Ethanim, the seventh month (1 Kings 8:2); and Bul, the eighth month (1 Kings 6:38). From these few mentions, some have assumed that the ancient Hebrew calendar was a strict lunar calendar. There is evidence, however, that the movement of the sun was also taken into account by the early Hebrews. The Gezer Calendar, dating from the 10th century BCE, the earliest written example of a Hebrew calendar so far found by archeologists, shows a twelve-month year which is correlated with the major agricultural seasons in ancient Israel—olive harvest, early grain planting, late grain planting, hoeing of flax, barley harvest, wheat harvest, and so on. That correlation of months to seasons confirms that the early Hebrew calendar was not exclusively lunar, but was instead lunisolar in practice, coordinated in some manner with the sun-regulated seasons in addition to the monthly waxing and waning of the moon, so as to keep the calendar aligned with the planting and harvest climatic requirements year after year.

After the Exodus, there were twelve months in the ancient calendar used by the Israelites, with months alternating between 29 and 30 days in length, which averages out to 29½ days per month. The resulting lunar year was composed of 354 days. Since that 354-day lunar year was eleven days shorter than the solar year, an adjustment by intercalation (probably a leap month added every three or four years, but the exact method is still unknown) was made to keep the seasons synchronized with the sun. While captive in Egypt, the Hebrews probably followed the Egyptian civil calendar, which had twelve months, each having 30 days, with five leap days added to prevent calendar creep, resulting in a year of 365 days, which is very close to the astronomically-correct 365¼-day year. There is no evidence that the Israelites ever adopted the 365-day Egyptian calendar for sacred purposes after the Exodus, though. Some Bible expositors have postulated a 360-day "prophetic year" that they claim can be used for interpreting biblical chronology and prophecies. However, the Bible itself does not stipulate any specific number of days in a Hebrew year, probably because its length had to be adjusted from time to time to reconcile the twelve lunar-determined Jewish festival months with their corresponding solar seasons.

Until the Exodus, the basic components of the Hebrew calendar were all derived from physical observation of the heavens—the day from the recurring rising of the sun, the month from the recurring crescent of the new moon, and the year from the recurring equinoxes and solstices. After the Exodus, the new nation of Israel was given a non-astronomical time unit to add to its calendar system, the week. Every seventh day was to be observed by the Israelites as a reminder of their deliverance from bondage, as recorded in Deuteronomy, chapter 5, verses 12-15: *"Keep the sabbath day to sanctify it, as the Lord thy God hath commanded thee. Six days thou shalt labour, and do all thy work: But the seventh day is the sabbath of the Lord thy God: in it thou shalt not do any work, thou, nor thy son, nor thy daughter, nor thy manservant, nor thy maidservant, nor thine ox, nor thine ass, nor any of thy cattle, nor thy stranger that is within thy gates; that thy manservant and thy maidservant may rest as well as thou. And remember that thou wast a servant in the land of Egypt, and that the Lord thy God brought thee out thence through a mighty hand and by a stretched out arm: therefore the Lord thy God commanded thee to keep the sabbath day"* (KJV). Thus, the seven-day week became a unit of time in Jewish life.

In addition to the sabbath day, festivals and religious days to be observed throughout the year were added to the calendar by God through Moses at Sinai, and sabbath and jubilee years were ordained. The Jewish new year was originally celebrated in the first month, as God had commanded, but when Israel became a kingdom there is evidence that a parallel civil year was instituted with its New-Year Day observed in the seventh month. In later times, the religious and civil new years were combined into one Jewish new-year observance on the first day of the seventh month, and that holiday is called *Rosh Hashanah* (literally, "head of the year") today. Other changes were to happen over time as well. The Exile in Babylon that began after Carchemish in 605 BCE resulted in major changes to the Hebrew calendar. The most obvious change was the adoption of Babylonian

Months of the Jewish Year

Number	Pre-Exilic Name	Post-Exilic Name	Length (days)	Gregorian Equivalent
1st	Abib	Nisan	30	March-April
2nd	Zif	Iyar	29	April-May
3rd		Sivan	30	May-June
4th		Tammuz	29	June-July
5th		Av	30	July-August
6th		Elul	29	August-September
7th	Ethanim	Tishri	30	September-October
8th	Bul	Heshvan	29 or 30	October-November
9th		Kislev	30 or 29	November-December
10th		Tevet	29	December-January
11th		Shevat	30	January-February
12th		Adar	29 (or 30 in LY)	February-March
13th (in LY)		Adar II	29	March-April

In a leap year (LY), the month of Adar II is inserted and all other months are moved back accordingly; a leap month is inserted in the 3rd, 6th, 8th, 11th, 14th, 17th and 19th years of the 19-year cycle.

names for the months, and those names are still being used today. The first month Abib became Nisan, the seventh month Ethanim became Tishri, and so on (see list of Jewish months above). More important for accuracy, the 19-year cycle of calendar synchronization (later called the Metonic cycle), with its schedule for adding leap months to seven specified years in every nineteen-year cycle, became standard, and it is found reflected in the chronology of the Book of Daniel.

The ancient Hebrew calendar had a high degree of accuracy. Before 70 CE, it was based on priestly observations from Jerusalem, the sighting of the new moon being the most important calendric event. All other Jewish calendars were coordinated with the Temple calendar, so that the festivals would be celebrated on the correct day everywhere. After the Temple was destroyed in 70 CE and the priesthood ceased to function, the calendar was maintained by rabbis in various locations. Since observations from the Temple were no longer possible, and since the Jewish people were becoming so widely dispersed that timely dissemination of calendric information was impossible from one central location, a Hebrew calendar employing mathematical calculation was developed by Rabbi Hillel II

Major Festivals on the Ancient Jewish Priestly Calendar			
Order	Post-Exilic Name	Day of Month and Festival	Pilgrimage
1st Month	Nisan	14th - Passover (Pesach) and 15th - 22nd - Feast of Unleavened Bread 16th - First Day, Feast of Weeks, First Fruits (barley)	✓
2nd Month	Iyar	14th - Second Passover	
3rd Month	Sivan	50th Day, Feast of Weeks (Shavuot), First Fruits (wheat)	✓
4th Month	Tammuz	- - -	
5th Month	Av	- - -	
6th Month	Elul	First Fruits (figs, pomegranates, dates)	
7th Month	Tishri	1st - New Year (Rosh Hashanah) 10th - Day of Atonement (Yom Kippur) 15th-22nd - Feast of Tabernacles (Sukkot), First Fruits (wine and oil)	✓
8th Month	Heshvan	- - -	
9th Month	Kislev	25th - Feast of Dedication (Hanukkah)	
10th Month	Tevet	- - -	
11th Month	Shevat	- - -	
12th Month	Adar	14th - Purim (with Fast of Esther)	
Since the creation of the State of Israel in 1948, the Chief Rabbinate of Israel has established four new Jewish holidays: Jerusalem Day (Yom Yerushalayim); Holocaust Remembrance Day (Yom HaShoah); Memorial Day (Yom Hazikaron); Israel Independence Day (Yom Ha'atzmaut).			

in the 4th century CE. A derivative of that universal calendar is used by many Jews today. It standardized the length of months and formalized the addition of leap months over the course of a 19-year cycle, so that the lunar calendar is regularly realigned with the solar year. The Hillel II calendar also ensured that Yom Kippur would not fall adjacent to a Sabbath and Hoshanah Rabba would not fall on a Saturday, extra-biblical prohibitions instituted by the rabbis. A day is added to the month of Heshvan or subtracted from the month of Kislev of the previous year to prevent those things from happening.

In reality, the rules for computing the Jewish calendar, both in antiquity and in more modern times, are much more detailed than has been outlined here, but this presentation covers all aspects that are important for using the ancient Hebrew calendar system as a tool for understanding the Bible.

Appendix One: Timekeeping in Ancient Israel

Sabbath and Jubilee Years

The Children of Israel were commanded to begin observing both sabbath and jubilee years (which, in practice, meant that they were to begin counting the number of memorial Passovers) once they had entered into and taken possession of the promised land, as recorded in Leviticus, chapter 25, verses 1-12:

"And the Lord spake unto Moses in mount Sinai, saying, Speak unto the children of Israel, and say unto them, When ye come into the land which I give you, then shall the land keep a sabbath unto the Lord. Six years thou shalt sow thy field, and six years thou shalt prune thy vineyard, and gather in the fruit thereof; But in the seventh year shall be a sabbath of rest unto the land, a sabbath for the Lord: thou shalt neither sow thy field, nor prune thy vineyard. That which groweth of its own accord of thy harvest thou shalt not reap, neither gather the grapes of thy vine undressed: for it is a year of rest unto the land. And the sabbath of the land shall be meat for you; for thee, and for thy servant, and for thy maid, and for thy hired servant, and for thy stranger that sojourneth with thee, And for thy cattle, and for the beast that are in thy land, shall all the increase thereof be meat. And thou shalt number seven sabbaths of years unto thee, seven times seven years; and the space of the seven sabbaths of years shall be unto thee forty and nine years. Then shalt thou cause the trumpet of the jubilee to sound on the tenth day of the seventh month, in the day of atonement shall ye make the trumpet sound throughout all your land. And ye shall hallow the fiftieth year, and proclaim liberty throughout all the land unto all the inhabitants thereof: it shall be a jubilee unto you; and ye shall return every man unto his possession, and ye shall return every man unto his family. A jubilee shall that fiftieth year be unto you: ye shall not sow, neither reap that which groweth of itself in it, nor gather the grapes in it of thy vine undressed. For it is the jubilee; it shall be holy unto you: ye shall eat the increase thereof out of the field" (KJV).

Leviticus, chapter 25, verses 20-22, clarified that the people of Israel would not go hungry because of their obedience to the commandment:

"And if ye shall say, What shall we eat the seventh year? behold, we shall not sow, nor gather in our increase: Then I will command my blessing upon you in the sixth year, and it shall bring forth fruit for three years. And ye shall sow

Diagram A - Relationship of Seasons to Sabbath and Jubilee Years

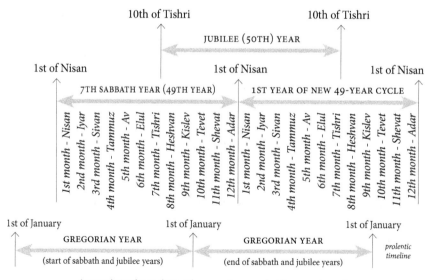

Jewish months are shown as numbers, with Nisan = 1; corresponding Gregorian months shown above.

Diagram B - Relationship of Sabbath, Jubilee, and Gregorian Years

(exact relationship to the Jewish year varies somewhat from year to year)

Appendix One: Timekeeping in Ancient Israel

the eighth year, and eat yet of old fruit until the ninth year; until her fruits come in ye shall eat of the old store" (KJV).

In practical terms, the people would sow barley and wheat in November of the fifth year, then reap the bounteous threefold "sixth-year" yield of both grains during the following March through June harvest months, then possibly sow barley again in November (the month for sowing) of the sixth year to harvest whatever they could harvest in early spring before the start of the seventh year on the 1st of Nisan (March-April). There would be no sowing at all in November of the seventh year, and thus no harvest of wheat or barley the following March through June in the eighth year. However, in November of the eighth year, both barley and wheat would once again be sown and then harvested in the spring and early summer of the ninth year. That schedule meant that there were two harvest seasons when no harvesting was done. Under that schedule, though, no additional provisions were needed for a sabbath-jubilee combination year since the jubilee ended on the 10th of Tishri (September-October in the eighth year), so sowing could still be done in November of the eighth year as during the sabbath-only years. Sabbath years were to be observed every seventh year, beginning on the 1st of Nisan, and were to extend until the following 1st of Nisan, whereas a jubilee year began on the 10th of Tishri in the forty-ninth year of a 49-year (seven sabbath-year) cycle, and it continued until the 10th of Tishri in the following year. Both sabbath and jubilee years began in one proleptic Gregorian year and ended in the following year. A jubilee year, although called a "fiftieth year," was not a separate year, but overlapped the last five months in the forty-ninth year and the first seven months in the first year in the next 49-year cycle, as shown in Diagram B on the opposite page.

Table of Sabbath and Jubilee Years from 1,700 CE to 2,037 CE							
JUBILEE	7th Sabbath	6th Sabbath	5th Sabbath	4th Sabbath	3rd Sabbath	2nd Sabbath	1st Sabbath
2037/2038	2037/2038	2030/2031	2023/2024	2016/2017	2009/2010	2002/2003	1995/1996
1988/1989	1988/1989	1981/1982	1974/1975	1967/1968	1960/1961	1953/1954	1946/1947
1939/1940	1939/1940	1932/1933	1925/1926	1918/1919	1911/1912	1904/1905	1897/1898
1890/1891	1890/1891	1883/1884	1876/1877	1869/1870	1862/1863	1855/1856	1848/1849
1841/1842	1841/1842	1834/1835	1827/1828	1820/1821	1813/1814	1806/1807	1799/1800
1792/1793	1792/1793	1785/1786	1778/1779	1771/1772	1764/1765	1757/1758	1750/1751
1743/1744	1743/1744	1736/1737	1729/1730	1722/1723	1715/1716	1708/1709	1701/1702

Table of Sabbath and Jubilee Years from 1 CE to 1,695 CE

JUBILEE	7th Sabbath	6th Sabbath	5th Sabbath	4th Sabbath	3rd Sabbath	2nd Sabbath	1st Sabbath
1694/1695	1694/1695	1687/1688	1680/1681	1673/1674	1666/1667	1659/1660	1652/1653
1645/1646	1645/1646	1638/1639	1631/1632	1624/1625	1617/1618	1610/1611	1603/1604
1596/1597	1596/1597	1589/1590	1582/1583	1575/1576	1568/1569	1561/1562	1654/1655
1547/1548	1547/1548	1540/1541	1533/1534	1526/1527	1519/1520	1512/1513	1505/1506
1498/1499	1498/1499	1491/1492	1484/1485	1477/1478	1470/1471	1463/1464	1456/1457
1449/1450	1449/1450	1442/1443	1435/1436	1428/1429	1421/1422	1414/1415	1407/1408
1400/1401	1400/1401	1393/1394	1386/1387	1379/1380	1372/1373	1365/1366	1358/1359
1351/1352	1351/1352	1344/1345	1337/1338	1330/1331	1323/1324	1316/1317	1309/1310
1302/1303	1302/1303	1295/1296	1288/1289	1281/1282	1274/1275	1267/1268	1260/1261
1253/1254	1253/1254	1246/1247	1239/1240	1232/1233	1225/1226	1218/1219	1211/1212
1204/1205	1204/1205	1197/1198	1190/1191	1183/1184	1176/1177	1169/1170	1162/1163
1155/1156	1155/1156	1148/1149	1141/1142	1134/1135	1127/1128	1120/1121	1113/1114
1106/1107	1106/1107	1099/1100	1092/1093	1085/1086	1078/1079	1071/1072	1064/1065
1057/1058	1057/1058	1050/1051	1043/1044	1036/1037	1029/1030	1022/1023	1015/1016
1008/1009	1008/1009	1001/1002	994/995	987/988	980/981	973/974	866/867
959/956	959/956	952/953	945/946	938/939	931/932	924/925	917/918
910/911	910/911	903/904	896/897	889/890	882/883	875/876	868/869
861/862	861/862	854/855	847/848	840/841	833/834	826/827	819/820
812/813	812/813	805/806	798/799	791/792	784/785	777/778	770/771
763/764	763/764	756/757	749/750	742/743	735/736	728/729	721/722
714/715	714/715	707/708	700/701	693/694	686/687	679/680	672/673
665/666	665/666	658/659	651/652	644/645	637/638	630/631	623/624
616/617	616/617	609/610	602/603	595/596	588/589	581/582	574/575
567/568	567/568	560/561	553/554	546/547	539/540	532/533	525/526
518/519	518/519	511/512	504/505	497/498	490/491	483/484	476/477
469/470	469/470	462/463	455/456	448/449	441/442	434/435	427/428
420/421	420/421	413/414	406/407	399/400	392/393	385/386	378/379
371/372	371/372	364/365	357/358	350/351	343/344	336/337	329/330
322/323	322/323	315/316	308/309	301/302	294/295	287/288	280/281
273/274	273/274	266/267	259/260	252/253	245/246	238/239	231/232
224/225	224/225	217/218	210/211	203/204	196/197	189/190	182/183
175/176	175/176	168/169	161/162	154/155	147/148	140/141	133/134
126/127	126/127	119/120	112/113	105/106	98/99	91/92	84/85
77/78	77/78	70/71	63/64	56/57	49/50	42/43	35/36
28/29	28/29	21/22	14/15	7/8	1 BCE/CE 1	---	---

Appendix One: Timekeeping in Ancient Israel

Table of Sabbath and Jubilee Years from 1 BCE to 1,393 BCE

JUBILEE	7th Sabbath	6th Sabbath	5th Sabbath	4th Sabbath	3rd Sabbath	2nd Sabbath	1st Sabbath
---	---	---	---	---	CE 1/1 BCE	7/8	14/15
21/22	21/22	28/29	35/36	42/43	49/50	56/57	63/64
70/71	70/71	77/78	84/85	91/92	98/99	105/106	112/113
119/120	119/120	126/127	133/134	140/141	147/148	154/155	161/162
168/169	168/169	175/176	182/183	189/190	196/197	203/204	210/211
217/218	217/218	224/225	231/232	238/239	245/246	252/253	259/260
266/267	266/267	273/274	280/281	287/288	294/295	301/302	308/309
315/316	315/316	322/323	329/330	336/337	343/344	350/351	357/358
364/365	364/365	371/372	378/379	385/386	392/393	399/400	406/407
413/414	413/414	420/421	427/428	434/435	441/442	448/449	455/456
462/463	462/463	469/470	476/477	483/484	490/491	497/498	504/505
511/512	511/512	518/519	525/526	532/533	539/540	546/547	553/554
560/561	560/561	567/568	574/575	581/582	588/589	595/596	602/603
609/610	609/610	616/617	623/624	630/631	637/638	644/645	651/652
658/659	658/659	665/666	672/673	679/680	686/687	693/694	700/701
707/708	707/708	714/715	721/722	728/729	735/736	742/743	749/750
756/757	756/757	763/764	770/771	777/778	784/785	791/792	798/799
805/806	805/806	812/813	819/820	826/827	833/834	840/841	847/848
854/855	854/855	861/862	868/869	875/876	882/883	889/890	896/897
903/904	903/904	910/911	917/918	924/925	931/932	938/939	945/946
952/953	952/953	959/960	966/967	973/974	980/981	987/988	994/995
1001/1002	1001/1002	1008/1009	1015/1016	1022/1023	1029/1030	1036/1037	1043/1044
1050/1051	1050/1051	1057/1058	1064/1065	1071/1072	1078/1079	1085/1086	1092/1093
1099/1100	1099/1100	1106/1107	1113/1114	1120/1121	1127/1128	1134/1135	1141/1142
1148/1149	1148/1149	1155/1156	1162/1163	1169/1170	1176/1177	1183/1184	1190/1181
1197/1198	1197/1198	1204/1205	1211/1212	1218/1219	1225/1226	1232/1233	1239/1240
1246/1247	1246/1247	1253/1254	1260/1261	1267/1268	1274/1275	1281/1282	1288/1289
1295/1296	1295/1296	1302/1303	1309/1310	1316/1317	1323/1324	1330/1331	1337/1338
1344/1345	1344/1345	1351/1352	1358/1359	1365/1366	1372/1373	1379/1380	1386/1387

1393/1394 - Land allotted to the twelve tribes in the first jubilee year after the Exodus

In the table for years BCE above, note that the land was allotted in the first jubilee year after the Exodus, 1394 BCE. The next year, 1393 BCE, started the sabbath cycle in the land of Canaan, and the next five years in that first sabbath cycle after the land was allotted were 1392 BCE, 1391 BCE, 1390 BCE, 1389 BCE, 1388 BCE (see diagram on page 137). Also, note that there was no year "0" (no year zero) when going from years BCE on this chart to years CE on the chart on the opposite page, since the year 1 BCE was followed by the year 1 CE as time moves forward in history.

Verifying the Sabbath and Jubilee Tables

After crossing the Jordan River in 1,402 BCE, the Children of Israel began the process of subduing the land of Canaan. In the forty-ninth year after the Exodus from Egypt (identified by counting forward in time for forty-nine Passovers, starting with the first Passover in Egypt; see page 163), the warfare had ended and the land of Canaan was at rest. It was at this time, in the forty-ninth year (essentially a first jubilee year after the Exodus) that the land was allotted to the twelve tribes. Once the land was allotted, the Children of Israel possessed the promised land and the sabbath-year count began, with 1,393 BCE marking the first year in the sabbath count in the land. Counting forward in time from that year in one-year increments reveals the proleptic Gregorian date for the first sabbath year observed by the Israelites in the land to be the year 1,387 BCE, calculated as follows:

- 1,394 BCE ... 49th year after Exodus, land allotted to the twelve tribes
- 1,393 BCE ... 1st year in the seven-year sabbath cycle
- 1,392 BCE ... 2nd year in the seven-year sabbath cycle
- 1,391 BCE ... 3rd year in the seven-year sabbath cycle
- 1,390 BCE ... 4th year in the seven-year sabbath cycle
- 1,389 BCE ... 5th year in the seven-year sabbath cycle
- 1,388 BCE ... 6th year in the seven-year sabbath cycle
- 1,387 BCE ... ***7th year, and first sabbath year observed in the land***

The first sabbath year is shown in the sabbath and jubilee table for years BCE on the previous page (see bottom row, far right column), and all subsequent sabbath and jubilee years from that first sabbath year down to the present day have been calculated from the date for that first sabbath year. The resulting sabbath and jubilee years are shown in the tables on pages 129-131. The validity of the tables can be verified by comparing the sabbath and jubilee years listed in them with other sabbath and jubilee events and chronological details mentioned in the Bible, the works of Josephus, the *Seder Olam*, and the *Talmud*.

Crosscheck #1 - The chronology of Caleb's jubilee year request ...

A first crosscheck of the sabbath-jubilee dates is provided by the chronology associated with Caleb as recorded in the Book of Joshua. In the year that the land was at rest and was ready to be allotted to each tribe, Caleb asked for his share of land that had been promised specifically to him because of his faithfulness at Kadesh-Barnea. That incident is recorded in Joshua, chapter 14, verses 7-10: *"Forty years old was I when Moses the servant of the Lord sent me from Kadesh-barnea to espy out the land; and I brought him word again as it was in mine heart. Nevertheless my brethren that went up with me made the heart of the people melt: but I wholly followed the Lord my God. And Moses sware on that day, saying, Surely the land whereon thy feet have trodden shall be thine inheritance, and thy children's for ever, because thou hast wholly followed the Lord my God. And now, behold, the Lord hath kept me alive, as he said, these forty and five years, even since the Lord spake this word unto Moses, while the children of Israel wandered in the wilderness: and now, lo, I am this day fourscore and five years old"* (KJV).

Caleb was forty years old when he was sent by Moses from Kadesh-Barnea into the land of Canaan as a spy, and he was eighty-five years old when he asked for his promised allotment as the land was ready to be assigned to the twelve tribes. Since the spies were sent from Kadesh-Barnea in the second year after the Exodus and thirty-eight years before the Israelites crossed the Jordan River in 1,402 BCE (Deuteronomy 2:14), that would mean they were sent in 1,440 BCE. Subtracting forty-five years (Passovers) from that year yields the year 1,394 BCE as the year that the land was at rest and Caleb made his request for his promised allotment of land. That result coincides with the year for the first sabbath year seven years later, namely 1,387 BCE, and it is a crosscheck on the accuracy of the sabbath-jubilee tables presented in this book. A diagram showing the years of Caleb is provided on page 137 (second column from right).

Crosscheck #2 - The destruction of Solomon's Temple ...

A second crosscheck is provided in the Babylonian Talmud. Tractate Arakin 12b says that Solomon's Temple was destroyed in the third year of a sabbath cycle. The Temple was destroyed by the Babylonians in 586 BCE, which would make the year 589 BCE a sabbath year, confirming the sabbath tables (see page 129-131).

Crosscheck #3 - The sabbath in the third year of Jehoshaphat ...

A third crosscheck is provided in 2 Chronicles, chapter 17, verses 7-9, which record that Jehoshaphat, in his third regnal year, sent his princes, accompanied by Levites and priests, to teach the Law to the people in the cities of Judah. That was in keeping with the commandment given by Moses in Deuteronomy, chapter 31, verses 10-13, for observing the sabbath year. The third regnal year of Jehoshaphat (r. 900-875) was 897 BCE, which was indeed a sabbath year (see page 131).

Crosscheck #4 - *The destruction of Herod's Temple in a sabbath year ...*

A fourth crosscheck is provided in the *Seder Olam*, which mentions that Herod's Temple and the city of Jerusalem were destroyed during a sabbath year.[1] Since we know from secular history that the destruction took place in August of the year 70 CE, that would mean that the Jewish year from Nisan 70 CE to Nisan 71 CE was a sabbath year, and that is in agreement with the sabbath and jubilee tables (see table for years CE on page 130, second row from bottom).

Crosscheck #5 - *The year Solomon's Temple was begun ...*

A fifth, albeit somewhat circumstantial, crosscheck on the observance of sabbath years in ancient times is provided in the *Seder Olam*, which provides two references for determining the year Solomon finished building the Temple. It refers to the major Temple renovations mentioned in the Bible, the first undertaken by Joash of Judah (see 2 Chronicles, chapter 24) and the second done by Josiah of Judah (see 2 Kings, chapter 22). Joash began his renovations in his twenty-third regnal year, 218 years before Josiah began his renovations, and 155 years after Solomon finished the Temple.[2] Josiah began his renovations in his eighteenth regnal year, which began in the year 623 BCE. Counting back 218 Passovers from that year gives the year 840 BCE for Joash's twenty-third regnal year. Counting back 155 Passovers identifies 996 BCE as the year Solomon finished building the Temple, in the eighth month of his eleventh regnal year. Since it took Solomon seven years to build the Temple, that means that the construction was begun after Passover in 1,002 BCE and completed in 996 BCE. Both were sabbath years when no agricultural work could be done, ensuring that ample manpower would have been available for starting and completing such a large construction project.

---

[1] Heinrich W. Guggenheimer, *Seder Olam: The Rabbinic View of Biblical Chronology* (Lanham, Maryland: Rowman & Littlefield Publishers, Inc., 1998, 2005), p. 264.
[2] Guggenheimer, *Seder Olam*, p. 161-162.

APPENDIX TWO

Synchronized Bible Timeline

The chronology embedded in the Book of Daniel provides a framework for the history of the Jewish people from the time of the reign of Solomon down to events occurring in modern times. Using chronological information from other books of the Bible together with the anchor date provided by the chronology in Daniel, chapter 4, a biblical timeline can be synchronized with the timeline of secular history all the way back to the birth of Abram in Ur.

Date of the Exodus

The anchor date revealed by the chronology of Daniel, chapter 4, is the year 964 BCE, the year that the kingdom of United Israel was rent from Rehoboam (see Timeline 2.1 on page 17). From that year, Solomon's reign can be located in time, and the year spanning 1,003-1,002 BCE can be identified as his fourth regnal year (see page 49). The fourth regnal year in Solomon's reign is an important year from a chronological standpoint, because that is the year when he began building the Temple, a month after Passover in 1,002 BCE, and all sacred chronology prior to the beginning of the kingdom period of Israel can be calculated from that event once the date for Solomon's fourth regnal year is known.

The key for extending biblical chronology back beyond the reign of Solomon is found in 1 Kings, chapter 6, verse 1, which says, *"And it came to pass in the four hundred and eightieth year after the children of Israel were come out of the land of Egypt, in the fourth year of Solomon's reign over Israel, in the month Zif, which [is] the second month, that he began to build the house of the Lord"* (KJV). Going back 480 years from the year 1,002 BCE, Solomon's fourth regnal year, would seemingly reveal the year of the Exodus to be 1,482 BCE. However, using the 480 years specified by the Masoretic text as the time span between the Exodus and Solomon's fourth regnal year creates chronological problems. The most serious problem is that the events in the timeline resulting from using the 480-year figure cannot be made to reconcile with the calendar of sabbath and jubilee years that can be generated from other sabbath-jubilee data provided in the *Tanakh* (OT), *B'rit Hadashah* (NT), *Seder Olam*, Josephus, and the *Talmud*. Thus, the accuracy of 480-year Masoretic figure must be questioned. As it turns out, the 480-year Masoretic figure is not universally documented. The Septuagint contradicts it in

3 Kings, chapter 6, verse 0, which says, *"And it came to pass in the four hundred and fortieth year after the departure of the children of Israel out of Egypt, in the fourth year and second month of the reign of king Solomon over Israel, that the king commanded that they should take great and costly stones for the foundation of the house, and hewn stones. And the men of Solomon, and the men of Chiram hewed the stones, and laid them for a foundation"* (LXX).[1] In the Septuagint, the 480-year Masoretic figure is replaced by a 440-year figure. That change moves the date for the Exodus forward in time from 1,482 BCE to 1,442 BCE, allowing events surrounding the Exodus to synchronize perfectly with the sabbath and jubilee dates calculated from the Bible and various related Jewish sources.

For determining the year of the Exodus, your author prefers to derive the date for that event by using the Septuagint's 440-year figure rather than the Masoretic text's 480-year figure. In this one instance, the figure recorded in the Septuagint produces a better synchronization with the strict chronological requirements of the sabbath and jubilee calendar, which have been verified by multiple chronological crosschecks, and it yields a timeline that agrees with the Masoretic verses describing the duration of Israel's conquest of Canaan (see Timeline A on the opposite page showing the various timelines from the Exodus to the first sabbath year in Canaan).[2]

Also, as an added benefit, a chronology for the life of Moses based on the 440-year Septuagint figure produces a timeline that fits into the historical narrative of Egypt's Dynasty 18 (see page 141). Another interesting synchronization results from locating the Exodus in the year 1,442 BCE. That places the initial allotment of the land of Canaan to the twelve tribes in the year 1,394 BCE. That means the allotment is revealed to have happened after the forty-ninth Passover, counting the Passover in Egypt as the first, or, in other words, the land was allotted in the first jubilee year, the symbolic fiftieth year after the Exodus, the year designated by God in the Law of Moses for returning land to its owners (see facing page).

---

[1] Sir Lancelot Brenton, *The Septuagint with Apocrypha; Greek and English* (Hendrickson, 1986).
[2] In the process of harmonizing the reigns of the kings of Israel and Judah (see pages 21-29), your author developed great confidence in the chronological information about the kings preserved in the Masoretic text. Chronological details and numerous crosschecks about the reigns given in the Masoretic text converge with other chronological elements derived from the biblical text to produce exact harmonization. However, that is not the case with the 480-year figure given in 1 Kings 6:1 for the duration of the time span between the Exodus and the fourth regnal year of Solomon. It cannot be made to fit the sabbath-jubilee calendar. Perhaps the 480 years was originally a measurement made from the time Moses fled from Egypt in 1,483 BCE.

Appendix Two: Synchronized Bible Timeline

Timeline A - Exodus to the First Sabbath Year in the Land of Canaan

(starting year of every sabbath/seventh year shown in bold type; all years BCE)

Gregorian years		Jubilee count (yrs.)	Caleb's age (yrs.)	Moses' age (yrs.)
1442	The Exodus from Egypt ←	1st		80
1441	Law given at Sinai	2nd	39	81
1440	Spies sent to Canaan ←	3rd	40	82
1439		4th	41	83
1438		5th	42	84
1437		6th	43	85
1436		7th	44	86
1435		8th	45	87
1434		9th	46	88
1433		10th	47	89
1432		11th	48	90
1431		12th	49	91
1430		13th	50	92
1429		14th	51	93
1428		15th	52	94
1427		16th	53	95
1426		17th	54	96
1425		18th	55	97
1424		19th	56	98
1423	*In the Wilderness*	20th	57	99
1422		21st	58	100
1421		22nd	59	101
1420		23rd	60	102
1419		24th	61	103
1418		25th	62	104
1417		26th	63	105
1416		27th	64	106
1415		28th	65	107
1414		29th	66	108
1413		30th	67	109
1412		31st	68	110
1411		32nd	69	111
1410		33rd	70	112
1409		34th	71	113
1408		35th	72	114
1407		36th	73	115
1406		37th	74	116
1405		38th	75	117
1404		39th	76	118
1403	d. Moses (120 years old) ←	40th	77	119
1402	Israel crosses Jordan River, ←	41st	78	120
1401	conquest of land begins	42nd	79	
1400		43rd	80	
1399		44th	81	
1398	*Conquest of the Land*	45th	82	
1397		46th	83	
1396		47th	84	
1395	Caleb (85 years old) asked for land,	48th	85	
1394	land apportioned at start of jubilee	49th / 50th Year	86	
1393	1st year in sabbath count	1st		
1392	2nd year in sabbath count	2nd		
1391	3rd year in sabbath count	3rd		
1390	4th year in sabbath count	4th		
1389	5th year in sabbath count	5th		
1388	6th year in sabbath count	6th		
1387	7th year; first sabbath year observed ←	7th		

FIRST JUBILEE CYCLE (jubilee year begins during 49th year)

FORTY YEARS IN WILDERNESS

Jubilee Year: 1394

– 137 –

Timeline B - Abraham to Solomon

▲ *denotes a pharaoh; using High Chronology* after 1,900 BCE*

BCE	
2162	— b. Abram in Ur, *Genesis 11*. [**Abraham = 1st generation**]
2087	— Abram (75 years old) left Haran, entered Canaan, *Genesis 12*.
2062	— b. Isaac (Abraham 100 years old), *Genesis 21*. [**Isaac = 2nd generation**]
2002	— b. Jacob (Isaac 60 years old), *Genesis 25*. [**Jacob = 3rd generation**]
1911	— b. Joseph (Jacob 91 years old), *Genesis 30*.
1897	— ▲ *Senusret II d. 1878 BCE.*
1894	— Joseph (17 years old) taken captive to Egypt, *Genesis 37*.
1881	— Joseph (30 years old) stood before Pharaoh, *Genesis 41*.
1878	— ▲ *Senusret III d. 1841 BCE.*
---	... *coregency with Amenemhat III ca.1860 BCE.*
1872	— Israel (aka Jacob, 130 years old) went to Egypt, *Genesis 47*.
---	... *Joseph about 39 years old (30+7+2), Genesis 41-42; sojourn of*
---	*Children of Israel in Egypt began* [**Children of Israel = 4th generation**]
1855	— d. Israel (147 years old); "blessing" given, *Genesis 47, 49*.
1842	— ▲ *Amenemhat III d. 1797 BCE (coreign after 858 BCE).*
1842	— 400 years of affliction began, *Genesis 15, Acts 7*.
1801	— d. Joseph (110 years old), *Genesis 50*.
1570	— ▲ *Ahmose I d. 1546 BCE.*
1551	— ▲ *Amenhotep I d. 1524 BCE.*
1524	— ▲ *Thutmose I d. 1518 BCE.*
1523	— b. Moses, *Exodus 2*.
1518	— ▲ *Thutmose II d. 1504 BCE.*
1516	— *Hatshepsut becomes a pharaoh (Thutmose II's 2nd year)*
1504	— ▲ *Thutmose III d. 1450 BCE (coreigned with Hatshepsut).*
1498	— ▲ *Hatshepsut d. 1482 (primary king after 1498 BCE).*
1486	— *Hatshepsut's sed year (her 30th year as a pharaoh)*
1483	— *Senenmut disappeared from history.*
1483	— Moses (40 years old) fled to Midian, *Exodus 2*.
---	... *see expanded timeline on page 141.*
1482	— *Thutmose III became sole ruler.*
1453	— ▲ *Amenhotep II d. 1419 BCE.*
1443	— Moses (80 years old) returned to Egypt.
1442	— **The Exodus** (late March), *Exodus 12*.
1441	— *Amenhotep II campaigned in Canaan in his 9th year.*
1419	— ▲ *Thutmose IV d. 1386 BCE.*
1403	— d. Moses (120 years old), *Deuteronomy 34*.
1402	— Joshua led Israelites across the Jordan River; *Joshua 3, 5*.
1394	— Jubilee year; Israelites alloted the promised land, *Joshua 12*.
1387	— Israelites observed first sabbath year in the promised land.
1002	— ♛ Solomon (4th year), began First Temple, *1 Kings 6*.

Annotations on right side:
- 130 years (Genesis 47:9)
- 430 years (Exodus 12:40; also, Genesis 15 as explained in Galatians 3:17)
- 400 years (Genesis 15:13, Acts 7:6)
- 453 years (Acts 13:20 - "about 450 years")
- 440 years (3 Kings 6:1 (LXX))

* from *Chronicle of the Pharaohs* by Peter A. Clayton (New York: Thames &Hudson; 2006)

Appendix Two: Synchronized Bible Timeline

Abraham to Solomon (2,162-1,002 BCE)

Once the year of the Exodus is known, the information provided in Exodus, chapter 12, verses 40-41, *"Now the sojourning of the children of Israel, who dwelt in Egypt, [was] four hundred and thirty years. And it came to pass at the end of the four hundred and thirty years, even the selfsame day it came to pass, that all the hosts of the Lord went out from the land of Egypt"* (KJV), can be used to calculate the year that Jacob (*aka* Israel) and his descendants (the Children of Israel) went down to Egypt. As shown on Timeline B on the opposite page, going back 430 years in time from the Exodus year 1,442 BCE yields the year 1,872 BCE as the date for the beginning of the sojourn of the Children of Israel in Egypt.[1]

From the year that the sojourn began, the year of the birth of Jacob can be calculated from the information given in Genesis, chapter 47, verses 8-9, *"And Pharaoh said unto Jacob, How old [art] thou? And Jacob said unto Pharaoh, The days of the years of my pilgrimage [are] an hundred and thirty years ..."* (KJV). Going back 130 years in time from 1,872 BCE gives the year 2,002 BCE as the year for the birth of Jacob. From the year of the birth of Jacob, the year of the birth of Isaac can be calculated from the information given in Genesis, chapter 25, verse 26, *"And after that came his brother out, and his hand took hold on Esau's heel; and his name was called Jacob: and Isaac was threescore years old when she bare them"* (KJV). Going back 60 years in time from 2,002 BCE gives the year 2,062 BCE as the year for the birth of Isaac. From the year of the birth of Isaac, the year for the birth of Abram (later renamed Abraham) can be calculated from the information given in Genesis, chapter 21, verse 5, *"And Abraham was an hundred years old, when his son Isaac was born unto him"* (KJV). Going back 100 years in time from 2,062 BCE gives the year 2,162 BCE for the birth of Abram, which places his birth as occuring in the last years of the Akkadian Empire.

Other time periods shown on the diagram can be calculated as follows: In Genesis, chapter 15, verse 13, Abraham is told by God, *"Know of a surety that thy*

---

[1] The 430-year figure for the period of sojourn in Egypt has been questioned by biblical scholars. The duration of the sojourn in Egypt has been shortened by some from 430 years to about 215 years, primarily for the purpose of trying to agree with archeological findings, such as those at Jericho that suggest a 13th-century BCE invasion of Canaan. That change is usually justified by asserting that the 400 years of affliction included the time of the patriarchs in Canaan before Jacob moved to Egypt. However, Psalm 105: 9-15, states in no uncertain terms that no oppression was experienced during the lifetimes of Abraham, Isaac, and Jacob while in Canaan. Both the 430-year and 400-year figures are correct.

seed shall be a stranger in a land [that is] not theirs, and shall serve them; and they shall afflict them four hundred years" (KJV). Going back in time 400 years from the Exodus in 1,442 BCE gives the year 1,842 BCE for the beginning of the affliction. That chronology from the *Tanakh* is verified by a comment made in the *B'rit Hadashah*, in the Book of Acts, chapter 13, verses 16-20, by the Apostle Paul, who studied the Hebrew Scriptures at the feet of the esteemed Rabbi Gamaliel, so it can be assumed that he is recounting the chronological understanding that was being espoused by the most authoritative Jewish scribes and Pharisees of the first century CE. Paul said: *"Men of Israel and you who fear God, listen. The God of this people Israel chose our fathers and made the people great during their stay in the land of Egypt, and with uplifted arm he led them out of it. And for about forty years he put up with them in the wilderness. And after destroying seven nations in the land of Canaan, he gave them their land as an inheritance. All this took about 450 years. And after that he gave them judges until Samuel the prophet"* (ESV).[1] From the time the fathers were chosen by Jacob when giving his death-bed blessing in 1,855 BCE until the Israelites crossed the Jordan River in 1,402 BCE yields a period of 453 years, which is, as Paul says, **about** (but not exactly) 450 years in duration.

The start of the 400-year period of affliction is shown by the timeline to have coincided with the first regnal year in the reign of the Amenemhat III (r. 1842-1797) as sole ruler after a sixteen coreign with his father Senusret III, the pharaoh who had made Joseph his second in command. That chronology conforms to the biblical text, which says that the affliction began in the reign of a new pharaoh, *"Now there arose up a new king over Egypt, which knew not Joseph"* (Exodus 1:8; KJV). Amenemhat obviously knew Joseph as a man, but did not continue to acknowledge (know) him as had his father, as second in command.

The chronological reference in Genesis, chapter 15, verse 16, which records what Abraham was told by God: *"But in the fourth generation they* [Abraham's seed] *shall come hither* [to Canaan] *again"* (KJV), gives insight as to the meaning of the word "generation" as applied to Israel as a people. The Bible lists at least twelve genetic generations of Israelites during the 430-year stay in Egypt prior to the Exodus, so it seems that the term "fourth generation" was used spiritually, with Abraham being the first generation, Isaac the second generation, Jacob the

---

[1] The translation for that verse from the ESV Bible quoted here is preferred, since the King James translation incorrectly indicates that the period of the judges was about 450 years in duration, a length of time that cannot be supported chronologically.

Appendix Two: Synchronized Bible Timeline

third generation, and all subsequent descendants of Jacob (the Children of Israel) thereafter referred to collectively as the fourth generation.

Moses in Egyptian History?

Moses was born in the second year of Thutmose I, the first Egyptian king to have the *nomen* (birth name) Thutmose ḏḥwty-ms 𓅝𓄟𓊃 (born of Thoth). Some have associated the name Moses with the last two hieroglyphs in the pharaoh's name, *ms* 𓄟𓊃, which mean "bear" as in "bear a child," and it is similar to the last syllables in the name Ramose (born of Ra), which was the name of the father of Hatshepsut's great steward Senenmut. Shown below is an expansion of Timeline B on page 138, which reveals some interesting chronological Senenmut-Moses correlations.

Expanded Timeline for Senenmut and Moses
▲ denotes a pharaoh; using High Chronology*

BCE	
ca. 1536	— b. Thutmose II (born at about the same time as Hatshepsut, see below).
ca. 1535	— b. Hatshepsut, daughter of the future Thutmose I (her birth calculated from
---	her estimated age of about 52 years old at her death in 1482 BCE).
1524	— ▲ Thutmose I became pharaoh, decreed death for all Hebrew male infants.
1523	— b. Moses, *Exodus 2*; found by pharaoh's daughter Hatshepsut (12 years old).
1518	— d. Thutmose I.
1518	— ▲ Thutmose II became pharaoh, with his sister Hatshepsut as wife-consort.
1516	— ▲ Hatshepsut recognized as pharaoh in the second year of Thutmose II's reign,
---	according to an inscription in the Chapelle Rouge, block 287, that describes
---	a festival of Amen during which Hatshepsut is made a pharaoh unified with
---	the Ka in the presence of an unnamed king (her husband Thutmose II).
ca. 1506	— b. Thutmose III, son of Thutmose II and a secondary wife, Iset.
1504	— d. Thutmose II.
1504	— ▲ Thutmose III became king as an infant (less than 2 years old).
1504	— Hatshepsut continued as pharaoh, coreigning with her step-son, Thutmose III,
---	who, at less than 2 years old, was too young to rule as king.
1498	— Hatshepsut assumes male pharaonic identity, ruling as primary king.
1486	— Hatshepsut celebrated her "sed year" (her 30th year as a pharaoh).
1483	— Hatshepsut's great steward Senenmut disappeared from history (inscriptions
---	place his disappearance in Hatshepsut's sixteenth year as king).
1483	— Moses (40 years old) fled to Midian, *Exodus 2*.
1482	— Thutmose III became sole ruler when Hatshepsut died.

* from *Chronicle of the Pharaohs* by Peter A. Clayton (New York: Thames &Hudson; 2006)

Hypothesis: Thutmose I became pharaoh in 1,524 BCE. The new king decreed that all male Hebrew infants be killed. The following year, in 1,523 BCE, his twelve-year-old daughter Hatshepsut rescued the infant Moses from the Nile with the intention of raising him as a member of her household. When Thutmose I died in 1,518 BCE, his son Thutmose II became pharaoh and his half-sister Hatshepsut became his wife and queen. In the second year of his reign, according to inscriptions on block 287 from the Chapelle Rouge, the deceased Thutmose I presided over a festival of Amen during which Hatshepsut was recognized as a pharaoh, *circa* 1516 BCE. Hatshepsut produced no male heir with Thutmose II, but he did sire a son, Thutmose III, with a secondary wife. When Thutmose II died in 1,504 BCE, Hatshepsut continued as a pharaoh, at first sharing her reign with her step-son Thutmose III, who, being less than two years old, was too young to rule. Seven years later, in 1,498 BCE, Hatshepsut assumed a masculine public identity and reigned as king of Egypt for the next seventeen years, with Thutmose III serving in a subordinate role. Sometime after her recognition as king, Hatshepsut elevated Senenmut to be her chief steward (top official), but Senenmut disappeared from history in 1,483 BCE, about a year before Hatshepsut's death and at precisely the same time that the biblical Moses fled to Midian after murdering an Egyptian. Was Senenmut the "Moses" who fled to Midian (unlikely), or did Moses kill Senenmut and then flee from Hatshepsut's wrath before returning to Egypt forty years later as the prophet Moses (possible)? The chronological correlations and historical details do allow such questions.

The Exodus to the Divided Kingdoms (1,442-961 BCE)

The periods of the judges and the kingdom of United Israel can be derived from the year of the Exodus, 1,442 BCE, as shown by Timeline C on the opposite page. One insight about the chronology of the period of the judges is worth a comment. The information given in Judges, chapter 11, verse 26, in which Jephthah the Gileadite, who was chosen to defend Israel when the king of Ammon demanded return of lands taken from them when the Israelites crossed the Jordan River, is recorded as taunting the king by asking, *"... Israel [has] dwelt in Heshbon and her towns, and in Aroer and her towns, and in all the cities that be along by the coasts of Arnon, three hundred years, why therefore did ye not recover them within that time?"* (KJV). Many chronologists, especially those who believe that the Exodus happened in the thirteenth century BCE instead of the fifteenth-century BCE date used in

Appendix Two: Synchronized Bible Timeline

BCE	**Timeline C - Exodus to the Divided Kingdoms**

1442 — **The Exodus from Egypt**, *Exodus 12.*
1402 — Israelites crossed Jordan River, *Joshua 3.*
1394 — Israelites inherited the promised land, *Joshua 21.*
--- ... in the 49th year after the Exodus (a jubilee year),
--- land allotted to the twelve tribes, also to Caleb.
1387 — First sabbath year *(observance not mentioned in Bible).*
1102 — Jephthah taunted king of Ammon, *Judges 11.*

<u>*First kingdom period*</u> ♛ <u>*King Saul*</u>

1086 — Saul anointed king of Israel, *1 Samuel 10, 13.*
1076 — b. David. *(birth not mentioned in Bible)*
ca. 1063 — David (13 years old?) anointed by Samuel, *1 Samuel 16.*
ca. 1060 — David (16 years old?) slayed Goliath; *1 Samuel 17.*
1046 — d. Saul slain by the Philistines; *1 Samuel 31.*

<u>*Second kingdom period*</u> ♛ <u>*King David*</u>

1046 — David (30 years old) anointed king of Judah, *2 Samuel 2.*
--- ... *reigns as king in Hebron for 7½ years.*
1039 — David anointed as king of Israel *2 Samuel 5.*
ca. 1037 — David captured Jerusalem, *2 Samuel 5.*
1006 — Solomon began short coreign with David, *1 Kings 1.*
1006 — d. David, *1 Kings 2.*

<u>*Third kingdom period*</u> ♛ <u>*King Solomon*</u>

1006 — *(from above)* Solomon made king by David, *1 Kings 1.*
1006 — Solomon reigned as sole king of Israel, *1 Kings 2.*
1002 — Solomon began First Temple (4th year), *1 Kings 6.*
--- ... *Temple construction began during sabbath/jubilee year.*
995 — Solomon dedicated First Temple; *1 Kings 8.*
--- ... *Temple dedicated during sabbath year.*
966 — d. Solomon, *1 Kings 11.*

<u>*Fourth kingdom period*</u> ♛ <u>*Divided Kingdom*</u>

966 — Rehoboam succeeded Solomon as king of United Israel, *1 Kings 11.*
964 — Jeroboam and the northern tribes rejected Rehoboam as king,*1 Kings 12.*
961 — 5th year of Rehoboam; Shishak took Temple treasures to Egypt, *1 Kings 14.*
... *Jeroboam king in the northern kingdom, established rival temple system.*
961 — Rehoboam became king of southern kingdom of Judah, *1 Kings 12.*

Side annotations:
- 300 years (*Judges 11:26*)
- 40 years (*Acts 13:21*)
- 40 years (*1 Kings 2:11*)
- 40 years (*1 Kings 11:42*)
- 440 years — *3 Kings 6:1 (LXX) - or 480 years measured from the time Moses fled from Egypt (1 Kings 6:1)*

this book, have voiced doubts about the accuracy of that statement, saying that there was not enough time between **their** date for the Exodus (*circa* 1,250 BCE) and **their** date for the beginning year of the reign of Saul (*circa* 1,045 BCE) so as to allow for a period of judges lasting more than three-hundred years, as Jephthah's boast to the king of Ammon obviously requires. However, when all of the available chronological information is correctly interpreted, placing the Exodus in the year 1,442 BCE, in the fifteenth century, and arranging the details as shown on the diagram on the previous page, a three-hundred-year-plus period for the judges is shown to fit within the biblical chronology exactly as the Bible says.

Hiram and the Kings of Tyre

Data about the reigns of the kings of Tyre in history is based solely on the chronological data recorded by Josephus in *Against Apion*, 1.17-18, which he said was a copy of an earlier chronology by Menander, who supposedly copied his data directly from the *Annals of Tyre*. It is assumed that the regnal figures recorded by Josephus and their lengths of reign are correct, as follows:

Hirom (Hiram I) – 34 years
Baleazarus (Baal-Ezer I) – 7 years
Abdastartos – 9 years
(eldest son) – 12 years
Astartus - 12 years
Aserymus (Astarymus) – 9 years
Pheles – 8 months
Ithobalus (Thobaal) – 32 years
Badezeros (Baal-Ezer II) – 6 years
Mategenus (Matten I) – 9 years
Pygmalion – 7 years (+ 40 years after Dido fled in 825 BCE)

Beyond the names of the kings and the length of their reigns, and the statement that Hirom's twelfth year synchronized with the fourth year of Solomon (a chronological tidbit that Josephus probably retained from his education as a member of a prominent priestly family), none of Josephus' chronology that uses the founding of Carthage as an anchor is worth serious consideration. Josephus probably believed that the dates he used for the founding of Carthage and Rome

Appendix Two: Synchronized Bible Timeline

to be true, but both events rely on non-chronological myths for establishing their chronology. As to how Josephus used the Tyrean regnal data, confusion results because of his math. When the Tyrean kings and their respective reigns are tabulated as recorded individually and the lengths of those reigns are totaled (see table below), the years from the start of Hirom's reign to the seventh year of Pygmalion (when mythology says that Dido supposedly fled from Tyre to found Carthage) add up to 137 years and 8 months. However, in *Against Apion*, Josephus says that the time span from the "whole time from the reign of Hirom, till the building of Carthage, amounts to the sum of one hundred fifty-five years and eight months." His figures contradict one another. Therefore, any chronological time span anchored by Josephus to the founding of Carthage must be considered highly suspect and of little historical value.

Using the regnal data for the kings of Tyre recorded by Josephus (the only data available to modern chronologists), and assuming that he was correct about the fourth year of Solomon and the twelfth year of Hirom being equivalent, the reigns of the kings of Tyre align in history as follows:

	Kings of Tyre	
YEARS (BCE)	NAME OF KING	LENGTH OF REIGN FROM JOSEPHUS
1014-980	Hirom (Hiram I)	34 years
... 1002	*12th year of Hirom's reign, Solomon began construction of the Temple*	
980-973	Baleazarus (Baal-Ezer I)	7 years
973-964	Abdastartus	9 years
964-952	(eldest son)	12 years
952-940	Astartus	12 years
940-931	Aserymus (Astarymus)	9 years
931-930	Pheles	8 months
930-897	Ithobalus (Ithobaal I)	32 years
897-891	Badezorus (Baal-Ezer II)	6 years
891-882	Mategenus (Matten I)	9 years
882-(875) 835	Pygmalion	7th year *(Dido fled to build Carthage, Pygmalion reigned forty more years)*
	TOTAL	**137 years 8 months**

The king of Tyre recorded on inscriptions as paying tribute to the Assyrian king Shalmaneser III under the name B'al-manzer in the year 871 BCE (the year of tribute payment according to the kings chronology in this book) may not have been a king at all. The late archaeologist W.F. Albright suggested that "manzer" could be translated as something like "religious votary", from *nzr*, "to vow."[1] It has been suggested by some that the phrase *Ba'li manzer Suraya*, which Albright translates as "Ba'li-Manzer the Tyrian", may also be translated as "Baal manzer of the Tyrians," or perhaps "Baal, priest of Tyre."

Date of Creation

The chronology in this book has been limited back in time to 2,162 BCE, back only to the birth of Abram. For your author, attempting to establish dates much further back in time seems futile, since Ecclesiastes, chapter 3, verse 11b, very clearly states, *"He has also set eternity in their heart, yet so that man will not find out the work which God has done from the beginning even to the end"* (NASB). As for creation, your author accepts the biblical account as inspired and accurate, and he also accepts as credible the empirical evidence that supports the scientific theory of creation, which posits a universe originating with a Big Bang that occurred 13.75 ± 0.12 billion years ago. He offers no apology for not attempting to reconcile the two creation accounts. Over the years, he has heard more than a few cosmologists repeating distortions of sacred texts in an attempt to discredit the biblical account of creation, and he has heard just as many young-Earth creationists repeating what can best be described as pseudo-science to explain away the findings of their assumed scientific adversaries, and he wishes to do neither. From personal experience, your author can certify that the Bible has always proven dependable and true for him, and that, using his technical training and God-given intellect, he has examined and found the chronological conclusions of modern science to be deserving of respect as well. When both the words of the Bible and the observations of science are correctly interpreted and fully understood, your author has no doubt that any truth revealed by one will agree with the truth revealed by the other since, ultimately, truth is an inherent attribute of God, who is, by definition, One.

---

[1] W. F. Albright, "The New Assyro-Tyrian Synchronism and the Chronology of Tyre" (*l'Annuaire de l'Institut de Philologie et d'Histoire Orientales et Slaves*, tome XIII, 1953; p. 4)

Index of Names

Abbreviations used: f = in a footnote, g = in a graphic, t = in a table

Abijah of Judah ... 8, 18t, 20t, 21t, 57-58, 98t, 99t, 111t

Abraham ... 1, 4, 132, 138g, 139, 139f, 140

Adad-nirari II ... 61, 99t, 111t

Adad-nirari III ... 24t, 74-76, 101t, 109-110, 113t, 114t

Ahab of Israel ... 8, 9, 13, 18t, 20t, 22t, 23t, 30-32, 63-66, 66f, 67-72, 87, 100t, 109, 112t

Ahaz of Judah ... 18t, 20t, 27t, 81-82

Ahaziah of Israel ... 18t, 20t, 23t, 67-68, 100t, 112t

Ahaziah of Judah ... 18t, 20t, 23t, 66, 68, 70-73

Akara ... 77, 79-80, 103t

Amaziah of Judah ... 18t, 20t, 24t, 25t, 75-78, 102t, 103t, 114t, 115t

Amenemnisu ... 45, 96t

Amenemope ... 50, 97t

Amenhotep II ... 138g, 141-142

Amon of Judah ... 18t, 20t, 29t, 89-90, 107t, 119t

Apries ... 92, 108t

Asa of Judah ... 18t, 20t, 21t, 22t, 36-37, 40, 58-62, 64, 66, 93, 99t, 100t, 111t, 112t

Ashurbanipal ... 87-89, 90, 93, 106t, 110g, 118t, 119t

Ashur-dan III ... 8, 30, 77, 79, 79f, 102t, 114t, 115t

Ashur-danin-pal ... vii, 32, 34, 71, 74, 109, 113t

Ashur-etil-ilani ... 91, 107t, 119t

Ashur-nasir-pal II ... 64, 67, 99t, 111t, 112t

Ashur-nirari V ... 77, 79, 103t, 115t

Ashur-uballit II ... 91, 108t, 120t

Athaliah of Judah ... 18t, 20t, 23t, 64-68, 70, 72-73, 101t, 113t

Azariah of Judah, see Uzziah of Judah

Baasha of Israel ... 18t, 20t, 21t, 22t, 37, 37f, 38, 39g, 40, 58-62, 99t, 111t

Bakenranef ... 87, 105t

Benhadad I ... 22t, 37-38, 39g, 40, 59-61

Benhadad II (*aka* Hadadezer) ... 65-66, 66f

Benhadad III ... 23t, 24t, 72, 74-75, 110, 114t

Black Obelisk ... 23t, 30, 32, 32f, 65, 69, 70, 109, 113t

Bûr-Saggilê eclipse ... vii, 7-9, 11, 13, 25t, 30-31, 33-34, 36, 64, 79, 79f, 103t, 109, 115t

Caleb ... 133, 137g, 143g

Champollion, Jean-François ... 5, 6, 13, 35, 40, 93

David of Judah and Israel ... (16), 41, 41f, 42t, 44-48, 49g, 50, 52-54, 58, 72, 83, 86, 88, 93, 96t, 97t, 143g, 145

Dynasty 18 ... 136, 141

Dynasty 20 ... 43, 93, 94g, 95t

Dynasty 21 ... 36, 40, 43, 45, 48, 57, 93, 94g, 96t, 97t, 98t

Dynasty 22 ... 36, 57, 93, 94g, 98t, 99t, 100t, 101t, 102t, 103t, 104t

Dynasty 23 ... 93, 94g, 102t, 103t, 104t, 105t

Dynasty 24 ... 93, 94g, 104t, 105t

Dynasty 25 ... 93, 94g, 103t, 104t, 105t, 106t

Dynasty 26 ... 93, 94g, 106t, 107t, 108t

Elah of Israel ... 18t, 20t, 22t, 60, 62-63, 82, 99t, 111t

Esarhaddon ... 28t, 87-88, 106t, 118t

Ethbaal, see Ithobaal

Hadadezer, see Benhadad II

Har-Psusennes II, see Psusennes II

Harsiese ... 101t

Hatshepsut ... 138g, 141-142

Hazael ... 69-72, 74

Hezekiah of Judah ... 18t, 20t, 27t, 28t, 83-84, 85g, 86-87, 104t, 105t, 110, 116t, 117t

Hiram I ... 144-145

Hoshea of Israel ... 18t, 20t, 27t, 28t, 81-82, 84, 86, 104t, 105t, 116t, 117t

Isaac ... 132, 138g, 139, 139f, 140

Ithobaal (Ithobalos) ... 144-145

Index of Names

Iuput ... 77, 79, 102t, 103t
Iuput II ... 82, 86, 104t
Jacob ... 132, 138g, 139, 139f, 140-141
Jehoahaz of Israel ... 18t, 20t, 24t, 74, 101t, 102t, 113t, 114t
Jehoahaz of Judah ... 18t, 20t, 29t, 91-92, 108t
Jehoash of Israel ... 18t, 20t, 24t, 25t, 74-76, 102t, 110, 114t
Jehoiachin ... 18t, 20t, 29t, 91-92, 108t
Jehoiakim of Judah ... 18t, 20t, 29t, 91-92, 108t
Jehoram of Ahab, see Joram of Israel
Jehoram of Israel, see Joram of Israel
Jehoram of Judah ... 18t, 20t, 23t, 66-70, 72, 100t, 101t, 112t, 113t
Jehoshaphat of Judah ... 8, 18t, 20t, 22t, 23t, 32, 65-67, 100t, 112t, 133-134
Jehu of Israel ... 18t, 20t, 23t, 24t, 68-72, 72f, 73-74, 101t, 109-110, 112t, 113t
Jeroboam of Israel ... 10, 18t, 20t, 21t, 35-36, 51-58, 61, 76f, 98-99, 111t, 143g
Jeroboam II of Israel ... 18t, 20t, 25t, 26t, 76, 76f, 77-80, 102t, 103t, 114t, 115t
Joash of Judah ... 18t, 20t, 23t, 24t, 72-75, 90f, 101t, 102t, 113t, 114t, 134
Joram of Judah, see Jehoram of Judah
Joram of Israel ... 18t, 20t, 23t, 63-64, 67-72, 100t, 101t, 112t, 113t
Joseph ... 52, 138g, 140
Josiah of Judah ... 18t, 20t, 24t, 29t, 73, 89, 89f, 90, 90f, 91-92, 107t, 108t, 119t, 120t, 134
Jotham of Judah ... 18t, 20t, 26t, 27t, 77, 79, 81-82, 104t, 116t
Kashta/Maatre ... 79, 81-82, 104t
Kurkh Monolith ... 23t, 30, 32, 64-65, 112t
Maatre, see Kashta/Maatre
Manasseh of Judah ... 18t, 20t, 28t, 29t, 85g, 87 87f, 88-89, 106t, 107t, 117t, 118t,119t
Manetho ... 7
Masoretic text ... viii, 4, 10 135, 136
Memphis Stele ... 142
Menahem of Israel ... 18t, 20t, 26t, 80-81, 103t, 104t, 115t, 116t

Mesha of Moab ... 63, 65, 69
Mesha Stele (Moabite Stone) ... 63, 69
Moses ... 48, 51, 56, 124, 127, 133-134, 136, 137g, 138g, 141-142, 144
Mukin-zeri eclipse ... 33-34
Nadab of Israel ... 18t, 20t, 21t, 58, 61-62
Nebuchadnezzar II ... 10, 15-16, 18t, 29t, 91-92
Necho II ... 29t, 91-92, 108t
Omri of Israel ... 18t, 20t, 22t, 62-64, 69-70, 99t, 109, 100t, 111t, 112t
Osochor ... 50, 97t, 98t
Orsorkon the Elder, see Osochor
Osorkon I ... 62-63, 99t, 100t
Osorkon II ... 100t, 101t
Osorkon III ... 77, 80-82, 103t Osorkon IV ... 82, 86, 96t, 104t, 105t
Pimay ... 77, 79-80, 103t, 104t
Pedubast ... 75, 77, 79, 102t
Pekah of Israel ... 18t, 20t, 26t, 27t, 81-82
Pekahiah of Israel ... 18t, 20t, 26t, 81-82, 104t, 116t
Piankhy/Piyi/Sneferre ... 81-82, 86, 104t
Psammetichus I ... 88-89, 91, 106t
Psammetichus II ... 108t
Psusennes I ... 45-46, 48, 52, 93-94, 96t, 97t
Psusennes II ... 57, 98t
Pul ... vii, 33-34, 77, 79, 80-82, 103t, 115t, 116t *(also, see Tiglath-pileser III)*
Qarqar (Battle of) ... 8, 9, 23t, 30-32, 64-66, 68, 100t, 109, 112t
Ramesses XI ... 43, 95t
Rawlinson, Sir Henry ... 7-8, 8f, 9-11, 13, 30-32, 36, 64, 79, 109
Rehoboam of Israel and Judah ... 6-10, 13, 13f, 14, 16, 17, 17g, 18t, 20t, 21t, 22t, 35-36, 36f, 37, 40-41, 47, 50-52, 54-55, 55g, 56, 56g, 57-58, 60, 64, 93, 98t, 135, 143g
Rudamon ... 82, 104t
Sargon II ... 10, 82, 87, 105t, 110, 117t
Saul of Israel ... 4, 41, 41f, 42, 42t, 43-45, 50, 54, 95t, 96t, 142, 143g

Index of Names

Seder Olam ... vii, 4f, 12f, 22t, 23t, 24t, 25t, 27t, 28t, 42, 46, 60, 60f, 63, 66f, 73, 73f, 74, 74f, 76, 76f, 77, 88, 90f, 93, 104t, 114t, 116t, 132, 134, 134f, 144, 144f

Senenmut ... 138g, 141-142

Sennacherib ... 28t, 84, 85g, 86-88, 105t, 110, 117t, 118t

Septuagint ... 4, 10, 35, 54, 136, 136f

Shabako ... 87, 105t

Shallum of Israel ... 18t, 20t, 26t, 80, 91, 103t

Shalmaneser III ... vii, 8, 9, 13, 23t, 30-32, 34, 64-65, 67, 69-72, 74, 100t, 109-110, 112t, 113t, 146

Shalmaneser IV ... 75-77, 79, 102t, 114t

Shalmaneser V ... 82, 87, 105t, 117t

Shamshi-adad V ... 32, 71, 74-75, 101t, 113t

Shebitku ... 87-88, 105t, 106t

Shishak ... 6, 7, 13, 17, 21t, 22t, 35-37, 40, 51-52, 54, 56g, 57, 60, 93, 143g

Shishak, also see Siamun

Shoshenq I ... 6, 7, 13, 22t, 35-38, 39g, 40, 57, 59, 60-62, 93-94, 98t, 99t

Shoshenq II ... 64, 67, 100t

Shoshenq III ... 74-76, 79, 102t, 103t

Shoshenq IV ... 77, 79, 103t

Shoshenq V ... 79-81, 103t, 104t

Shoshenq VI ... 87, 106t

Siamun ... 21t, 37, 40, 50, 52, 54, 57, 60, 94, 98t

Sin-sar-ishkun ... 91, 107t, 119t, 120t

Sin-shumu-lishir ... 91, 107t, 119t

Smendes I ... 43, 45, 95t, 96t

Sneferre, see Piankhy/Piyi/Sneferre

So ... 82

Solomon of Israel ... 3, 6, 24t, 29t, 35-36, 41, 41f, 42t45-48, 49g, 50, 50f, 51-54, 55g, 57, 73, 76, 83, 90f, 93-94, 97t, 98t, 134-136, 138g, 139, 142, 143g, 144

Taharqa ... 88, 106t

Takeloth I ... 64, 67, 69, 100t

Takeloth II ... 8f, 71, 74-75, 101t, 102t

Takeloth III ... 81, 82, 104t

Tanutamani ... 88, 106t

Taylor Prism (Sennacherib's Prism) ... 84

Tefnakht ... 82, 86, 104t, 105t

Tel-al-Rimah Stele ... 75, 114t

Tel Dan Stele ... 71-72, 72f

Tel Gezer ... 50f

Thiele, Edwin R. ... 9, 9f, 10, 11, 12f, 12t, 13, 86, 144

Thutmose I ... 138g, 141-142

Thutmose II ... 138g, 141-142

Thutmose III ... 138g, 141-142

Thutmose IV ... 142

Tiglath-pileser III ... vii, 27t, 32-34, 77, 79-81, 87, 109-110, 103t, 104t, 115t, 116t, 117t

Tikulti-ninurta ... 62-63, 99t, 111t

Ussher, Archbishop James ... 3f, 4, 4f, 5, 12f, 12t

Uzziah (Azariah) of Judah ... 18t, 20t, 25t, 26t, 75-82, 102t, 103t, 104t, 114t, 115t, 116t

Zachariah of Israel ... 18t, 20t, 26t, 80, 103t, 115t

Zedekiah ... 18t, 20t, 29t, 91-92, 108t

Zimri of Israel ... 18t, 20t, 22t, 62-63, 99t, 111t

Additional publications by Dan Bruce ...

DANIEL UNSEALED *(re-released 2013)*
An exposition revealing what the seven chrono-specific predictive prophecies in Daniel say about the history of the Jews, Jerusalem, and the Anointed One of Israel; paperback, 224 pages (6 x 9); ISBN 978-1489505415; available as a print-on-demand book from CreateSpace at https://www.createspace.com/4288792.

SYNCHRONIZED CHRONOLOGY OF ANCIENT KINGDOMS
Comparing the Regnal Chronologies of Israel, Egypt, Assyria, Tyre, Babylon, and Urartu between 1,006 BCE and 560 BCE; paperback, 86 pages (8½ x 11); ISBN 978-1489557773.

THE FIRST COMING OF JESUS CHRIST (forthcoming)
Explaining the life of Jesus from his baptism to his ascension, with his words and deeds presented chronologically in a first-century Jewish milieu.

THE HAND OF GOD IN THE HISTORY OF ISRAEL (forthcoming)
The remarkable story of one man's faith, one people's struggles, and how God's promises to them will one day be fully fulfilled by the Anointed One of Israel.

INTO THE MIND OF THE GOD OF HEAVEN (forthcoming)
Explaining what the Bible says about the loving relationship between God and mankind, and how each man and woman on Earth can experience that love.

Visit our website at www.prophecysociety.org

Printed in the USA
CPSIA information can be obtained
at www.ICGtesting.com
LVHW052207121023
760994LV00033B/674